THE IR FARMERS HANDBOOK 2003

Compiled by

Martin O'Sullivan B.Agr. Sc M.A.C.A.

with contributions from

Michael O'Sullivan, Dip. For. Man. M.S.I.F.
Richard Rea, B.Agr.Sc.. Dip.E.I.A.,Mgmt.,MACA

Published by

O'Sullivan Consulting
Farm and Forestry Consultants

Bank House,,
Carrick-on-Suir,
Co. Tipperary.
Tel (051) 640397: Fax (051) 640932

Published by
O'Sullivan Consulting

Published 2002 by
O'Sullivan Consulting
Farm and Forestry Consultants
Bank House
Carrick-on-Suir
Co. Tipperary
Tel 051-640397
E mail skos@eircom.net

© O'Sullivan Consulting 2002

ISBN 0 9534826 5 D

This book is intended as an aid to farmers and those involved in providing services to the farming community and is based on our understanding of current law and practice. While every effort has been made to ensure accuracy, the authors or publisher will not accept any liability for loss, distress or damage resulting from any errors or omissions.

Origination by O'Sullivan Consulting

Printed by Kilkenny People Printing Ltd.

THE AUTHOR

The author, **Martin O'Sullivan** is one of the longest serving private Agricultural Consultants in Ireland having commenced practice in 1978. Prior to setting up practice he served as an Agricultural Advisor under the Co.Wexford Committee of Agriculture (now Teagasc). Apart from his involvement in farm consultancy he is also a partner in the accountancy firm Skelly O'Sullivan based in Carrick on Suir.

Over the last two decades the role of the agricultural consultant has changed substantially from the traditional one of advising farmers on crop and animal production methods. Today's consultant is more concerned with matters such as accounts and taxation, finance, legal claims, premiums and subsidies and the emerging area of environmentally sensitive farming methods. With the benefit of experience of solving farmers problems on a day to day basis and also the ongoing feed back from the first nine editions of The Irish Farmers' Handbook, the author has attempted to provide a practical working aid that will benefit not alone the farmer but also the many professionals dealing with farmers.

THE CONTRIBUTORS

Michael O'Sullivan Dip.For. Man. M.S.I.F.
A practising private forestry consultant since 1996, he worked as a Coillte District Manager prior to setting up in consultancy. He is a member of the Society of Irish Forester and is a partner in O'Sullivan Consulting, Farm & Forestry Development Services, Carrick on Suir.

Richard Rea B.Agr.Sc. Dip.E.I.A.,Mgmt.,MACA
One of the pioneers of private agricultural consultancy, he has practised from Tipperary Town since 1975. His contribution to this years handbook particularly in the area of Compulsory Acquisition Orders draws on his specialist knowledge of the area allied to the benefit of many years experience gained in private practice. Richard is the principal of Martin & Rea (Tipperary) Ltd. Agricultural Consultants and is also a partner in Rea Clarke & Associates, Agriculture & Environmental Consultants.

Foreword by Minister Joe Walsh

I am delighted once again to welcome the 2003 edition of the Irish Farmers' Handbook, which is now an essential reference booklet to all in the farming and agri-business community.

It is not surprising that primary agriculture remains more important to Ireland that to most other EU Member States. The agri-food sector accounts for around 9% of GDP and employment and 7% of Irish exports. Because of its very low import content, agri-food contributes about one quarter of our total net foreign earnings from merchandise exports.

The commitment of the Government to Irish agriculture, food and rural development is clearly underlined by a very high level of public expenditure. Total public expenditure on the agri-food sector each year is around 2.7 billion, of which over fifty six percent comes from the EU.

The Government is committed to the long-term development of Irish agriculture, food and rural development. The core of this policy is maintaining the greatest possible number of family farms and to preserving the rural environment as the basis of a thriving rural community.

The importance of competitiveness was underlined in the Agri Food 2010 report. Much of the work of my Department is designed to improve the competitive position of the agri-food sector through research and training, encouraging the land mobility and ensuring productive on-farm investment. In my opinion, everyone involved in the sector - farmers, the food industry and policymakers need to focus on improving competitiveness, in order to meet challenges and opportunities in the years ahead.

The coming year will present many challenges for all of us in the Agricultural Sector, among them the mid-term review of Agenda 2000. The CAP, which has been so beneficial to Irish Agriculture, is facing a number of challenges and the proposals in the Review are for a far more significant reform of the CAP that was anticipated. The agenda 2000 agreement represented a favourable outcome for Ireland and I am completely dedicated to the defence of Ireland's agricultural interests. I look forward to meeting those challenges along with the continuing WTO negotiations, enlargement of the EU and the Irish Presidency of the EU in the first half of 2004.

In conclusion I would like to take the opportunity to wish all involved in the agriculture and food sector a healthy and prosperous year ahead.

Joe Walsh T.D.　　　**Minister for Agriculture, Food and Rural Development**

ACKNOWLEDGEMENTS

Bryan Barry, I.F.A..
Jim Bourke, O'Sullivan Consulting.
Michael Brady, Agricultural Consultant.
Jim Devlin, I.F.A.
Anthony Dowd, Forest Service
Sean Foley, Department of Agriculture, Food and Rural Development
Dan Gahon, Department of Agriculture, Food and Rural Development
Gerry Gunning, I.F.A.
Eamon Hayes, Solicitor, Clonmel Road, Carrick on Suir.
Harvey Jones, I.F.A.
Health & Safety Authority
Eamonn Keane, Department of Agriculture, Food and Rural
Development
Kevin Kinsella, I.F.A.
Catherine Lascurettes, I.F.A.
Brendan Lee FBD.
Nuala MacNamara, FBD Insurance
John McNamera, Kildalton, Agricultural College..
David Meagher, Murphy Bros., Agricultural Contractors.
Christine Mullins, O'Sullivan Consulting.
Louise O'Meara, Skelly O'Sullivan & Company.
Hugh O'Neill, Agricultural Consultant.
Skelly O'Sullivan Staff
FRS People Placement.
Pat Smith, I.F.A.
Michael Treacy, Farm Development Service
David Walsh, Agricultural Consultant.

The authors particularly wish to acknowledge the assistance given by the staff of The IFA, Teagasc and the Department of Agriculture, Food and Rural Development. Without their most willing co-operation the completion of this handbook would not have been possible.

CONTENTS

Useful Tables & Charts

"Today's been hard work, but it's an investment in my future"

It's what you do now that helps you provide for the future. So, if you've got funds available to invest, talk today to AIB Bank. Our dedicated Investment Advisors will offer practical advice on every aspect of your investment needs. Helping you to maximise returns on all the work you're putting in today.

Business life is full of possibilities.

Your nearest AIB branch can help you with the practicalities.

Be with AIB.

CONTENTS (Continued

"creating the perfect environment for growth"

ACCBANK offers a wide range of banking services for our Agri-Business customers including:

Agricultural & Rural Development Finance

Farm Machinery & Car Finance

Quota Loans

Deposits & Investments

Forestry Loan Fund

Mortgages

Agri - Tourism

Life Insurance & Pensions

please contact your local branch for details

CONTENTS (Continued)

Independent Merchant Group

 **Kevin Cooney** Group

QUINNS of BALTINGLASS LTD.

GRENNAN BROS.

 **McDonnell Bros.** (AGRICULTURAL SUPPLIERS) LTD *GENERAL GRAIN AND AGRICULTURAL MERCHANTS*

B∎LGER

LIFFEY✦MILLS

 **Brett**

Family Businesses Serving Family Farms

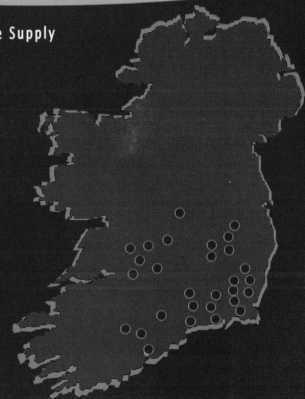

- Our CORE Business is the Supply of Farm Inputs

- Extensive Network of Trading Outlets

- Providers of Comprehensive Technical Support

- Purchaser of over 300,000 Tonnes of Irish Grain Annually

- NATIVE Cereals Included in Our Feeds

- Committed To Local Communities

Delivering Real Competition
Tel: 00353 52 27646 Fax: 00353 52 27647
E-Mail: info@independentmerchants.ie

2003 Year Planner

JANUARY

1	W
2	T
3	F
4	S
5	S
6	M
7	T
8	W
9	T
10	F
11	S
12	S
13	M
14	T
15	W
16	T
17	F
18	S
19	S
20	M
21	T
22	W
23	T
24	F
25	S
26	S
27	M
28	T
29	W
30	T
31	F

FEBRUARY

1	S
2	S
3	M
4	T
5	W
6	T
7	F
8	S
9	S
10	M
11	T
12	W
13	T
14	F
15	S
16	S
17	M
18	T
19	W
20	T
21	F
22	S
23	S
24	M
25	T
26	W
27	T
28	F

MARCH

1	S
2	S
3	M
4	T
5	W
6	T
7	F
8	S
9	S
10	M
11	T
12	W
13	T
14	F
15	S
16	S
17	M
18	T
19	W
20	T
21	F
22	S
23	S
24	M
25	T
26	W
27	T
28	F
29	S
30	S
31	M

JULY

1	T
2	W
3	T
4	F
5	S
6	S
7	M
8	T
9	W
10	T
11	F
12	S
13	S
14	M
15	T
16	W
17	T
18	F
19	S
20	S
21	M
22	T
23	W
24	T
25	F
26	S
27	S
28	M
29	T
30	W
31	T

AUGUST

1	F
2	S
3	S
4	M
5	T
6	W
7	T
8	F
9	S
10	S
11	M
12	T
13	W
14	T
15	F
16	S
17	S
18	M
19	T
20	W
21	T
22	F
23	S
24	S
25	M
26	T
27	W
28	T
29	F
30	S
31	S

SEPTEMBER

1	M
2	T
3	W
4	T
5	F
6	S
7	S
8	M
9	T
10	W
11	T
12	F
13	S
14	S
15	M
16	T
17	W
18	T
19	F
20	S
21	S
22	M
23	T
24	W
25	T
26	F
27	S
28	S
29	M
30	T

APRIL	MAY	JUNE
1 T	1 T	1 S
2 W	2 F	[2] M
3 T	3 S	3 T
4 F	4 S	4 W
5 S	[5] M	5 T
6 S	6 T	6 F
7 M	7 W	7 S
8 T	8 T	8 S
9 W	9 F	9 M
10 T	10 S	10 T
11 F	11 S	11 W
12 S	12 M	12 T
13 S	13 T	13 F
14 M	14 W	14 S
15 T	15 T	15 S
16 W	16 F	16 M
17 T	17 S	17 T
[18] F	18 S	18 W
19 S	19 M	19 T
20 S	20 T	20 F
[21] M	21 W	21 S
[22] T	22 T	22 S
23 W	23 F	23 M
24 T	24 S	24 T
25 F	25 S	25 W
26 S	[26] M	26 T
27 S	[27] T	27 F
28 M	28 W	28 S
29 T	29 T	29 S
30 W	30 F	30 M
	31 S	

OCTOBER	NOVEMBER	DECEMBER
1 W	1 S	1 M
2 T	2 S	2 T
3 F	3 M	3 W
4 S	4 T	4 T
5 S	5 W	5 F
6 M	6 T	6 S
7 T	7 F	7 S
8 W	8 S	8 M
9 T	9 S	9 T
10 F	10 M	10 W
11 S	11 T	11 T
12 S	12 W	12 F
13 M	13 T	13 S
14 T	14 F	14 S
15 W	15 S	15 M
16 T	16 S	16 T
17 F	17 M	17 W
18 S	18 T	18 T
19 S	19 W	19 F
20 M	20 T	20 S
21 T	21 F	21 S
22 W	22 S	22 M
23 T	23 S	23 T
24 F	24 M	24 W
25 S	25 T	[25] T
26 S	26 W	[26] F
[27] M	27 T	27 S
[28] T	28 F	28 S
29 W	29 S	29 M
30 T	30 S	30 T
31 F		31 W

The Irish Farmers' Association
Members' Services/Benefits

**Effective Representation
on the Issues of
Concern to Irish Farmers**

Access to IFA's
Premium/Headage/Tillage Aid
Payment Problem Section

Strong Representation
of Farmers with EU
Government & Agri-Business

Livestock prices and
Valuation Services

Professional Advice &
Support Services

Farm Product Price
Monitoring &
Reporting Service

Leadership that Delivers
the Best Possible Results

Democratic Structure that
Facilitates Everybody's
Point of View

Members can access key
information through our
interactice website www.ifa.ie

**The Farmer's Voice
outside the Farm Gate**

MEMBERS' VALUABLE BENEFITS PACKAGE

includes

- Up to 30% off home phone calls with Esat BT
- 10% VHI discount with Easy Payments Options
- €30 FBD Insurance discount voucher
- 40% savings on your mobile phone bill with the IFA/O_2 group deal
- €125 IFAC discount (new accounts/tax clients only)
- €100 Kingswood Herd Manager computer software discount
- Free travel insurance for package holidays with Co-op Travel
- 10% discount on ferry crossings to Britain by car with Irish Ferries
- Other special discounts negotiated during the year

Members' Personal Accident Insurance

All fully paid-up members of IFA between the ages of 18 and 74 years inclusive are automatically insured for Personal Accident benefits with FBD Insurance plc. as outlined below.

In the event of accidental:	Benefit
1) Death	€20,000
2) Total loss by physical severance at or above the wrist of one or both hands.	€10,000
3) Total loss by physical severance at or above the ankle of one or both feet.	€10,000
4) Total and irrecoverable loss of all sight in one or both eyes.	€10,000
5) Permanent total disablement from pursuance of gainful employment of any or every kind.	€10,000
6) Sustaining bodily injury - for period in hospital(excluding the first three days) for up to one year.	€275 *per week*

Full details including exclusions in membership pack

The Irish Farmers' Association

IFA is working hard on the critical issues affecting farm families:

- Applying intense pressure to increase farm product **prices** and rebuild our **market share** in EU and international markets
- Defending our interests in the Fischler **CAP Reform** proposals and in the **WTO**
- Resisting unfair or impractical **environmental regulations,** which would unnecessarily damage dairy, beef and tillage farmers
- Promoting structural reform and **competitiveness**
- Demanding improvements in the **farm grant schemes**
- Insisting **payment deadlines** negotiated by IFA are met
- Attacking **red tape** and unnecessary form-filling
- Tackling unidentified and untraceable **imports** and developing **Feile Bia.**

The challenges facing Irish Farmers can be met by uniting behind IFA, which has the voluntary commitment, experience and professional support to deliver results at home and in Europe.

John Dillon,
IFA President

UNITY - STRENGTH - DELIVERY

www.ifa.ie

Tables & Charts

CHART 1 - INCOME TAX ALLOWANCES

	1999/00	2000/01	2001	2002	2003
	IR£	IR£	IR£	Euro €	Euro €
Personal Allowance	Allce.	Allce.	Tax Credit	Tax Credit	Tax Credit
Single person	4,200	4,700	814	1,520	1,520
Married couple	8,400	9,400	1,628	3,040	3,040
Widowed person (in year of bereavement)	8,400	9,400	1,628	3,040	3,040
Widowed person (subsequent years)	4,700	5,700	962	1,820	1,820
Widowed with dependent child *(additional)*					
First year after bereavement	5,000	10,000	2,000	2,600	2,600
Second year after bereavement	4,000	8,000	1,600	2,100	2,100
Third year after bereavement	3,000	6,000	1,200	1,600	1,600
Child Allowance					
Incapacitated	800	1,600	238	500	500
Widow, Widower etc.	4,200	4,700	814	1,520	1,220
Single parent - additional	4,200	4,700	814	1,520	1,220
Other Allowances /Credits					
Dependent relative allowance	110	220	33	60	60
Blind person	1,500	3,000	444	800	800
Both spouses blind	3,000	6,000	888	1,600	1,600
Age Allowance - Single / widowed	400	800	119	205	205
- Married man	800	1,600	238	410	410
Employee allowance	1,000	1,000	296	660	800
Home Carer			444	770	770

CHART 2 - INCOME RATES

1995/'96 Single/Widow(er) IR£ 8,900 @ 27% Bal @ 48% Married Couple IR£ 17,800 @ 27% Bal @ 48%	1998/'99 Single/Widow(er) IR£ 10,000 @ 24% Bal @ 46% Married Couple IR£ 20,000 @ 24% Bal @ 46%	2001 Single/Widow(er) IR£ £20,000 @20 % Bal @ 42% Married Couple IR£ (a)[1]£29,000 @20% (b)[2]£40,000 @20% Bal @ 42%
1996/'97 Single/Widow(er) IR£ 9,400 @ 27% Bal @ 48% Married Couple IR£ 18,800 @ 27% Bal @ 48%	1999/'00 Single/Widow(er) IR£ 14,000 @ 24% Bal @ 46% Married Couple IR£ 28,000 @ 24% Bal @ 46%	2002 € Single/Widow(er) €28,000 @ 20% Bal. @ 42% Married Couple IR£ (a)[1]€37,000 @20% (b)[2]€56,000 @20% Bal @ 42%
1997/'98 IR£ Single/Widow(er) 9,900 @ 26% Bal @ 48% Married Couple IR£ 19,800 @ 26% Bal @ 48%	2000/01 IR£ Single/Widowed 17,000 @22% Bal. @ 44% Married/Couple IR£ (a)[1]28,000 @22% (b)[2]34,000 @22% Bal @ 44%	2003 € Single/Widow(er) €28,000 @ 20% Bal. @ 42% Married Couple IR£ (a)[1]€37,000 @20% (b)[2]€56,000 @20% Bal @ 42%

[1] (a) denotes single income couples [2] (b) denotes two income couples

15:00, Hamra, Sweden

Your herd may not notice the name change, but they will notice the difference.

More than a simple name change, the transformation of Alfa Laval Agri to DeLaval signals our total commitment to the dairy farmer. Throughout the day, around the world, DeLaval people and equipment are actively at work. More than a valued supplier, we aim to expand our role to get even closer to farmers and continue to drive progress in milk production. It's no small job. But then DeLaval is no ordinary company.
For more information please contact your local DeLaval dealler or DeLaval Limited at Clover Hill Industrial Estate, Clondalkin, Dublin 22. Telephone 01-4136300 or Fax 01- 4136319 or visit www.delaval.com DeLaval is a member of the Tetra Laval Group.

⚡ DeLaval

CHART 3 - INCOME TAX EXEMPTION LIMITS

	2001 £	2002 €	2003 €
Under 65 years:			
married persons (assessed jointly)	6,068	10,420	10,420
others	3,034	5,210	5,210
Over 65 year and over:			
married persons (assessed jointly)	12,500	30,000	30,000
others	6,290	15,000	15,000
Increase in exemption limit in respect of			
1st and 2nd child	450	575	575
3rd and subsequent children	650	830	830
Marginal Relief			
(where income exceeds but is not more than twice the exemption limit)	40%	40%	40%

CHART 4 - CAPITAL ACQUISITION TAX THRESHOLDS

Relationship to person granting the gift or inheritance	2001	2002
	€	€
Son, daughter or favourite niece or nephew	316,800	422,148
Brother, Sister, Niece, Nephew or Grandchild	31,680	42,215
Others	15,840	21,108

"If anything goes wrong
I know I won't be left carrying the can"

Stephen Corry, Ardcath, Garristown, Co. Meath

When you're in business you have to expect the unexpected.
In dairy farming things are no different. I spend a lot of my time
planning my business, monitoring the farm plan, updating the
herd records, checking market prices and so on.

But even the best laid plans can go astray which is where
FBD come into their own.

At FBD they've thought about my business and it shows.
I review my insurance cover with them once a year. After that
I don't worry about it because I trust them.

After all, they've been designing their policies around farmers'
needs and budgets for as long as I can remember. Sure anyway,
doesn't the cream always rise to the top?

Peace of mind at the right price

tel: (01) 409 3200 email: info@fbd.ie

website: www.fbd.ie

CHART 5 - CAPITAL GAINS TAX INDEXATION FACTORS

Indexation factors for capital gains tax

Year of Expenditure	Year of disposal					
	1997/98	1998/99	1999/00	2000/01	2001	2002
1974/75	6.112	6.215	6.313	6.582	6.930	7.180
1975/76	4.936	5.020	5.099	5.316	5.597	5.799
1976/77	4.253	4.325	4.393	4.580	4.822	4.996
1977/78	3.646	3.707	3.766	3.926	4.133	4.283
1978/79	3.368	3.425	3.479	3.627	3.819	3.956
1979/80	3.039	3.090	3.139	3.272	3.445	3.570
1980/81	2.631	2.675	2.718	2.833	2.983	3.091
1981/82	2.174	2.211	2.246	2.342	2.465	2.554
1982/83	1.829	1.860	1.890	1.970	2.074	2.149
1983/84	1.627	1.654	1.680	1.752	1.844	1.911
1984/85	1.477	1.502	1.525	1.590	1.674	1.735
1985/86	1.390	1.414	1.436	1.497	1.577	1.633
1986/87	1.330	1.352	1.373	1.432	1.507	1.562
1987/88	1.285	1.307	1.328	1.384	1.457	1.510
1988/89	1.261	1.282	1.303	1.358	1.430	1.481
1989/90	1.221	1.241	1.261	1.314	1.384	1.434
1990/91	1.171	1.191	1.210	1.261	1.328	1.376
1991/92	1.142	1.161	1.179	1.229	1.294	1.341
1992/93	1.101	1.120	1.138	1.186	1.249	1.294
1993/94	1.081	1.099	1.117	1.164	1.226	1.270
1994/95	1.063	1.081	1.098	1.144	1.205	1.248
1995/96	1.037	1.054	1.071	1.116	1.175	1.218
1996/97	1.016	1.033	1.050	1.094	1.152	1.194
1997/98	-	1.017	1.033	1.077	1.134	1.175
1998/99	-	-	1.016	1.059	1.115	1.156
1999/00	-	-	-	1.043	1.098	1.138
2000/01	-	-	-	-	1.053	1.097
2001					-	1.037

Note 1: The Tax year end changed to the 31st. December in 2001

Note 2: Indexation relief will only apply to the period of ownership up to 31 December 2002

AGRI AWARE

PROMOTING IRISH AGRICULTURE'S PIVOTAL ROLE IN...

AGRI AWARE

Agri Aware
Waverley Office Park,
Old Naas Rd.,
Bluebell,
Dublin 12.
Tel. (01) 460 1103
Fax. (01) 460 1097
E-mail:
info@agriaware.ie
Website:
www.agriaware.ie

- SUPPORTING 300,000 IRISH JOBS

- PRODUCING QUALITY FOOD

- MEETING THE HIGHEST FOOD SAFETY STANDARDS

- CARING FOR THE NATION'S LIVESTOCK 365 DAYS OF THE YEAR

- SUSTAINING THE RURAL ECONOMY

- PRESERVING OUR RURAL ENVIRONMENT

TABLE 6 - PENSIONS & BENEFITS

	To Jan 2003	From Jan. 2003
	€	€
Old Age Contributory Pension		
(i) Under 80:- Weekly Rate		
Personal rate	147.30	157.30
Person with qualified adult under 66	245.40	262.10
Person with qualified adult 66 or over	261.10	278.80
(ii) 80 or over:- Weekly Rate		
Personal Rate	153.70	163.70
Person with qualified adult under 66	251.80	268.50
Person with qualified adult 66 or over	267.50	285.20
Widow's/Widower's Contributory Pension		
Under 66- Weekly Rate	123.30	130.30
66 and under 80	144.80	155.80
80 and over	151.20	162.20
Old Age Non Contributory Pension:		
(i) Under 80:- Weekly Rate		
Personal rate	134.00	144.00
Person with qualified adult under 66	222.50	239.20
(ii) 80 or over:		
Personal Rate	140.40	150.40
Person with qualified adult under 66	228.90	245.60
Farm Assist		
Personal Rate- Weekly Rates	118.80	124.80
Person with qualified adult	197.60	207.60
Child Benefit - Monthly Rates	From 1/4/02	From 1/4/03
First and second children	€117.60 ea.	€125.60 ea.
Third and subsequent children	€147.30 ea.	€157.30 ea.

permanent tsb
AGRI FINANCE

AGRI FINANCE FOR TODAY'S FARMER

The Sales Team

Ollie McGuire
Area: Wexford, Wicklow, Carlow
Mobile: 087 6691757
Office: Ardkeen, Waterford
Tel: Margaret (051) 844990

Sean O' Leary
Area: Cork
Mobile: 087 6349024
Office: Douglas, Cork
Tel: Eleanor (021) 4365003

Clem Power
Area: Cork
Mobile: 087 6691755
Office: Douglas, Cork
Tel: Eleanor (021) 4365003

Seamus Salmon
Area: Mayo, Galway, Roscommon, Sligo, Donegal
Mobile: 087 6691758
Office: Ellison St, Castlebar Co. Mayo
Tel: Marguerite (094) 34550

John Moran
Area: Limerick, Clare, North Tipperary, Kerry
Mobile: 087 6172567
Office: Upper William St, Limerick
Tel: Celine (061) 211080

Tom Fives
Area: Waterford, Kilkenny, South Tipperary
Mobile: 087 6691754
Office: Ardkeen, Waterford
Tel: Margaret (051) 844990

Roy Matthews
Area: Offaly, Laois, Kildare, Westmeath
Mobile: 087 6691759
Office: Ellison St, Castlebar Co. Mayo
Tel: Marguerite (094) 34550

John Murtagh
Area: Longford, Leitrim, Cavan, Monaghan
Mobile: 087 6691760
Office: Head Office, St. Stephen's Green, D2
Tel: Anne-Marie 1850 211811 (01) 6695262

Sinead Delaney
Area: Meath, Louth, Dublin
Mobile: 087 6691756
Office: Head Office, St. Stephen's Green, D2
Tel: Anne-Marie 1850 211811 (01) 6695262

permanent tsb Agri Finance Ltd are the team to work with you and your business. Our very experienced Agri Sales team are very pleased to share their farming business knowledge and finance expertise. Our representatives specialise in advising you on equipment and machinery lease and hire, fixed/variable rate loans and car finance.

For all-round guidance and excellent lending rates call your local sales executive now or log onto our website www.**permanenttsb**.ie and you can apply online for an Agri Finance quote or loan. There's information on our sales team, a map locator, competitions and the Easy calc to work out quotes.

CHART 7 - TABLE OF HALF YEARLY REPAYMENTS

Six monthly loan repayments per €1,000 borrowed						
Term in Years	**4%**	**5%**	**6%**	**7%**	**8%**	**9%**
2	263	268	272	276	281	284
3	179	183	187	190	194	197
4	137	141	142	145	148	151
5	111	115	116	122	124	128
6	95	98	100	103	106	110
7	83	86	88	92	95	98
8	74	77	79	82	86	89
9	67	71	75	76	80	83
10	61	64	66	70	74	77
11	57	60	63	66	70	73
12	53	56	59	62	65	69
13	50	53	57	60	63	67
14	47	51	54	57	60	64
15	45	48	52	55	59	62
16	43	47	50	53	56	60
20	37	40	43	46	50	54

McQUINN
CONSULTING

Oakview, Brewery Road, Tralee, Co. Kerry.
Tel.: 066-7129355/7129397 Fax: 066-7129404
E-mail: info@mcquinnconsulting.com Website: www.mcquinnconsulting.com

AGRI/BUSINESS

Income Tax Returns

CAT/CGT/VAT

PAYE/PRSI Returns

Business Development and Management

Company Formation

FARM CONSULTANCY

Expert Witness Reporting

CPO Claims & Negotiations

Loss Assessment

Farm Retirement Scheme

E.U. Schemes

ENVIRONMENTAL SERVICES

REPS Approved Planners

Nutrient Management Planning

Environmental Impact Statements

PROPERTY SERVICES

Property Dealing

Leases

Valuations

Quota Trading

FINANCIAL SERVICES

Lending Advice

Investment Advice

Loan Applications

Pensions & Life Assurance

Credit Negotiations

Share Dealing

Business Start Ups

TABLE 8 - CURRENT RATES OF PREMIUMS & SUBSIDIES

	RATE (€)
LIVESTOCK PREMIUMS	
Suckler cow premium	224.19 / head
National Envelope - Suckler Cow Premium (2002 payment)	Approx. 76.2 / head
Special beef premium	150.00 / head
Bull Beef Premium	210.04 / head
Extensification premium	Low 40.00 / head High 80.00 /head
Slaughter premium	80.00 / head
Ewe premium	21.00 / head
Rural world premium (disadvantaged areas)	7.00 / head
ARABLE AID	
Cereals	383.04 / ha
Maize (base area dependant)	365.40 / ha
Proteins	440.80 / ha
Oilseeds	383.10 / ha
Linseeds	383.10 / ha
Set-asisde	383.04 / ha
DISADVANTAGED AREAS PAYMENTS	
Mountain Areas	101.58 on first 10 ha 88.88 thereafter up to a max. of 45ha,
More Severely Handicapped	88.88 up to 45 ha
Less Severely Handicapped	76.18 up to 45 ha

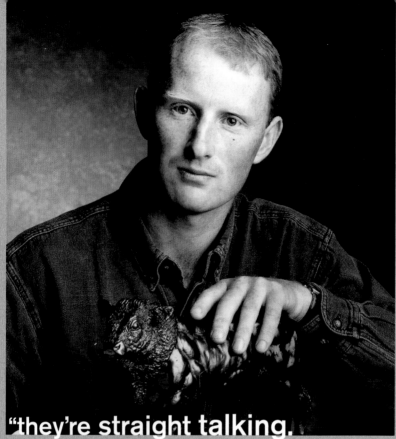

"they're straight talking, they leave the bull in the field"

Michael Clarke, Farmer, Turloughmore, Athenry, Co. Galway

You get a lot of time to think, working on a farm. And heaven knows, there's plenty to be thinking about these days.

On top of worrying about your stock, equipment, vet's bills, hygiene and employees, there's the market to think about. Make no mistake about it - farming is a business.

At FBD they've thought about my business and it shows. FBD's range of policies is designed to meet farmer's needs and farmer's budgets. When they talk, they talk turkey, not bull.

Peace of mind at the right price

tel: (01) 409 3200 email: info@fbd.ie
website: www.fbd.ie

TABLE 9 - CONVERSION FACTORS

To Convert	Multiply By	To Convert	Multiply By
inches to centimetres	2.54	cu. cm. to cu. inches	0.06102
centimetres to inches	0.3937	cu. feet to cu. metres	0.02831
feet to metres	0.3048	cu. metres to cu. feet	35.3147
metres to feet	3.2808	cu. yards to cu. metres	0.7646
yards to metres	0.9144	cu. metres to cu. yards	1.3079
metres to yards	1.09361	cu. inches to litres	0.1638
miles to kilometres	1.60934	litres to cu. inches	61.03
kilometres to miles	0.62317	gallons to litres	4.545
sq. in. to sq. centimetres	6.4516	litres to gallons	0.22
sq. cm. to sq. inch	0.15499	ounces to grams	28.3495
sq. metres to sq. feet	10. 7638	grams to ounces	0.03528
sq. feet to sq. metres	0.092903	pounds to grams	453.592
sq. yards to sq. metres	0.836103	grams to pounds	0.03528
sq. metres to sq. yards	1.19599	pounds to kilograms	0.4536
sq. miles to sq. km.	2.5899	kilograms to pounds	2.2046
sq. km. to sq. miles	0.386103	tons to kilograms	1,016.05
acres to hectares	0.40468	kilograms to tons	0.00098
hectares to acres	2.47105		

Outlook for Agriculture Policy in 2003

Michael Berkery, General Secretary, IFA

The year gone by has been a most difficult one for IFA and for farmers. Product prices for the main products, milk, cattle, pigs and grain are all unacceptably low. The summer weather was extremely bad, which increased costs and depressed production. At EU policy level, the substantial changes to the CAP contained in the Commission's mid-term review have added to uncertainty amongst farmers about the future. At year-end, the cut-backs in public expenditure threaten a number of schemes of importance to farmers at a time when farm incomes are under pressure. Thus farmers are not entering 2003 from a position of prosperity or in a mood of confidence. Much of the policy agenda for the coming year, both at EU and national level, is already well signalled, and I will outline the main issues.

CAP MID-TERM REVIEW

The proposals from Commissioner Fischler last July went far beyond a review of the CAP and would involve a major reform, particularly the plans to "modulate" direct payments, i.e. cut them by 20%, and to "decouple" payments, i.e. break the link between the direct payment and the level of production on farms. However, the EU Summit decisions in October on the funding of the CAP after 2006 remove the case for an early reform of CAP. IFA's position has been that the Agenda 2000 decisions should have been allowed to run their full course, and indeed it made no sense for the EU to be planning further cuts to the CAP at least before the WTO negotiations were concluded in a few years time.

While there continues to be some uncertainty about the timetable, it is now likely that modulation is off the agenda until 2006 or 2007. Fischler is still battling to have his decoupling proposals kept on the table, but the Council of Ministers is more likely to defer this as well. The Council of Ministers will have to make up its mind early in the New Year on the CAP review because the EU is obliged to set out its stall in detail in the WTO by the end of March (see later).

Also, it must not be forgotten that the Agenda 2000 decisions to cut milk support prices by 15% in the 2005 – 07 period, with some limited compensation, is still facing us. IFA is making the case that this should be deferred for a further period which would make sense in CAP budget terms, but that would require a new decision by the Council of Ministers.

WTO NEGOTIATIONS

The EU countries are amongst the 140 countries that are members of the World Trade Organisation. Over a year ago, a new round of WTO negotiations was launched at Doha. The EU negotiates as a unit and the negotiations are led by the Commission on behalf of the member states. The terms of reference are to continue the process of reducing protection and support for agriculture. All three "pillars" of support are subject to negotiation: import tariffs, export subsidies and internal supports, and also what are termed "non-trade concerns" which includes issues such as animal welfare, the environment and use of artificial growth promoters.

All the participants in the WTO are required to put forward their general proposals to achieve the Doha objectives by 31 March next. A positive development from our perspective is that the recent US Farm Act is highly supportive of their own farmers, and this should mean that the WTO negotiations will be slow and difficult. Also, the EU approach is far from unified; between the Fischler view that we should rush for decoupled direct payments and phase down price supports, and the French Government view that further reform should be gradual and that farm incomes are an important consideration in deciding future CAP policy. However, we must also be aware that there is pressure on the EU both from the underdeveloped countries and from the food exporting countries such as Australia and New Zealand to gain greater access to the EU food market.

The present deadline is that the WTO negotiations on agriculture would be completed by January 2005, but that seems unlikely to be met. Any new agreement would be subsequently phased in over a period of 5 or 6 years.

EU ENLARGEMENT

It is decided that ten countries of Central and Eastern Europe will become members of the EU from May 2004, assuming that their peoples vote in favour of membership. As regards the extension of the CAP to the new members, the accession negotiations are due to be completed by the end of 2002. Most of the big decisions are already made. The new members will have to accept supply management (quotas, premium quotas and base areas) based on recent historic production levels. They will benefit from full CAP price supports on entry, and the direct payments will be phased in, starting at 25% in 2004, 40% by 2007 and reaching parity with the EU level in 2013.

The CAP budget for the EU of 25 has recently been agreed by the EU Summit. It will increase from about €43 billion in 2004 to €45.7bn in 2007 to €48.6bn by 2013, and about €5bn of the 2013 total is allocated for direct payments in the 10 new states. At least there is now reasonable certainty about the funding of CAP for the next decade. While the budget is tight, the challenge is to devise a CAP structure that can provide reasonable support to farmers through a combination of market prices and direct payments within this budget.

MID-TERM REVIEW OF THE NATIONAL DEVELOPMENT PLAN

The National Development Plan 2000-06 (NDP) covers a range of schemes of importance to farmers. These include the four "CAP Rural Development" measures namely REPS, Early Retirement, Disadvantaged Areas, and Forestry, and the on-farm investment measures including Farm Waste Management and Dairy Hygiene, and also the Installation scheme. In the case of most of these measures the expenditure in the first three years is well lower than provided for in the NDP. This has been due to a number of factors including the late introduction of some schemes, the disruption due to Foot and Mouth disease in 2001 and the income pressure on farmers. IFA's priority in the mid-term review will be to seek to retain the level of funding for these measures in the NDP and to utilise the underspent allocation to-date to make improvements to the schemes.

THE ENVIRONMENT / NITRATES DIRECTIVE

IFA is particularly concerned about the increased pressure likely to come on farmers in 2003 to comply with the terms of the EU Nitrates Directive. While negotiations with Government on this issue have not yet been completed, it is clear that farmers will be particularly reliant on two schemes: REPS and Farm Waste Management.

IFA is proposing improvements to REPS which should encourage many more farmers to participate in the scheme and thereby meet the terms of the Nitrates Directive. The current level of participation at less than 40,000 is far below the Government's own projections in the NDP. As regards grant aid for farm investment, the allocation in the 2003 Book of Estimates at only €31m is a cut of 44% on the allocation for 2002. This is unacceptable to IFA and we will insist on adequate funding to keep the scheme open in the event of demand increasing substantially in 2003.

PRODUCT PRICES, PRICE SUPPORTS, PROCESSING COSTS AND MARKETING

The price levels for the main sectors of agriculture, particularly milk and beef, which account for two-thirds of total agricultural output, have a major impact on farm income. The EU beef market has made a very strong recovery from the last BSE crisis of late 2000 and is now back in balance. In 2002, Ireland is exporting 250,000 tonnes or over half of production to the high-priced UK market. Going forward, we must consolidate our position in the UK, increase our product level on retail shelves, and grow our export levels to other EU country markets. The target must be to move Irish cattle prices off the bottom of the EU price league, to at least the average EU price which is €2.80/kg or £1/lb.

In the dairy sector, commodity prices continue to be weak. Farmers have had to live on lower margins in 2002 and it is time that the dairy processors also cut their costs including further rationalisation in the industry. The EU Commission also needs to change its policies in order to allow dairy products to trade above the intervention price and enable markets to recover. It needs to adopt a more targeted and aggressive policy on export refunds and internal market aids to allow more stable trading conditions for milk producers in the EU.

SCALE AND COMPETITIVENESS AT FARM LEVEL
While many farmers are opting for an off-farm job as the only realistic means of earning a viable family income, others wish to remain in full-time farming on a commercial basis. Both groups of farmers need supportive policies. The Government's National Spatial Strategy recently published is intended to promote more balanced regional development and thereby provide a better spread of employment opportunities around the country.

For those farmers who wish to stay full-time in farming, many need to increase their scale and efficiency to provide a reasonable income. A key requirement is access to more land at a reasonable price. That is why IFA is making a major push in the negotiations with Government for incentives, through tax relief and social welfare dis-allowances, to encourage medium-term land leasing at an affordable price.

2 December 2002.

Agricultural Consultants Association of Ireland
A.C.A.
www.agriculturalconsultantsassociation.com

The Agricultural Consultants Association (A.C.A.) is the professional body representing the majority of private agricultural consultants . Members hold a B. Agr. Sc. or an equivalent qualification and have at least two years experience.

Services Provided

- Farm Financial Advice
- Farm Accounts & Taxation
- Agri Litigation and Loss Reporting
- Environmental Impact Consultancy
- REPS Planning

- Farm Management Advice
- C.P.O. Compensation Reporting
- Professional witness reporting
- Forest Management Consultancy
- Rural Development Projects

Munster

Ken Baker, Drummin, Ardnacrusha, Co. Clare.	Ph. 061-328774
John G. Barlow, 14 Davis St, Tipperary Town.	Ph. 062 - 33888
Michael Brady, Corran, Waterfall, Near Cork.	Ph. 021-4885699
Tom Butler, Farm Business Advisors Ltd, FBA Hse, Cork Rd, Fermoy.	Ph. 025-31244
Anthony D. Cleary, Bantis House, Cloughjordan, Co. Tipperary.	Ph. 067-29073
John Collins, Ballinastona, Kilmallock, Co. Limerick.	Ph. 061-382217
John Crowley, Rathroon, Bandon, Co. Cork.	Ph. 023-49854
Patrick Fitzsimons, 32 Grand Parade, Cork.	Ph. 021-4276366
Thomas Hanrahan, Kilworth, Fermoy, Co. Cork	Ph. 025-27123
James Kennedy, Kennedy & Assoc., West Inch, Annascaul, Co. Kerry.	Ph. 066-9157327
Eamon Larkin , 3 Willow Grove, Old Cratloe Road, Limerick.	Ph: 061-451483.
William Martin, 16 St.Patrick's Hill, Cork.	Ph. 021-4501338
Tom McMahon, 1 Church St., Newcastlewest, Co. Limerick,	Ph. 069-62219
Eddie McQuinn, Oak View, Brewery Road, Tralee, Co. Kerry.	Ph. 066-7129355
Terence Morrissey, 87 O'Connell St., Dungarvan, Co. Waterford	Ph. 05844995
Larry Murnane , Ballymacreese, Ballyneety, Co. Limerick.	Ph. 061-351286
Gerard O'Brien, Ambleside, Clongower, Thurles, Co.Tipperary..	Ph. 0504-21834
Philip O' Dwyer, Foxfort, Causeway, Co. Kerry.	Ph: 066-7131952.
Dan O'Keefe, Unit 9, Robert Scott House, Cork.	Ph. 021-4551638
Martin O'Sullivan, O'Sullivan & Co., Bank Hse, Carrick-on-Suir, CoTipp.	Ph. 051 - 640397

Munster contd.,

Richard Rea, Martin & Rea Ltd. 8 Grattan St., Tipperary	Ph. 062-52166
Charles Smyth, 35 Bridgefield ,Lewis Rd, Killarney, Co.Kerry	Ph.064 - 37414
David Walsh, Kilmacogue, Oola, Co. Limerick.	Ph: 062-47657.

Leinster

Francis Ashe, Ashe Rountree & Co., 24 Mountjoy Sq., Dublin 1.	Ph. 01-6785900
Dr. N. Bielenberg, Stewarts Ltd., 47 Laverty Court, Dublin 2.	Ph. 01-6760964
John Britton, ACE Consultancy Services, Tober, Dunlavin, Co.Wicklow.	Ph. 045-401344
Michael Cahill, 9 Connawood Grove, Old Connaught Ave, Bray, Co.Wicklow.	Ph. 01-2821793
James Carton, Philip Farrelly & Partners, 23 Willowbrook, Mullingar, Co. Westmeath.	Ph. 044-44710
Ultan Conway, ,Moatstown, Kildalkey, Navan, Co. Meath.	Ph. 046-35142
Enda Cullinan, Curravanish, Tinahely, Co. Wicklow.	Ph. 0402-38578
Thomas Dolan, Loughfield, Baltrasna, Moate, Co. Westmeath.	Ph. 0902-81799
Andy Dunne, Shamrock House, Abbeyleix Rd, Portlaoise, Co. Laois.	Ph. 0502-20157
Andy Egan, 21 Main Street, Longford, Co. Longford.	Ph. 043-45720
Philip Farrelly, Philip Farrelly & Partners, 2 Kennedy Road, Navan, Co. Meath.	Ph. 046-23934
Joseph Harte, Danesbrook, Laracor, Trim, Co. Meath.	Ph. 046-31432
Frank Hevey, Killyon, Hill of Down, Enfield, Co. Meath.	Ph.046-71818
Michael Kelly, Monteen, Thomastown,Co.Kilkenny.	Ph. 056-24655
James Kirwan, Clongowney, Banagher, Co. Offaly	Ph. 0509-51365
Patrick Minnock, The Stream, Dublin Road, Carlow.	Ph. 0503-43780
Peadar Moynihan, Oldtown, Johnstown, Navan, Co. Meath.	Ph.046-71262,
Bridget Murray, Newcastle Farm, Newcastle, Co. Dublin.	Ph. 01-4589335
Niall O'Keefe, Corbertstown, Killucan, Co. Westmeath.	Ph. 044-74192
John Rountree, Ashe Rountree & Co, 24 Mountjoy Sq. Dublin 1.	Ph. 01 6785900
Jim Ryan, Jim Ryan & Ass's, Headstown, Castletown, Navan, Co. Meath.	Ph. 046-52499
Aidan Wall, Aidan Wall & Associates, Bective Square, Kells, Co. Meath.	Ph. 046-40961

Connaught/Ulster

Thomas Canning, Ballyvary, Castlebar, Co.Mayo.	Ph. 094-31675
Brian Carroll, The Deanery, Main St., Swinford, Co.Mayo.	Ph. 094-53742
Anne-Marie Clarke, Rea Clarke & Assoc., Clare St. Ballina Co. Mayo	Ph. 096-72776,
Vincent Costello, New Inn, Ballinasloe, Co. Galway.	Ph. 0905-75606
Oliver Crowe, Castle Street, Killeshandra, Co. Cavan.	Ph. 049-4334462
Brian Dolan, Cashelmane, Creeslough, Co.Donegal.	Ph. 070-38322

Connaught/Ulster contd.,

Justin Feeney, Dromore West, Co. Sligo.	Ph. 096-47350
Noel Feeney, Philip Farrelly & Partners, Bridge St, Carrick on Shannon, .	Ph. 078-21920
Michael Finn, Ballycahalan, Peterswell, Co. Galway.	Ph. 091-631434
Pauric Henry, Mayville, Roselawn Drive, Castlerea, Co. Roscommon.	Ph. 0907-20130
John Kenny, Pearse St, Ballina, Co. Mayo.	Ph. 096-21996
Pauraic Larkin,P.Larkin & Assoc. Clooneen, Athleague, Co. Roscommon.	Ph. 0903-63304
Peter Martyn, Carrick Hill, Breaffy, Castlebar. Co. Mayo.	Ph. 094-22737
John McLoone, Lower Main Street, Glenties, Co. Donegal.	Ph. 075-51234
Michael Moloney, Pollavaddy, Balla, Castlebar, Co.Mayo	Ph. 094-66943
John O'Connor, Credit Union Bld., Dublin Rd, Tuam, Co. Galway	Ph. 093-24809
Ned O'Connor, 16 Kildallogue Heights, Strokestown, Co. Roscommon.	Ph. 078-33243
Andrew Roohan, Clyhore, Ballyshannon, Co. Donegal.	Ph. 072-52756
Liam Walsh, 30 Corcoran Terrace, Ballina, Co. Mayo.	Ph. 096-72791
William Walsh, Main Street, Ballinrobe, Co. Mayo.	Ph 092-41711

FOREST MANAGEMENT CONSULTANTS

Padraig Dolan, Derrybeg, Killeagh Tullamore, Co. Offaly.	Ph. 0506-52609
Paddy Donovan, Prospect, Maree, Oranmore, Co. Galway.	Ph. 091-792392 ,
Paul Finnegan, Newline, Ballycrissane, Ballinasloe, Co. Galway	Ph. 0905-75287
Donal Fitzpatrick, Lifford House, Ennis, Co. Clare	Ph. 065-6821518
Dermot Houlihan, 27 Bushy Park, Circular Road, Galway.	Ph. 091-527580
Peter O'Brien, Glenmore Hse., The Spa, Tralee, Kerry.	Ph. 066-7136506
Patrick Purser, 36 Fitzwilliam Square, Dublin 2.	Ph. 01-6625621
Fionan Russell, Dunderry, Navan, Co. Meath.	Ph. 046 38588
Colman Young, "Ashlu" Newpark Portlaoise Co. Laois.	Ph. 0502-21678

Further information from:
Ann Marie Clarke,
Hon-Secretary, ACA,
8 Grattan St.,
Tipperary.
Ph. 062-52166

Part 1 - Dealing with the Department

ACCESS TO THE DEPARTMENT

OPENING HOURS
All Department offices are open to the public from 9.30 a.m. to 12.30 p.m. and from 2.00 p.m. to 5.00 p.m. in the evening.

TELEPHONE QUERIES
Table 1.1 sets out all of the various sections of the Department that farmers may need to contact. Telephone calls are charged at the rate of a local call if the lo-call numbers are used as set out below.

Table 1.1 Department contact numbers

Office	Lo-call Number
Agriculture House - Head Office	1890 200 510
Accomodation/Co-ordination/Health/Safety	1890-200-510
Appeals Unit	1890 200 510
Area Aid Unit - Cork, Kerry, Limerick	1890 200 503
Area Aid Unit - Clare, Galway, Roscommon	1890 200 502
Area Aid Unit - Donegal, Mayo, Sligo	1890 200 504
Area Aid Unit - Carlow, Dublin, Kildare, Kilkenny, Tipperary, Laois.	1890 200 505
Area Aid Unit - Cavan, Leitrim, Longford, Louth, Meath, Monaghan, Offaly, Westmeath	1890 200 498
Area Aid Unit - , Waterford, Wexford, Wicklow	1890 200 505
Farm Retirement Scheme	1890 200 509
Installation Aid Scheme	1890 200 508
Milk Policy Division	1890 200 510
Organic Farming	1890 200 509
REPS	1890 200 509
Special Beef Premium Unit - Portlaoise	1890 200 506

PROBLEMS WITH APPLICATIONS

LIVESTOCK AND ARABLE SCHEMES

ROUTINE PROBLEMS

The Department of Agriculture, Food and Rural Development undertake that problems with applications that are identified as a result of administrative checks will be drawn to the attention of the applicant as soon as possible after discovery. The maximum response time for alerting applicants to problems with the various scheme applications is set out hereunder:

Table 1.2: Maximum response time for routine problems

Scheme	Maximum Response Time
Suckler Cow Premium	Within 4 weeks of discovery
Special Beef Premium	Within 4 weeks of discovery
Ewe Premium	Within 3 weeks of discovery
Slaughter Premium	Notified to producers through quarterly producer statements. Responses will be processed within 4 weeks of receipt and the results will be incorporated in the producers next quarterly statement.
Area Aid	Majority of problem applications notified to the farmer by 15 September. All problems should be notifed not later than 30 September. If the applicant responds within 14 days, thereby clarifying the problem, the application should be processed by 16 October.

PROBLEMS AS A RESULT OF AN INSPECTION

Problems with applications which are identified as a result of an inspection must be drawn to the attention of the farmer or their representative at the time of inspection. The applicant should be given an opportunity to provide an explanation. Alternatively, the applicant can provide a written clarification within seven days of the inspection. This explanation or clarification should be taken into account before a decision is made by the inspector.

PROCEDURE FOR DEALING WITH PROBLEMS

Table 1.3: Procedure for dealing with problems

Stage	Action by Department	Action by Farmer
1. Problem identified in course of administrative checks or inspection	**Notification** Letter to applicant setting out nature of problem and likely consequences if not resolved	Applicant has 14 days to respond providing an explanation or clarification of the problem
2. Applicant does not respond within 14 days	**Reminder** Reminder letter to applicant as in step 1 above and allowing a further 14 days for reply	Applicant has further 14 days to respond providing an explanation or clarification of the problem
3. Applicant either responds to letter or reminder or does not respond within 14 days to reminder	**Notice of Decision** Letter to applicant setting out decision on application based on information available to the Department. Where the applicant has responded the response will be taken into consideration.	Applicant either accepts the decision or may apply to have the decision reviewed within 14 days of the date of notice of the decision. Alternatively, applicant may appeal the Agricultural Appeals Office.

The Department will specify the reply date on the correspondence where they decide that a query will take an applicant more that 14 days to deal with.

EARLY RETIREMENT SCHEME AND REPS

Table 1.4: Maximum response time for ERS and REPS problems

Stage	Maximum Response Time
Early Retirement Scheme	
administrative validation check	Within 4 weeks of receipt of application
prepayment inspection	Within 4 weeks of the inspection
REPS	
prepayment inspection	Within 4 weeks of inspection
annual compliance check	Within 4 weeks of inspection

29

EARLY RETIREMENT SCHEME

Applications for the retirement scheme are submitted to the Early Retirement Section in Wexford where they are initially subjected to an administrative check to ensure that all relevant documents are not missing. If some documents are missing the Section will grant the applicant 10 working days in which to rectify matters, otherwise payment will only commence from the date that all documentation has been submitted..

Complete applications will be passed on to the relevant FDS local offices for processing. A sample of these application will be selected for prepayment inspection.

RURAL ENVIRONMENT PROTECTION SCHEME

Applications for the REPS scheme will be submitted to local FDS offices. Applications for second and subsequent payments will be sent to participants prior to their anniversary dates. The responsibility lies with the applicant to ensure that application is returned on time.

SPLIT HOLDINGS

There are a number of EU directives that govern the splitting of holdings. In particular the EU and the Department of Agriculture, Food and Rural Development are trying to ensure that farms are not split for the purpose of receiving more subsidies or premium payments. Where they are suspicious that such has been the case Department of Agriculture, Food and Rural Development inspectors will assess each case on it's individual merits. However, in general the following criteria, if all present should satisfy an inspector that two holdings constitute individual units:

- Legally separate, i.e. separate ownership or held under a properly executed lease,
- Separate management, i.e. not managed as part of a joint enterprise with another holding.

The following characteristics are deemed to constitute evidence of separate management:

- Separate herd numbers
- Herds kept separately, i.e. no intermixing,
- Herds handled separately in separate handling facilities
- Separate Area Aid applications
- Separate REPS applications, where applicable

- Stock-proofed boundaries between such holdings, where they are adjoining, with no access other than through a public access
- Separate farm accounts / farm profiles / receipts as applicable
- Separate PPSN number for each applicant

In the event of a dispute the case may be referred to the Agricultural Appeals Office, once operational.

INSPECTIONS

LEVEL OF INSPECTION

All schemes require the inspection of a minimum number of applications. For the area aid schemes the applications are selected for inspection on the basis of risk analysis. For the livestock schemes inspections are based on risk analysis and random selection. For on-farm investment schemes all applications are subject to inspections. The minimum level of inspections for the various schemes are set out on page 33.

LIVESTOCK AND ARABLE INSPECTION PROCEDURES

INSPECTORS' OBLIGATIONS

When notice is give of an inspection, the period of notice cannot exceed 48 hours. Inspectors, on arrival should introduce themselves, produce identification and state the purpose of the visit. They should then explain the inspection procedure and satisfy themselves that the applicant understands it. If the applicant or any representative is not present, the inspection will proceed anyway. In this case the inspector should leave written notification that an inspection has taken place including the inspector's name and phone number. If an inspector is unduly delayed at a previous inspection the applicant should be contacted as soon as possible and not later than one hour before the appointed time for the inspection. If the inspection cannot be carried out that day an alternative arrangement will be made in agreement with the applicant

On completion of the inspection if noncompliance is found the applicant or their representative should be informed of what has been found and how the findings do not comply with the requirements of the scheme. The applicant should then be invited to provide an explanation of the noncompliance either at the time of the inspection or within seven days of the date of the inspection. Any explanation tendered will be noted in the inspector's report. The farmer should also have the opportunity to write their comments on the inspector's report.

FARMERS' OBLIGATIONS

If the farmer cannot be present he/she can arrange for a representative to attend on his/her behalf. If the applicant fails to cooperate with the inspection the application will be rejected.

LIVESTOCK INSPECTIONS

For livestock inspections a notification card is send out to the farmer detailing the scheme to be inspected and the animals that should be available.

The following points are worthy of note:

- The farmer is obliged to present and handle each animal as required by the inspector
- Disinfectant facilities should be available
- Hogget ewes should be penned separately for Ewe Premium
- Special Beef Premium inspections require a check of all male animals on the holding
- Suckler Cow Premium inspections necessitate a check of all female animals
- Extensification Premium inspections require a check of all animals on the holding
- Slaughter Premium inspectors check all the slaughter receipts and the herd register
- The herd register should be fully up to-date and available for all livestock inspections

ARABLE / AREA AID INSPECTIONS

Arable aid inspections will normally be carried out before August 10 each year, i.e. commencement of the harvest. Where the area of a parcel of land is in dispute the inspector will carry out field measurements on site.

Table 1.5: Inspection rate

Scheme	Applications to be Inspected
Suckler Cow Premium	10%
Special Beef Premium	10%
Ewe Premium	10%
Extensification Premium	10% (integrated with other inspections)
New Slaughter Premium	10% (integrated with other inspections)
Disadvantaged Areas Compensatory Allowances	5% for Area Based Scheme
Arable Aid / Area Aid	5%
Early Retirement Scheme	• Prepayment inspection 10% • Annual compliance inspection 10%
Rural Environment Protection Scheme - Application for admission to scheme - Application for Annual Payment	• Applications from previous participants in the REPS 5% • Applications from first time participants 10% • Annual compliance inspection 25% • Annual plan check and farm visit 5%
Farm Waste Management Scheme	• Pre-approval inspection 100% • On completion of work, prepayment inspection 100%
Dairy Hygiene Scheme	• Pre-approval inspection 100% • On completion of work, prepayment inspection 100%
Alternative Enterprise Scheme	• Pre-approval inspection 100% • On completion of work, prepayment inspection 100%
Installation Aid	• Pre-approval inspection 10%

FARM DEVELOPMENT INSPECTION PROCEDURES

- All REPS, ERS and Installation Aid inspections are required to be unannounced. The date and time for inspections relating to On-Farm Investment schemes should be arranged with the applicant.
- On arrival the inspector should present identification, state the purpose of the visit and explain the inspection procedure to the farmer. The inspector should be satisfied that the farmer understands the procedure.

33

- In the case of prearranged inspections the applicant can arrange to be represented by another person. However, if either the applicant or any representative is absent the inspection will take place anyway. In this case the inspector should leave written notice that the inspection has taken place. They should also leave the name and phone number of the inspector and note whether any problems were identified.
- In the case of a REPS or ERS inspection, where the inspector considers that an inspection may be imposed the applicant should be informed, if present. The decision to apply a penalty should be notified to the applicant within four weeks of the inspection. The applicant will then have ten days to submit their comments from the date on the letter of notification.

PAYMENT AND DECISION DEADLINES

SUCKLER COW PREMIUM
Advance payments of 60% will commence on 16 October of the year of application. Where the retention period is completed by 16 October all eligible advance payments will be made by 1 December. In other eligible cases the advance payments will be made within 30 days of the end of the retention period.

Balancing payments will commence early in the following year with a view to paying all clear cases by 28 February. Payment in all problem cases subsequently found eligible will be made by 30 June.

SPECIAL BEEF PREMIUM
The advance payments of 60% should commence on 16 October. Where the retention period is completed by 16 October all eligible advance payments will be made by 1 December. In other eligible cases the advance payments will be made within 30 days of the end of the retention period. Payment of the balance due should commence in the following year when the full quota usage for the year has been determined. However, payment of all eligible cases should be made by 30 June.

EWE PREMIUM
Payment of the Ewe Premium will be made in October of each year.

SLAUGHTER PREMIUM
As with the Special Beef Premium the 60% advance should commence on 16 October. The balancing payment will be made the following year once the national quota usage is determined. Eligible payments should be completed by 30 June in line with EU rules.

EXTENSIFICATION PREMIUM
All extensification payments should be made in June of the year following the year for which eligibility is established.

ARABLE AID
Payment in eligible cases should be made in the first payment run which commences on 16 November. In cases where there are still outstanding queries payment will be made by 31 January, provided that any response received is sufficient to clarify the problems that existed.

DISADVANTAGED AREAS COMPENSATORY ALLOWANCES
The Area Based Compensatory Allowance Scheme which commenced in 2001 is paid annually in one installment in September.

EARLY RETIREMENT SCHEME
Under the Early Retirement Scheme all applications not selected for prepayment inspection will be approved for payment within 10 weeks. Where an application is selected for inspection an additional two weeks should be allowed. Once applications are approved the issue of payment should follow within six weeks. Payments will be made monthly thereafter for the duration of the pension period. It is important to note that initial payments will be back dated to the date that a valid application was received by the Department of Agriculture, Food and Rural Development.

RURAL ENVIRONMENT PROTECTION SCHEME
New applicants who are applying for the first time should have their applications approved within twelve weeks, provided that no prepayment inspection is due. If an inspection is required the application should be processed within fourteen weeks. The

payment normally issues within one month of approval. Where the applicant is applying for a second or subsequent payment the application should be processed within ten weeks with payment following a month afterwards. Under the proposed new scheme it is envisaged that applications for second or subsequent payments will not be held up if inspections are due. The inspection may even take place after the payment is made. If a penalty is to be applied it will be deducted from the following years payment or from other subsidies in the case of final year applicants.

FARM WASTE MANAGEMENT SCHEME, DAIRY HYGIENE SCHEME AND ALTERNATIVE ENTERPRISE SCHEME

The initial approval for the grant should be forthcoming within three months of submission of a valid application. In order for payment to be cleared the applicant must submit notice of completion of the works with supporting documentation. Approval should be forthcoming within three months of the submission of this documentation. The payment should then issue within six weeks of the approval for payment.

INSTALLATION AID

If the application is not selected for a prepayment inspection it should be approved for payment within ten weeks of the 'application for payment'.. If an inspection is required approval should still be forthcoming within twelve weeks. The applicant will usually receive the actual payment within six weeks of approval.

APPEALS

The Government plans to provide an independent appeals office to adjudicate upon appeals from farmers who are dissatisfied with decisions taken by the Department of Agriculture, Food and Rural Development. This new office will be called the Agriculture Appeals Office. The remit of this office will extend to schemes including REPS, Early Retirement Scheme, Installation Aid as well as all the livestock headage and premium schemes.

This office will be fully independent of the Department of Agriculture, Food and Rural Development and it's officials. The appeals officers will have the power to conduct oral hearings, to call witnesses and to take evidence on oath, if necessary. The decisions of the appeals officers will be binding on the Department.

TRANSITIONAL ARRANGEMENTS

Pending the establishment of the Agriculture Appeals Office the headage and premium appeals unit will continue to operate. This will also be the case with the REPS Appeals Office.

APPEALS PROCEDURE

Before taking an appeal to the Agriculture Appeals Office the applicant must first exhaust all avenues of appeal within the section that deals with the scheme involved. For example if a farmer had a problem with a penalty that was imposed on his or her farm following a REPS inspection the farmer would first have to appeal the imposition of the penalty to his own local FDS office. Only when this appeal is rejected can the farmer appeal to the REPS appeals office. In some cases farmers may have to make appeals to two levels of Department officials before they can apply to the appeals office.

COMPLAINTS

Farmers have a right to complain if they feel that they have not received an appropriate level of service. Complaints should be made initially to the senior officer in charge of the area to which the complaint relates. This complaint can be made in person or in writing. Where the farmer is not satisfied with the response they may pursue the matter with the Quality Services Officer. The Quality Services Officer should then have the matter fully investigated. This should be done impartially by an officer who was not involved in the matter giving rise to the complaint.

The Quality Services Officer may be contacted at the Quality Services Unit, Department of Agriculture, Food and Rural Development, Agriculture House, Kildare Street, Dublin 2. Tel: 01-6072694 or Lo-Call 1890 20 05 10 ext. 2694.

Finally if a farmer is still unhappy with the service provided he can contact the office of the Ombudsman at 18 Lower Leeson Lane, Dublin 2. Tel: 01-6785222 or Lo-Call 1890 22 30 30.

Part 2 - Farm Investment Grants

FARM WASTE MANAGEMENT SCHEME

The Farm Waste Management Scheme (FWM) replaces the Control of Farmyard Pollution Scheme and will have funding of €18.2m per year available up until 2007.

ELIGIBLE APPLICANTS

The scheme is open to farmers who:

- have more than 30 income units and less than 200. Calculation of these income units takes into account each applicant's farming activities and off-farm activities at the rate of €254 gross off-farm income per unit. At least 20 of the income units must be derived from farming.
- who are landowners or lease holders of lands on which it is proposed to carry out the development.
- if born after 01/01/75, hold a certificate in farming, or has received at least 180 hours recognised training in agriculture or horticulture and has at least three years farming experience. In the case of applications from joint herdowners or partnerships only one of the parties involved need meet the trining requirements.
- if born before 01/01/75 has been engaged in farming for at least five years .
- whose lands have been declared for area aid.
- Undertake to follow good farming practice.

ELIGIBLE INVESTMENT

The scheme aims to control farm pollution by providing grant aid to farmers for animal housing, farm yards and storage facilities for silage and agricultural wastes. The following are some of the proposed activities that the new scheme will cover.

- Slatted houses, loose houses, cubicle houses, isolation houses, sheep housing
- Hay barns, silage slabs, concrete silo (unroofed), silo walls to existing silo bases
- Waste storage facilities, dungsteads, lagoons (lined), effluent tanks
- Roofs for livestock feeding areas
- Fixed slurry pumps, agitators, protective fending, yard drains, automatic scrapers.

- Sheep accommodation, roofed and unroofed. Sheep dipping tanks, cattle crushes
- Mobile equipment, including slurry tankers, slurry injection systems, rotary spreaders and dual spreaders

With regard to mobile equipment grant aid of 20% will be available within an investment limit of €7,620.

INCOME UNITS
Income units are calculated for the various farm enterprises as follows:

400 gallons milk	1 Units
All bovines (excl. dairy cows) over 2 yrs.	1 Unit
Bovines 6 mths. to 24 mths.	0.6 Units
Ewes	0.15 Units
Horses	1 Unit
Fallow/sitka deer	0.15 Units
Red deer	0.3 Units
Sows breeding only	0.8 Units
Sows breeding and finishing	1.1 Units
Tillage per hectare (e.g.. cereals)	1 Unit
Intensive tillage per hectare (incl. beet and potatoes)	2 Units
Forestry per hectare	1 Unit
Off farm income (each €254 gross income)	1 Unit

PLANNING PERMISSION
If planning permission is necessary, it must accompany the application. In general, a building is exempt from planning where the floor area does not exceed 300 square metres and the total floor area of all buildings within a class does not exceed 450 square metres (animal housing; or other waste producing buildings) or 900 square metres (dry buildings). Buildings within 10 metres of a public road, or within 100 metres from a neighbouring dwelling or school may require planning permission.

GRANT RATES

Table 2.1 Rates of Farm Waste Management Grants

Investment	Applicants with not more than 150 IU's	Applicants with 150 to 200 IU's
Waste storage facilities. Animal housing (sheep & bovines). Silage storage facilities. Associated facilities.	40%	20%
Mobile equipment for application of farm wastes. (there must be adequate waste storage facilities present on the farm).	20% max. investment of €7,618.	20% (max. investment of €7,618)

The maximum amount of investment eligible for grant aid is €50,790 per holding.

YOUNG FARMER TOP-UP

The grant rate will be increased in respect of all investments, except mobile equipment, by 15% in disadvantaged areas and 5% in non-disadvantaged areas for farmers under 35 years of age at the date of application who have satisfied the following conditions:

- if the applicant was born after 1 January 1975 he/she must hold a Certificate in Farming.
- if born before 1 January 1975 he/she must have completed a Teagasc 180 hour training course and have at least three years farming experience.
- must have commenced farming in the previous five years i.e. must have first become registered for a herd number within five years of making an application for the scheme.

To qualify for the disadvantaged area rate, at least half of the land owned/leased must be in a disadvantaged area.

FARM WASTE MANAGEMENT SCHEME - IMPORTANT POINTS

- Farmers who have drawn down grant aid under a previous Control of Farmyard Pollution Scheme will be allowed to receive the maximum grant under this scheme.
- Farmers may also receive aid under the Dairy Hygiene Scheme
- Farmers must be in REPS or abide by the Good Farming Practice criteria.
- The Department of Agriculture, Food and Rural Development have undertaken to review the standard costings annually.
- The grant aided investment cannot lead to an increase in the level of production on the farm.
- The applicant shall use the building for five years after receiving the grant or otherwise the grant will be recouped.
- Where a contractor is employed to carry out the work they must hold a current C2 or Tax Clearance Cert.
- Applicants must have a Tax Clearance Cert. if payment is in excess of €6,349.

After receiving approval for grant aid farmers cannot commence work, or purchase equipment, without first notifying the Department.

YOUNG FARMERS INSTALLATION AID

This scheme was introduced in 2001 and is intended as an aid to young farmers to become established in farming. It is available to farmers under the age of 35. The grant aid is available as a once-off payment of **€9,523** and is fully funded by the National Exchequer. A total of €36.5m has been allocated to the scheme which runs until 2007..

ELIGIBILITY FOR INSTALLATION AID
Then following criteria apply:

- Applicants must be over 18 and less than 35 years of age.
- Must be first set up after 1 January 2000 on a holding of at least 5 hectares of utilised agricultural land.

- For applicants born after 01/01/75, the Certificate in Farming will be required or a Farm Apprenticeship Board Certificate or a Degree in Agricultural Science or Veterinary. Persons with two years post secondary cycle training and 180 hours agricultural training will also meet the training requirements.
- Applicants born before 1/1/75 require 180 hours of training and three years farming experience.
- Must have incurred setting up costs and provide proof that some or all of these costs remain to be discharged. Such costs include legal, accountancy or consultancy, stamp duty or family settlements.
- The farm must be capable of having 20 income units from farming at the time of set up and have a total minimum of 50 income units within 2 years of setting up.
- The farm must have less than 150 income units with at least 20 income units coming from farming which means that off farm income cannot exceed €33,020.
- Applicants must be first registered as a herd, flock or cereal number sole user after the date of setting up.
- Applicants must get full title to lands through outright ownership or a lease with a minimum term of five years to run.
- Applicants must remain in farming at least 5 years from time of installation.

PAYMENT
The grant will be €9,523 in all qualifying cases.

APPLICATION PROCEDURE
The application is in two stages. Firstly you must make an **Application to Enter the Scheme.** This is done within six months of set up i.e. date of lease or transfer. You are required to submit the following:

- - Application Form
- - Original Birth Cert
- - Cert from DVO confirming herd/flock number.
- - Evidence that some set up costs remain to be discharged.
- - Ccpy of Transfer or Lease (stamped or unstamped).

Secondly you make an **Application for Payment** which is generally made at the end of the first year after set up, but in any event within thirty months from the date of setting up. At this point you will have satisfied the income unit conditions and all of the legal documentation will be in order. The following documents will need to accompany the Application for Payment:

- • - Application form completed and certified by Agricultural Consultant/Advisor
- • - Current Tax Clearance Cert
- • - Income Tax Assessment
- • - Area Aid Form
- • - Stamped Deed of Transfer/Lease, along with Folio(s) and Land Registry Dealing Number.
- • - Where some lands are rented, a rental agreement or auctioneers certificate.

IMPORTANT POINTS

- • Only transfers of land after 01/01/2000 are eligible.
- • In the case of transfers of land, a land registry dealing number will be sufficient to prove transfer of land.
- • Young farmers must be in REPS or alternatively undertake to carry out farming under the rules of Good Farming Practice.

DAIRY HYGIENE SCHEME

This scheme is designed to help farmers fund the necessary investment to bring their on-farm facilities up to the standards set by the EU milk hygiene directive. Funding amounting to €45.4m is available towards the scheme which will run until 2007.

ELIGIBLE APPLICANTS

The scheme is open to farmers who;
- • have more than 30 income units and less than 200. Calculation of these income units takes into account each applicant's farming activities and off-farm activities at the rate of €254 gross off-farm income per unit. At least 20 of the income units must be derived from farming.
- • who are landowners or lease holders of lands on which it is proposed to carry out the development.
- • if born after 01/01/75, hold a certificate in farming, or have 180 hours of recognised training as well as three years farming experience.
- • if born before 01/01/75 have at least five years farming experience.

- whose lands have been declared for area aid.

ELIGIBLE INVESTMENTS

Investment eligible for aid covers dairy premises new or up-grades, bulk milk tanks, new milking machines, dairy washings collection tank, plate coolers, provision of plumbed in water supply, water treatment/heating systems, electrical installations and wash up facilities.

GRANT RATES

Table 2.2 Rates of grant for dairy hygiene scheme

Investment	Applicants with not more than 150 IU's	Applicants with 150 to 200 IU's
Dairy/Milking premises (new or upgraded)/milk cooling equipment	40%	20%
Milking Machines (new or upgraded)	40% (max. investment of €10,1580	20% (max. investment of €10,1580)
Bulk Milk Tanks	40% max. investment of €10,158.	20% (max. investment of €10,1580

The maximum amount of investment eligible for grant aid is €31,743 per holding.

YOUNG FARMER TOP-UP

The grant rate will be increased in respect of all investments, except for upgrading milking machines and bulk tanks, by 15% in disadvantaged areas and 5% in non-disadvantaged areas for farmers under 35 years of age at the date of application who have satisfied the following conditions:

- if the applicant was born after 1 January 1975 he/she must hold a Certificate in Farming.
- if born before 1 January 1975 he/she must have completed a Teagasc 180 hour training course and have at least three years farming experience.

- must have commenced farming in the previous five years i.e. must have first become registered for a herd number within five years of making an application for the scheme.

To qualify for the disadvantaged area rate, at least half of the land owned/leased must be in a disadvantaged area.

DAIRY HYGIENE SCHEME - IMPORTANT POINTS

- Farmers who have drawn down grant aid under a previous Dairy Hygiene Scheme will be allowed to receive the maximum grant under this scheme.
- Farmers may also receive aid under the Farm Waste Scheme.
- Farmers must be in REPS or abide by the Good Farming Practice criteria.
- The Department of Agriculture, Food and Rural Development have undertaken to review the standard costings annually.

SCHEME OF INVESTMENT AID IN ALTERNATIVE ENTERPRISES HOUSING AND HANDLING FACILITIES

The objective of this scheme is to promote and maintain agricultural enterprises not in surplus by providing grant aid to farmers for investment in housing/handling facilities for horses, deer, rabbits, goats and other acceptable non quota species.

ELIGIBLE APPLICANTS

The scheme is open to farmers who;

- have more than 30 income units and not more than 200. Calculation of these income units takes into account each applicant's farming activities and off-farm activities at the rate of €254 gross off-farm income per unit. At least 20 of the income units must be derived from farming.
- who are landowners or lease holders of lands on which it is proposed to carry out the development.
- if born after 01/01/75, hold a certificate in farming, or 180 hours of recognised training and at least three years farming experience.
- if born before 01/01/75 have at least five years farming experience.

- Must have completed a minimum of 20 hours of recognised training, relevant to the particular enterprise. This training may form part of or be additional to the training requirements set out above.
- whose lands have been declared for area aid.

BUSINESS PLAN

A business plan will be required for assessment of the economic viability of the enterprise and the planned investment project.

GRANT AID

The rate of grant aid payable is 40% for participants with less than 150 IU's or 20% for those with between 150 and 200 IU's. The maximum amount of investment eligible for grant aid is €31,743 per holding in respect of horses or deer and €6,349 in respect of other species. Investment items eligible for aid are as follows:

Sportshorses
- Housing, associated concrete, feed storage facilities
- Lunging/exercise areas (suitable all weather surfaces), including gates and fencing, water supply and fencing (perimeter and internal)

Deer Farming
- Housing, associated concrete, feed storage facilities and waste storage facilities
- Handling facilities (including gates and fencing)
- Fencing (perimeter and internal) and water supply

Goats
- Housing, associated concrete, milking facilities, feed storage facilities and waste storage facilities, Fencing (perimeter and internal)
- Water supply for milking facilities

Rabbits
- Housing, cages and fittings.

Other Species
- Housing and handling facilities for other species excluding greyhounds..

GRAIN STORAGE SCHEME

This scheme is to provide grant aid for the upgrading of existing grain storage facilities and the installation of a limited number of new storage facilities on farm. An allocation of €9.52 is available from the National Exchequer.

ELIGIBLE PERSONS
- Farmers who have a minimum of 30 ha. of tillage including set aside in the preceding three years including year of application.
- Farmers must comply with Good Farming Practice as well as Code of Practice laid down in the Grain Assurance Scheme.

ELIGIBLE INVESTMENTS
- Projects involving construction of new storage facilities or upgrading of existing storage facilities will be eligible for aid.
- On completion a store must have minimum capacity of 200 tonnes and adequate aeration and/or drying facilities for the capacity of the store

GRANT AID
Grain Stores - 40% subject to a minimum investment of €32,000 and a maximum investment of €238,000.
Dryers - 30% subject to a minimum investment of €32,000 and a maximum investment of €238,000.

APPLICATION FORMS
May be had from Crop Production and Safety Division, Department of Agriculture, Food and Rural Development, Agriculture House, Kildare St., Dublin 2.

COMMERCIAL HORTICULTURE SCHEME

This scheme is intended to assist in the development of the horticulture sector.

ELIGIBLE PERSONS/PROJECTS
- Persons who have a minimum of 30 income units with at least 20 from farming.
- Persons must have the necessary skill and competence for running the business.
- The project must be shown to be viable by furnishing a comprehensive business plan and most recent accounts.

ELIGIBLE INVESTMENTS
Aid is targeted towards the entire industry including mushrooms and bee keeping.

GRANT AID
General - 35% subject to a minimum investment of €10,000 and a maximum investment of €1.27m. over the period of the scheme.
Beekeeping - 35% subject to a minimum investment of €2,000.

APPLICATION FORMS
May be had from Crop Production and Safety Division, Department of Agriculture, Food and Rural Development, Agriculture House, Kildare St., Dublin 2.

POTATO SECTOR GRANT SCHEME

This scheme is intended to assist in the development of the potatoe sector. An allocation of €5.07m. has been provided for the scheme under the National Development Plan.

ELIGIBLE PERSONS/PROJECTS
- Persons must have the necessary skill and resources to undertake the project.
- The project must be shown to be viable by furnishing a comprehensive business plan.

ELIGIBLE INVESTMENTS
New storage (min. 100 tonnes) and handling facilities
Refurbishing existing facilities.

Equipment for grading, cleaning, weighing, packing and labelling.
Obtaining planning and drawing up plans. (max 5% of total expenditure).

GRANT AID
Up to 35% of approved costs subject to a maximum grant €52,500 and a minimum expenditure limit of €10,000.

APPLICATION FORMS
May be had from Crop Production and Safety Division, Department of Agriculture, Food and Rural Development, Agriculture House, Kildare St., Dublin 2.

SCHEME OF GRANT AID FOR DEVELOPMENT OF THE ORGANIC SECTOR

This scheme which is approved under the National Development Plan is intended to assist towards investment in equipment and facilities for the production, preparation, grading, packing and storage of organic products. Both on-farm and off-farm projects are eligible.

GRANT AID
For on farm investment projects costing over €2,540 the Department will provide 40% grant assistance up to a maximum of €50,790. For off-farm investments investment projects costing over €2,540 the Department will provide 40% grant assistance up to a maximum of €253,948.

LOCAL ROADS IMPROVEMENT SCHEME

This scheme is operated by the local authorities in accordance with conditions laid down by the Department of the Environment, whereby local people can get together with the Council to improve non-public roads. The work must be for the joint benefit of two or more parcels of land occupied by different persons or serve the public e.g. bog roads. Applications are made to the County Council and the amount of contribution from the applicants is determined on the basis of rateable valuations.

Part 3 - Livestock and Arable Schemes & Subsidies

THE INTEGRATED ADMINISTRATION AND CONTROL SYSTEM (IACS)

The Integrated Administration and Control System is a means of applying checks and controls on applications by farmers for various financial aids. The requirements are set out in EU Council Regulation 2508/92 and 2419/2001 and apply throughout all EU Member States. IACS consists of the following elements:

- Aid Applications
- Computerised databases
- An Integrated control system
- A Land Parcel Identification System
- A system for the identification and registration of bovine animals known as the Cattle Movement and Monitoring System (CMMS).

The Land Parcel Identification System (LPIS) records details of land area and usage. The Cattle Movement and Monitoring System better known as the CMMS is a computerised database of all calf birth registrations and animal movements.

APPLYING FOR AREA AID

Farmers are required to submit an Area Aid application each year if they wish to participate in any of the following:

- Arable Aid
- Area Based Compensatory Payments
- Special Beef Premium
- Suckler Cow Premium
- Ewe Premium (if you wish to claim the Rural World Premium)
- Extensification Premium
- Rural Environmental Protection Scheme (REPS)
- Scheme of Investment Aid for Farm Waste Management
- Scheme of Investment Aid for the Improvement of Dairy Hygiene Standards
- Scheme of Investment Aid in Alternative Enterprises
- Early Farm Retirement Scheme

FIRST TIME APPLICANTS
Farmers applying for Area Aid for the first time will be subject to an inspection to verify that they are operating independently from any other farmer. When submitting the area aid form they should include maps with their application, outlining clearly the boundaries of the farm.

SAME LAND AS PREVIOUS YEAR
When making an area-aid application the preprinted form should be used. Where the same area of ground is been farmed the farmer will simply have to re-declare the use of each parcel and will not need to resubmit maps. It is important to note that the areas printed on the form are gross areas. Each applicant should therefore, deduct the necessary area of waste to arrive at the net area for each parcel.

ADDITIONAL LAND
If new land has been acquired or additional land has been rented the farmer should endeavor to obtain the Land Parcel Identification Number for that parcel from the previous applicant. Failing that, an original Ordnance Survey or Land Registry map should be submitted, identifying the parcel concerned. These new plots or blocks must be clearly defined on the map and should be numbered individually.

TRANSFER OF THE ENTIRE HOLDING
Where the entire holding is transferred from one farmer to another and the transferor has lodged an Area Aid Application but all of the conditions for receiving aid have not been met no aid will be paid. However the aid applied for by the transferor can be paid to the transferee if the Department are notified immediately and a request for payment is made.

LATE LODGMENT
In the case of applications involving permanent pasture only a 0.5% reduction applies to any related aid payable for each working day that application is late. After 1 July applications will not be accepted. For all other applications a 1% reduction applies for up to 25 days. After 25 days an application will not be accepted.

PENALTIES

Where the area found on inspection is less than the area declared on the area aid form aid will be based on the area found. Where the area found is greater than the area declared on the form the area declared will be used to calculate payments.

The following penalties also apply, except in the case of force majeure:

- the area found on inspection will be reduced by twice the difference found where that difference is more than 3% or 2 hectares, whichever is the lesser.
- if the difference found is more than 20% then no payment will issue.
- if the over declaration related to a plot of seaside then in addition to the penalty applied for over declaration of setaside, the area of arable crops will also be reduced proportionately to maintain the original setaside percentage declared.
- where a farmer makes a false declaration through serious negligence, they will be excluded from the relevant aid scheme for 2003.
- where an applicant intentionally makes a false declaration they shall be excluded from the relevant scheme for the current and following year.

EXCEPTIONAL CIRCUMSTANCES (FORCE MAJEURE)

If for certain unforeseen reasons applicants are unable to comply with the conditions of a scheme they may still be entitled to payment. Such situations might include:

- Long term illness of the applicant.
- Death of the applicant
- A severe natural disaster affecting the farm
- The accidental destruction of livestock buildings on the farm
- An epizootic disease affecting part or all of the farm

If any of the above circumstances arise the Department should be immediately notified.

Table 3.1: Summary of premium and disadvantaged areas payments 2003

SCHEME	RATE (€)	DETAILS
LIVESTOCK PREMIUMS		
Suckler Cow premium	224.19 / head	
Beef National Envelope - Suckler Cow Premium	76.20/head (2002 payment)	Additional top up on replacement heifers
Special beef premium	150.00/head	12 applications 1 Jan. to 31 December
Bull Beef Premium	210.04 / head	
Extensification premium	Low 40.00 / head High 80.00 /head	Census dates to be decided
Slaughter premium	80.00 / head	Bulls, steers, cows
	80.00 / head	Heifers
Beef National Envelope - Slaughter Premium	Approx. 76.2 / head (2002 payment)	Additional top-up on replacement heifers - max. Limited to 20%
Ewe premium	21.00/head	One payment in October
National Envelope - Ewe Premium	1.22/head (2002 payment)	No application necessary
Rural world premium (disadvantaged areas)	7.00/head	No application necessary
ARABLE AID		
Cereals	383.04 / ha	Oilseed payment may be subject to adjustment for world price and maximum guaranteed area.
Maize silage	365.40 / ha	
Proteins	440.80 / ha	
Oilseeds	383.10 / ha	
Linseed	383.10 / ha	Maize silage payment is subject to base area limit
Set-aside	383.04 / ha	
DISADVANTAGED AREAS PAYMENTS		
Mountain Areas	57.14 up to 60 ha	Area-aid application closing date .
More severely handicapped	88.88 up to 45 ha	
Less severely handicapped	76.18 up to 45 ha	

Note: Payments rates and application closing dates may be subject to alteration.

ARABLE AID SUBSIDIES

As a result of the agreement for reform of the Common Agricultural Policy which included measures to reduce cereal prices substantially, a support system has been adopted to compensate producers for the expected income loss. Arable producers can apply for area-aid on eligible land used to grow cereals, oilseeds, linseeds and protein crops.

ELIGIBLE LAND
Area-aid can be claimed only on crops grown on eligible land. Eligible land is any land that was sown to crops with a view to harvest in any of the years from 1 January 1987 to 31 December 1991.

ELIGIBLE CROPS
The following crops are eligible for area payments:
Cereals: Barley, wheat, durum wheat, oats, rye, maize, sorghum, triticale, buckwheat, millet and canary seed.
Oilseeds: Rapeseed, soya beans and sunflower seed. Aid payments for oilseed rape will be made only on certain varieties and crops of a specified end use.
Proteins: Peas (harvested in a dry state), field beans and sweet lupins.
Linseeds: These have been included in the area-aid payments since 1994.

Area-aid payments cannot be claimed on other crops such as fodder beet, sugar beet or potatoes. However fodder crops such as fodder beet, kale, turnips and swedes can be entered in one's area-aid form as forage area. It is worth noting that a producer can elect to enter crops eligible for area-aid as forage area and forego the area-aid payments.

CROP HUSBANDRY
All crops must be sown by 15 May in accordance with normal husbandry standards. This means that the land must be prepared and seed sown in a way and at a rate which would be expected to produce a normal marketable crop. The crop must then be maintained until the flowering stage. In the case of oilseeds, linseeds and protein crops these crops must be maintained until at least 30 June unless harvested at full maturity prior to this date. Crops may not be planted for the sole purpose of claiming arable aid. Normal husbandry standards include harvesting at full maturity, where appropriate.

APPLICATION PROCEDURES

The application for arable aid subsidies is made annually by filling out an area-aid application form and declaring the crops for which aid is sought. Aid will be paid on eligible crops declared, and failure to submit this form will result in exclusion from the scheme. Area-aid application forms must be submitted to the Department of Agriculture and Food. Each field submitted must be adjusted to take account of lands lost to headlands, roadways, paths, ponds, electricity pylons or rock outcrops.

EXCHANGE OF LAND ELIGIBILITY

The Department of Agriculture and Food allow the exchange of land eligibility between different fields. This enables the grower to rotate crops between eligible and ineligible plots without the loss of cereal aid. It will also act to encourage good agronomic practices which will aid in disease and weed control and help maintain soil structure.

APPLICATION PROCEDURE

Any grower who wishes to exchange land eligibility must submit the relevant application form to the Department of Agriculture and Food, Area Aid Unit (Arable Crops Section), Hume House, Ballsbridge, Dublin 4, before the specified closing date which is usually mid February. Up until 2001 farmers could apply for a transfer for more than one year or 'until further notice' but this option is no longer available and farmers are now required to apply for eligibility transfer every year .

ROTATION PRACTICE

Eligibility of land can be transferred in order to facilitate the following rotations:

- Potatoes to cereals and vice versa
- Sugar beet to cereals and vice versa
- Seed production to cereals and vice versa
- Grass to cereals and vice versa

REASONS FOR EXCHANGE

When filling out the application form to transfer eligibility the applicant must specify the reasons for the exchange. If a reason other than those listed is stated then a brief explanation should be given. The following are the reasons listed:

- Prevent the build up of disease or pest infection
- Improve the soil structure
- Eliminate wild oats, perennial weeds etc.
- Arrest organic matter decline
- Remedy or prevent adverse environmental situations
- Other

CONDITIONS OF TRANSFER

Exchanging eligibility must not increase the area of eligible land on the holding. Where the field receiving eligibility is larger than that which is losing eligibility, area payments can be claimed only for the eligible area which has been transferred. The remaining area can be used to grow crops, without area aid. Eligibility can not be exchanged between holdings.

CONACRE AND RENTED LAND

All land which is being farmed by an applicant in a particular year, including conacre land, can be regarded as part of the holding for that year for the purpose of eligibility exchanges.

Exchange of eligibility will be permitted for one or more cropping years. In the case of rented land producers are advised to obtain, and to retain for reference, written agreement of the land owner to transfer eligibility, and the duration of the transfer. In the event of disputes, oral agreement between the landowner and the producer relating to exchange of eligibility will not be accepted as proof of any such agreement.

SET-ASIDE

Land which receives eligibility under the exchange arrangement may be used for set-aside provided that it fulfills the other requirements for set-aside i.e. that it was cultivated with a view to harvest in the previous year, and that it was farmed by the applicant in the two preceding years.

ARABLE AID SCHEMES

A single arable scheme has replaced the General and Simplified Schemes with all producers receiving the same rate of aid. The categorisation of large and small producers will still continue with large producers claiming more than 15.13 hectares. Such producers are obliged to set aside a minimum of 10% of the area claimed plus the set aside area. However both categories can voluntarily set aside up to 40% of the total area in 2003.

ARABLE AID RATES
The rates of payment of aid under this scheme are as follows:

Table 3.2 Arable Aid Rates

CROP	€/Ha. 2001	€/Ha. 2002/2006
CEREALS	383.04	383.04
MAIZE (subject to base area limit)	365.4	365.4
PROTEINS	440.8	440.8
OILSEEDS	466.06	383.1
LINSEEDS	459.83	383.1
SET-ASIDE	383.04	383.04

SET-ASIDE

Producers claiming Area Aid on more than 15 hectares are obliged to set aside a minimum of 10% of the area claimed plus the set aside area. In 2003 all growers may voluntarily set aside up to 40% of the total area.

ELIGIBLE SET-ASIDE LAND
The following conditions apply to set aside land:
- Lands in set-aside must be eligible land.
- The area set-aside will not include trees, pylons, ponds or ditches or other areas of waste.

- Land to be used for set aside must cover an area of at least 0.3 hectares in one block and have a width of at least 20 metres. Smaller areas will be considered if they occupy whole fields with permanent boundaries or parcels at least 10 metres wide along permanent watercourses or lakes and subject to special controls aiming in particular to ensure compliance with environmental objectives.
- Where eligible land is planted with trees under the forestry grants scheme on or after 22 June 1995, the land in question may be counted towards the obligatory set aside but not the voluntary set aside. In such circumstances the afforestation premium will only be paid and no payment will be made in respect of set aside.

SET-ASIDE MANAGEMENT

In order to be eligible for aid payment, land set aside must be maintained in accordance with determined criteria. The penalties for breach of these management regulations can be quite severe. The set-aside period and the permitted uses of set-aside land apply throughout the twelve month period from 15 January to the following 14 January. During the 'core' set-aside period from 15 January to 31 August it is forbidden to use land in set-aside for any type of agricultural production or for any other lucrative use. Certain types of non-food crops can be grown. A list of these is available from the Department of Agriculture and Food. The management of set-aside land can best be outlined in accordance with the time of year.

HARVESTING TO 15 JANUARY

A green cover must be established before 15 January in all cases except where a late harvested root crop has been sown. Light cultivation immediately after harvesting to promote natural regeneration is permitted provided a green cover is established by 15 January.

Where harvesting is delayed due to adverse weather conditions or in the case of late harvested root crops, thus preventing the sowing of a green cover, no action such as cultivation or spraying should be taken which would impede natural regeneration

During the period 1 September to the 14 January farmers are permitted to use the green cover on their set aside to feed their own animals either by grazing it or harvesting it as hay or silage

FROM 15 JANUARY TO 15 APRIL

Where a green cover has been established it should be retained until 15 April.

FROM 16 APRIL TO 31 AUGUST

Ploughing of set-aside land is not permitted during this period except for the following purposes:

- from 16 April to establish a green cover
- from 16 July to prepare land for sowing of crops for harvesting not earlier than 15 May

The green cover must be cut at least once during the period 16 July to 15 August, to leave a covering of 10 cm or less. The cuttings must be left undisturbed on the land. If it is necessary to cut the green cover during the period 16 April to 15 July, in order to control weeds or to maintain an acceptable visual appearance, it must be cut at a height of at least 20 cm.

Where a green cover has been established the application of fertiliser or lime or the control of weeds is allowed after 16 April. Weed control can be by way of shallow cultivation or by the use of non-residual herbicides.

FROM 1 SEPTEMBER TO 14 JANUARY

During this period farmers are permitted to use set-aside land to feed their own animals either by grazing or as hay or silage.

CALCULATION OF MINIMUM SET-ASIDE REQUIREMENT

A farmer can calculate the area necessary for set-aside as follows (where the set-aside requirement is 10%):

TOTAL AREA x 10 ÷ 100 = SET-ASIDE.

If a producer knows the set-aside area and wants to calculate the amount of land permissible for arable aid, the following calculation is used:

SET-ASIDE x 90 ÷ 10 = SOWN CROP AREA.

Where a producer knows the sown crop area and wants to find out how much land should be set aside, the following calculation is used:

AREA SOWN x 10 ÷ 90 = SET-ASIDE.

It is important to note that the set-aside requirement is a percentage of the total area including the set-aside and not a percentage of the area actually sown to crops.

LIVESTOCK SUBSIDIES - STOCKING DENSITIES

There are two separate types of stocking densities, calculated in different ways:

- **Stocking density for Premium purposes**
- **Stocking density for Extensification purposes**

These are outlined separately hereunder.

STOCKING DENSITY FOR PREMIUM PURPOSES

The number of animals qualifying for the special beef premium and the suckler cow subsidy is restricted by the application of a farm stocking density limit.

LIVESTOCK UNIT EQUIVALENTS
The stocking density is calculated by reference to the forage area declared on the annual area-aid form and:

- The number of livestock units represented by the number of ewes, suckler cows and male animals for which a premium application has been submitted in the calendar year
- The number of dairy cows necessary to produce the milk quota allocated to the applicant on 31 March each year

The number of livestock units calculated is divided by the forage area on the area-aid form to give the stocking density.

It should be noted that the reference date now used for determining milk quota is the 31st. March and not the 1st. April. In practice this means that farmers who are leasing temporary milk will have to include this quota in their calculations.

The following livestock unit equivalents are used to calculate the stocking density for premium purposes:

Table 3.3 Livestock units for Premium Purposes

Animals	Livestock Units
Suckler Cow	1 L.U.
Heifers less than 24 months on which suckler cow premium is applied	0.6 L.U.
Male Cattle 24 months or less	0.6 L.U.
Male Cattle over 24 months	1 L.U.
Ewes for premium purposes	0.15 L.U.
Dairy cows	Milk Quota ÷ 876= L.U.

Note: Where a dairy farmer is engaged in an officially recognised milk recording scheme, the recorded average milk yield can be used in the calculation of livestock units for stocking density purposes, instead of the national herd average of 876 gallons. It is also worth noting that in calculating the stocking density for premium purposes, heifers are not counted, nor are any suckler cows, male cattle or ewes that are omitted from the premium applications.

STOCKING DENSITY AND SUCKLER COWS

The following points should be noted:

- A female bovine which is under 24 months but has calved is a cow and is therefore 1 livestock unit.
- Where an applicant applies for Suckler Cow or Ewe Premium in excess of his or her quota the number of animals taken into account for stocking density purposes is equal to that of the quota.
- In the case of the Suckler Cow Premium Scheme it is the livestock unit value of the animals originally applied on and not the livestock unit value of any replacements that is taken into account for stocking density purposes. For example, if a heifer under two years is used to replace a cow the livestock unit value of the cow will be taken for stocking density purposes.

FORAGE AREA

The forage area is the area available for rearing bovine animals and sheep. In the case of owned land it must be available for at least seven consecutive months starting from any date between 1 January and 31 March. Where forage area is rented or leased it must be available for use for at least four consecutive months between 1 April and 30 September. Forage area can include:

- rough grazing, shares in commonage, certain grazing rights
- tillage crops such as fodder beet, turnips, mangolds, kale
- cereal, oilseed and protein crops on which aid for arable crops is not claimed.

It does **not** include:

- areas under roads, paths, buildings, farmyards, woods, scrub, ponds, lakes, sand or areas of bare rock, areas used for turf-cutting, quarrying etc.
- areas fenced off to exclude livestock under a REPS plan, etc.
- areas used for permanent crops or horticultural crops
- areas used for the aid scheme for dried fodder (grass meal production)
- areas under cereal, oilseed and protein crops which are declared for arable aid
- areas in a national or community set-aside scheme
- areas used as sportsfields, golf courses, pitch and putt courses, etc.
- commonage areas which are required to be totally de-stocked under a Commonage Framework Plan.

STOCKING DENSITY LIMITS

The stocking density limit for premium purposes in 2003 is 1.8 L.U./ha. (down from 1.9 in 2002). Farmers who exceed the stocking density limit will not be paid premiums on the excess of suckler cows, male cattle or ewes submitted for subsidy. However, these animals will be considered to have claimed the premiums.

EXAMPLES OF STOCKING DENSITY CALCULATIONS

Example 1: A mixed-enterprise farmer has 26 suckler cows, 40 male cattle under 24 months of age, 120 ewes, a milk quota of 12,600 gallons and 49 forage hectares (121.08 acres.) The number of livestock units on his farm is calculated as follows:

Table 3.4: Example to calculate total livestock units

ANIMALS	LIVESTOCK UNITS
SUCKLER COWS (26 x 1)	= 26 L.U.
DAIRY COWS (12,600 ÷ 876 and rounded up)	= 15 L.U.
MALE CATTLE (40 x 0.6)	= 24 L.U.
EWES (120 x 0.15)	= 18 L.U.
TOTAL	**= 83 L.U.**

The stocking density is calculated by dividing his total livestock units by the forage area as follows:

$$\text{STOCKING DENSITY} = \text{L.U.} \div \text{FORAGE AREA}$$
$$= 83 \div 49$$
$$= 1.69 \text{ L.U./HECTARE. } (0.69 \text{ L.U./Acre})$$

This farmer is not restricted by the stocking density limit of 1.8 L.U./Ha. and therefore will be paid on all the animals applied for.

STOCKING DENSITY FOR EXTENSIFICATION PURPOSES

Extensification Premium is payable on animals which qualify for either the Special Beef Premium or the Suckler Cow Premium in cases where the stocking density on the holding is below certain limits. This stocking density is based on the actual numbers of bovines on the farm as opposed to the number of animals that appear on an application form. The definition of forage area for Extensification Premium purposes is different to the definition used in determining eligibility for the other premiums. Whether or not a person has a milk quota is irrelevant for the Extensification Premium calculation.

FORAGE AREA FOR EXTENSIFICATION PURPOSES

The forage area of a holding for the purpose of calculating stocking density for Extensification Premium differs from that used to calculate the stocking density for premium purposes.

It can include:

- rough grazing
- share in commonage
- certain grazing rights
- tillage crops such as fodder beet, turnips, mangolds, kale

It **cannot** include:

- areas under roads, paths, buildings, farmyards, woods, scrub, ponds, lakes, sand or areas of bare rock, etc.
- areas used for turf-cutting
- areas used for quarrying
- areas fenced off to exclude livestock under a REPS plan, etc.
- areas used for permanent crops or horticultural crops
- areas used for the aid scheme for dried fodder (grassmeal production)
- areas under cereal, oilseed and protein crops **whether or not** declared for arable aid
- areas in a national or Community set-aside scheme
- areas used as sportsfields, golf courses, pitch and putt courses, etc.
- commonage areas which are required to be totally de-stocked under a Commonage Framework Plan.

LIVESTOCK UNIT EQUIVALENTS FOR EXTENSIFICATION

Table 3.5: Livestock unit equivalents for extensification

Animal Category	L.U. Equivalent
Suckler cows and dairy cows, irrespective of age	1
Male bovines and heifers over 24 months	1
Male bovines and heifers over 6 months and under 24 month	0.6
Ewes and ewe hoggets (on which premiums are applied)	0.15

Note: A female bovine which is under 24 months but has calved is a cow and is therefore 1 livestock unit.

LIVESTOCK SUBSIDIES

EU EWE PREMIUM

To qualify for ewe premium an applicant must:
- Be a registered herd owner
- Hold a ewe premium quota
- Have at least 10 ewes that have lambed at least once or will be one year by the end of the retention period.
- Maintain the ewes applied on for 100 days after the closing date for receipt of applications.
- Be able to establish ownership and identification of the sheep applied onto the Department's satisfaction .
- Comply with the requirements of the National Sheep Identification System.

RATE OF PREMIUM
The rate of premium was previously calculated by reference to prevailing market prices within the E.U. But since 2002 this is no longer the case and producers are now paid a fixed rate of €21 per ewe in October of each year. A further top from the National Envelope may also be granted. In 2002 this top up amounted to €1.22.

APPLYING FOR PREMIUM
Applications for premium are normally accepted from early December to early January, the exact dates will appear on the application form. The ewes must then be maintained for 100 days after the application closing date.

APPLYING FOR LEASE OR TRANSFER OF QUOTA
The closing date for transfer and leasing Ewe Premium Quota is the same closing date as the premium application date.

NATIONAL RESERVE
Quota can be allocated from the National reserve firstly to producers with less than 20 livestock units and the balance going to producers with over 20 livestock units. No other conditions apply in either category. The closing date for applications from the National Reserve is generally August in the year prior to the year in which the quota is intended for use.

Ewe Premium – *Important* Points

- To qualify for the rural world premium a producer must have at least half of his land situated in a disadvantaged area and must have submitted an area aid form. It is not necessary to apply separately for this premium.
- The definition of an eligible ewe is 'a female animal which has lambed at least once or which is at least 12 months of age by the end of the 100-day retention period.'
- The applicant must have at least 10 ewes that have lambed once or are visibly in lamb and held on the farm at the time of application.
- The ewes must be maintained on the farm for 100 days from the closing date for receipt of applications.

EU SUCKLER COW PREMIUM SCHEME

This scheme applies to two categories of farmers:

- Farmers with suckler cows producing calves for meat production and who are not engaged in milk production.
- Farmers with milk quotas of not more than 35,470 gallons (Small-Scale Milk Producers Scheme) with suckler cows producing calves for meat production.

INDIVIDUAL QUOTAS

Individual quotas were introduced in Ireland in 1993 and were based on the number of suckler cows eligible for premiums in the reference year, 1992, less a reduction for the national reserve. In order to apply for the premium the farmer must first hold Suckler Cow Quota. Payments will only be made on cows up to the number of quota units held by the farmer. These quotas may be traded between farmers by lease or purchase.

APPLICATION PROCEDURE

In 2003 farmers can make an application for suckler cow premium anytime during the period 2 January to 29 June. The application form is similar in style to the beef premium form in that there will no longer be a requirement to fill in the ear-tag number of each cow unless the herd is restricted under the BTE Schemes at the date of application. Instead, the Cattle Identity Cards of those animals being applied for should be enclosed with the application.

However, it will still be necessary to write down the ear-tag numbers of any heifers on which premium is being applied.

CONDITIONS OF THE SUCKLER COW SCHEME

The applicant must:

- have a suckler cow quota.
- be a registered herd-owner.
- be 18 years or older.
- use cows for rearing calves and meat production.
- on the date of application, own, possess and maintain the suckler cows or heifers being applied for a six month period after receipt of the application by the Department..
- if applying for premium on 14 or more animals there must be at least 15% heifers (maiden or in calf) and at most 40% included in the application and these animals must be retained throughout the retention period.
- a heifer must be at least 8 months old at the date of application.
- a heifer replacing a suckler cow already applied for must be at least 8 months at the date of replacement.

PAYMENT RATE

The rate per cow/heifer applied for is €224.15. In addition to the basic premium was a top-up payment of €76 out of the National Envelope in 2002 on heifers which replaced other heifers on which premium has been applied for and which did not calve in the calendar year (maximum number of top ups payable limited to 15%). The top is also payable on heifers which did calve in 2002 and on which premium was applied for (maximum number of top ups payable limited to 20%).

DEFINITION OF A SUCKLER COW

To qualify for the suckler cow premium the cow must belong to a recognised beef breed or be born of a cross with a beef breed and belong to a herd intended for rearing calves for meat production.

DRY HEIFER REQUIREMENTS

From 2002 onwards producers are obliged to keep a minimum of 15% heifers subject to a maximum of 40% of the total number of premiums being applied for. It will not be possible to fulfill this requirement by using replacement heifers as the animals can not have calved within the six month retention period. This requirement does not apply to producers with less than 14 cows.

PENALTIES AND RESTRICTIONS

Payment of premiums will only be made up to a stocking density of 1.8 Livestock Units per hectare, calculated by reference to the number of overall premium applications made, milk quota held and the forage area declared on an area aid form.

Late Applications: applicants will suffer a penalty of 1% per working day that they are late up to 25 calendar days. Applications that are more than 25 calendar days late will receive no payment.

Non compliant animals (less than 10% of total): claiming for non compliant animals will attract no payment and will also result in payment on the other animals claimed being reduced by an amount which equals the percentage of rejected animals. For example if 5% of animals are rejected then the payment due on the other animals will be reduced by 5%. It should be noted that rejected animals will be accumulated across all cattle schemes i.e. Suckler Cow, Special Beef and Slaughter Premium and the percentage reduction will be applied at the end of the scheme year.

Non compliant animals (10% - 20%): payment on the other animals claimed for Suckler Cow, Special Beef and Slaughter Premium will be reduced by an amount which equals twice the percentage of rejected animals.

Non compliant animals (over 20%): no payment will be made on the other animals claimed.

Non compliant animals (over 50%): no payment will be made on the other animals claimed and in addition an amount equaling the amount claimed will be deducted from premium entitlements over the next two years..

Intentional fraud involving over 20% of animals claimed: no payment will be made on the other animals claimed and in addition an amount equaling the amount claimed will be deducted from premium entitlements over the next three years..

SUCKLER COW PREMIUM - IMPORTANT POINTS

- If a producer is eligible and applies for the extensification premium he will be paid an extra €40 (or €80 high rate) on each of the suckler cows on his application.
- Replacement of suckler cows during the retention period by other eligible cows or replacement heifers can be made within 20 days of the disposal or loss. The replacement animal must be entered in the Herd Register ten days of the replacement.
- A female bovine which is under 24 months but has calved is a cow and is therefore 1 livestock unit.
- Where an applicant applies for Suckler Cow or Ewe Premium in excess of his or her quota the number of animals taken into account for stocking density purposes is equal to that of the quota.
- In the case of the Suckler Cow Premium Scheme it is the livestock unit value of the animals originally applied on and not the livestock unit value of any replacements that is taken into account for stocking density purposes. For example, if a heifer under two years is used to replace a cow the livestock unit value of the cow will be taken for stocking density purposes.
- Producers must at all times comply with the 15% heifer requirement during the retention period. If a heifer calves, she must be replaced within 10 days with a heifer which should be at least 8 months.
- Heifers should be at least 8 months at the date of application.

EU SPECIAL BEEF/ BULL PREMIUM SCHEME

The premium is intended to compensate beef producers for the projected market price reductions as a result of the change in the price support systems. It is payable on all male cattle over 7 months. The EU has introduced a limit of 1,028,153 animals which can qualify. If the limit is exceeded nationally the number of eligible animals will be reduced proportionately.

ELIGIBILITY FOR PREMIUM

The premium may be claimed twice in the lifetime of each male bovine animal. The 1st. installment can be claimed on eligible animals between 7 and 19 months of age (inclusive), while the second installment can be claimed at 20 months or over.

Example:
If a bullock was born on 13 February 2003 it would not be eligible for the first beef premium if the application was lodged on 5 September 2003. However, it would be eligible if the application was lodged after the 13 September 2003.

APPLICATION PROCEDURE
Applications for the beef premium and bull premium are all made on a single simplified application form. Each farmer can make a total of twelve such applications in the year up to 31 December. There is no need to write in the animals BTE number when applying for bullocks. This number will be scanned from the cards. However, if applying for bulls the ear tag number should be entered in the spaces provided. The Department of Agriculture and Food will also allow the applicant to rectify errors on the application, without penalty, provided that the farmer makes the amendment before the Department notice the error.

PAYMENT RATES

Table 3.7: Rates of beef / bull premium

Year	Rate
2001	€136 per eligible **bullock**
2002	€150 per eligible **bullock**
2001	€185 per eligible **bull**
2002	€210 per eligible **bull**

The rates of payment shown for Special Beef and Bull Premium may be reduced somewhat if the national quota for the Special Beef/Bull Premium is breached.

STOCKING DENSITY RESTRICTIONS
Payment of livestock subsidies to farmers is restricted by a farm stocking density limit of 1.8 L.U./ per hectare (see Stocking Density For Premium Calculations) The livestock unit equivalents of cattle for the beef/bull premium are as follows:

Male cattle 7-24 months at date of application   0.6 Livestock Units
Male cattle over 24 months at date of application   1.0 Livestock Units

Therefore cattle eligible for the second installment of the Special Beef Premium should where possible be applied for at under 24 months of age, thus maximising the number of animals that can be applied for within the stocking density limit.

APPLICATION LIMITS

The upper limit for both the first and the second premium is 180 head This means than an individual producer can apply on up to 180 for the first premium **and** 180 for the second premium. In the event that there is an overshoot in the national quota, smaller producers with applications for less than 50 head will be exempted from any reduction in premium payments.

PENALTIES AND RESTRICTIONS

Payment of premiums will only be made up to a stocking density of 1.8 Livestock Units per hectare, calculated by reference to the number of overall premium applications made, milk quota held and the forage area declared on an area aid form.

Late Applications: applicants will suffer a penalty of 1% per working day that they are late up to 25 calendar days. Applications that are more than 25 calendar days late will receive no payment.

Non compliant animals (less than 10% of total): claiming for non compliant animals will attract no payment and will also result in payment on the other animals claimed being reduced by an amount which equals the percentage of rejected animals. For example if 5% of animals are rejected then the payment due on the other animals will be reduced by 5%. It should be noted that rejected animals will be accumulated across all cattle schemes i.e. Suckler Cow, Special Beef and Slaughter Premium and the percentage reduction will be applied at the end of the scheme year.

Non compliant animals (10% - 20%): payment on the other animals claimed for Suckler Cow, Special Beef and Slaughter Premium will be reduced by an amount which equals twice the percentage of rejected animals.

Non compliant animals (over 20%): no payment will be made on the other animals claimed.

Non compliant animals (over 50%): no payment will be made on the other animals claimed and in addition an amount equaling the amount claimed will be deducted from premium entitlements over the next two years..

Intentional fraud involving over 20% of animals claimed: no payment will be made on the other animals claimed and in addition an amount equaling the amount claimed will be deducted from premium entitlements over the next three years..

EU SLAUGHTER PREMIUM

This premium is not to be confused with the Deseasonalisation Slaughter Premium which is only available certain years and only for certain times of the year. The Slaughter Premium Scheme was first introduced in 2000 and is available all year round and can be claimed on all bovines over the age of 8 months for slaughter within the E.U. and live exports to non E.U. countries..

RATES OF PAYMENT
The premium is subject to a National Quota Ceiling of 1.777 million rights and if this figure is exceeded the amount of premium will be reduced accordingly. The rate of premium is €80. A National Envelope top up payment on beef breed heifers may also be paid. In 2002 the top up amounted to €22.85.

Payment will be made by way of a 60% advance payment payable after 16 October with the balance being paid the following year

ELIGIBLE ANIMALS
The premium is available for all bulls, steers, cows and heifers from the age of 8 months that are slaughtered at licensed meat export premises and abattoirs and animals exported to a third country.

RETENTION PERIOD
Producer must hold animal for a minimum period of 2 months ending less than one month before slaughter or export.

THE EXTENSIFICATION PREMIUM

There are two rates of payment of Extensification Premium. The extensification premium of €40 per head is payable on suckler cows and male cattle eligible for subsidy where the farm stocking density is less than 1.8 L.U. / ha. The premium of €80 is paid on the same categories of animals where the stocking rate is less than 1.4 L.U. / ha The higher premium rate is paid instead of the lower rate, not in addition to it.

CALCULATING EXTENSIFICATION STOCKING DENSITY

The method of calculating the stocking density for extensification purposes is very different to the calculation used in determining eligibility for the Beef Premium or Suckler Cow Premium. In determining eligibility for Extensification Premium, **all** male bovine animals and heifers over the age of six months and **actual** cows present on the holding during the year concerned together with the ewes for which premium claims have been submitted in the calendar year are taken into account.

DATABASE SYSTEM

The Department has a computer record of all animals present on holdings, born into holdings, and moved onto and off holdings. This computer record known as CMMS (Cattle Movement Monitoring System) will enable the Department to calculate automatically a farmer's average number of bovine livestock units throughout the year based on the number of days each bovine animal over six months old is present on his or her holding. From 2003 onwards it will no longer be necessary to complete the census forms as the CMMS system will enable the Department to determine the numbers of animals on the farmer's holding.

SIMPLIFICATION OF APPLICATION

The system which required the farmer to opt for either the high or the low rate of Extensification Premium, or for the simplified or census system will no longer apply from 2003 onwards. Farmers who are interested in obtaining extensification will be required to confirm their interest on the 2003 Area Aid Form.

CENSUS SYSTEM OF DETERMINING ENTITLEMENT

While it will not be necessary to complete census forms, this basis of determining entitlement will still apply. The Department will choose five dates, spread throughout the year and the CMMS computer will identify the number of animals on hand at these dates. The five dates are chosen at random and farmers will be issued with herd profiles for each of the census dates so that they can check that the numbers of animals being taken into account are correct, and that they can monitor the position in regard to stocking densities as the year progresses. The number of animals to be taken into account for Extensification Premium purposes is converted by the Department into livestock units for each census date and the average is taken into account in the calculation of stocking density. The other elements to be taken into account in the calculation will be the number of ewes on which a farmer has applied for Ewe Premium, or his Ewe Premium Quota if lesser, and the forage area available. Stocking density for Extensification Premium purposes is calculated by dividing the average number of bovine livestock units plus the livestock unit value of the ewes entered for the Ewe Premium Scheme by the net eligible forage area in hectares.

The net forage area is the forage area declared on the area-aid application form, excluding arable crops declared as forage area.

GAINING ELIGIBILITY FOR EXTENSIFICATION PREMIUM
Once a farmer has determined the total number of Livestock Units on the farm it is then possible to calculate the stocking density for extensification purposes (see stocking density calculations page 65). The final figure used by the Department will be the average figure from the five census dates. Farmers should be aware of their average throughout the year so that proper planning decisions can be made.

Example:
Using average figures for the year a mixed enterprise farmer with 45 milking cows has submitted 30 male cattle over 24 months of age for the 21-month special beef premium in January. He has a further 40 male cattle eligible for the 9-month special beef premium and intends to submit these in June. He also has 30 heifers (under 2 years old), 40 calves (less than 6 months old) and a 3 year old bull. In January he also applied on 100 ewes for premium. He has a grassland forage area of 72 hectares. The total number of livestock units could be calculated as follows:

Table 3.7: Example stocking density calculation

Animal Category	Number	L.U. Equivalent	Total L.U.
Cows	45	1	45
Bullocks Under 2 yrs	40	0.6	24
Bullocks over 2 yrs	30	1	30
Heifers	30	0.6	18
Calves	40	0	0
Bull	1	1	1
Ewes	100	0.15	15
		Total	133

In this case his stocking density is 1.84 L.U. / Ha. (133 ÷ 72), just outside the limit for Extensification Premium. It would be worth looking at reducing numbers slightly in order to qualify. A reduction of four livestock units over the year would be sufficient to gain extensification payment on the 70 cattle eligible for beef premium in which case the resultant premium would be €2,800..

PAYMENT RATES

Table 2.10: Extensification premium rates

Year	Rate	Stocking Limit
2003	€40	between 1.4 and 1.8 L.U./Ha. (inclusive)
	€80	less than 1.4 L.U./Ha.

APPLICATION PROCEDURE

There is no formal application process but farmers will be required to indicate on the 2003 Area Aid form if they wish to be considered for receipt of extensification premium.

AREA BASED DISADVANTAGED AREAS PAYMENTS

An area based Disadvantaged Areas Compensatory Allowance Scheme came into effect in 2001. It replaced the Cattle, Beef Cow, Sheep and Goat Headage schemes in Disadvantaged Areas. The principal alteration is that the method of payment will move from a payment per head to a straight acreage payment. The motive behind this change is that there will no longer be an incentive for farmers to carry extra livestock in order to maximise disadvantaged areas payments.

PAYMENT RATES

Table 3.8: Payment rates under the area based disadvantaged scheme

Category	Rate (€)	Max. Payment (€)
Mountain-type grazing	101.58 on 1st.10 Ha. 76.18 on next 35 Ha.	3,682
More Severely Handicapped-lowland	88.88 up to 45 Ha.	4,000
Less Severely Handicapped-lowland	76.18 up to 45 Ha.	3,428

Where farmers have a combination of categories of land they will be paid on the mountain land firstly, lowland in the More Severely Handicapped Areas next and lowland in the Less Severely Handicapped Areas next.:

COMPENSATION SCHEME

While it was envisaged that most farmers will benefit from the implementation of this new scheme there will be some farmers whose payments will be less than the payments that they received heretofore. The Department have, therefore introduced a compensation scheme to minimise the impact of these losses in the first three years of the new scheme. This compensation takes the form of an additional top-up payment based on the amount of money lost on the changeover. It is calculated on the basis of a percentage of the difference received under the new scheme and the average received in the years 1998, 1999 and 2000. The top-up rates are calculated as follows:

Table 3.9: Rates of top-up compensation scheme

Year	% of Loss due to Changeover
2002	80%
2003	50%
2004 onwards	0%

CONDITIONS OF THE SCHEME

- The recipient must be 18 years or over.
- Must be a herdowner with a herd number.
- Must have a minimum of 3 Ha within the disadvantaged areas
- Must reside within 70 miles of the farm if resident outside the disadvantaged areas.
- To be eligible for the full top up farmers cannot reduce their forage area.
- Must commit to farm for the next five years
- Must comply with Good Farming Practices standards.

SPLIT HOLDINGS

Farmers with holdings split inside and outside the disadvantaged areas will not be at a handicap under the new system. The payment is based on the acreage within the disadvantaged areas regardless of whether the applicant also has land in a non disadvantaged area.

STOCKING RATE

Applicants must meet a minimum stocking level of 0.15 livestock units equivalent per forage hectare in the calendar year preceding application. This limit will not apply where agri-environmental or other recognised environmental measures require a lower stocking density.

APPLICATION METHOD

The payment of disadvantaged areas entitlements will be based on the area aid application. It is expected that payments will be made in September each year.

DISEASE ERADICATION SCHEMES

The control and eventual eradication of Bovine T.B. and Brucellosis is essential for the well being and future development of the industry. The eradication schemes currently in operation have seen substantial revision in recent times and the following are the main features of the schemes currently in operation:

- annual testing of the national herd and/or designated categories of animals, with primary responsibility for arranging testing, negotiating terms and paying for certain tests assigned to farmers.
- follow up and focused strategic additional testing, including the use of blood testing in certain circumstances.
- a comprehensive programme to expedite the lifting of movement restrictions on certain herds.
- a comprehensive research programme aimed at preventing the spread of disease by wildlife.
- improved epidemiology and feedback to farmers.
- continuing research on developing blood tests, vaccines and other technological tools.
- A national Forum to advise and make recommendations to the Minister on the operation of the Schemes.

COMPENSATION BASED ON LIVE VALUATIONS

Under the Programme for Prosperity and Fairness (PPF) agreement was reached in relation to the introduction of an On Farm Market Value Scheme. From 2 April 2002 the scheme became fully operable.

The main features of the live valuation system include:

- valuations will be carried out by suitably qualified valuers within prescribed timescales and by reference to guidelines laid down by the Department.
- A ceiling of €2,540 (inclusive of factory salvage price) will apply to payment in respect of any single animal, except in respect of one pedigree stock bull per farm where a ceiling of €3,175 (inclusive of factory salvage price) applies.
- Where the farmer or the Department do not accept the initial valuation, they can appeal to another valuer on the panel. The party making the appeal will carry the full cost involved.

- If there is no agreement after appeal the matter is referred to an Arbitration Panel whose decision will be final.
- Following completion of the on-farm valuation process the reactors are removed from the farm by the Reactor Collection Service on the next available occasion.

INCOME SUPPLEMENT

An income supplement is payable where disease breakdown results in the removal of more than 10% of animals in the herd and where depopulation is deemed not appropriate. Payment is in respect of each animal removed as a reactor from the herd, subject to a maximum of 100 animals qualifying for payment. Income supplement eligibility will cease in the event of:

- animals being purchased or moved into a restricted holding. other than a replacement bull or a bull in a newly established suitable enterprise with the permission of the DVO.
- the farmer failing to cooperate with veterinary inspectors or authorised officers in carrying out their duties under the Disease Eradication Schemes.
- Depopulation of the herd being deemed appropriate by the Department.

Table 3.10 T.B Income Supplement Monthly Rates

	Pedrigree	Non-Pedrigree	Transient
Suckler cows	€38.09	€38.09	nil
Dairy cows / Other Animals	€25.39	€25.39	nil

Table 3.11 Brucellosis Income Supplement Monthly Rates

	Standard Rate	Standard Plus	Transient
Suckler cows	€38.09	€38.09	nil
Dairy cows / Other Animals	€25.39	€25.39	nil

DEPOPULATION GRANT

Farmers whose herds are depopulated totally or partially in the interests of disease control may qualify for Depopulation Grants. Grants are paid for each animal removed in the depopulation measure and also for those removed as reactors since the holding was restricted.. Payment is conditional on the farmer's agreement to the depopulation. Payment is made in respect of each month of the rest period.

Table 3.12: TB depopulation grant rates

Animal Category	Payment per month (max 4 months)		
	Pedigree	Non Pedigree	Transient
Dairy cows & in-calf heifers, pedigree bulls > 12 months	€57.13	€57.13	-
Other cows / in-calf heifers	€31.74	€31.74	-
Other animals	€19.04	€19.04	-

Table 3.13 : Brucellosis depopulation grant rates

Animal Category	Maximum payment for 4 Months		
	Standard Rate	Standard Rate Plus	Other Rate
Dairy cows & in-calf heifers, pedigree bulls > 12 months	€126.97	€228.55	-
Other cows / in-calf heifers	€126.97	€126.97	-
Other animals	€38.09	€76.18	-

Note: Depopulation grant rates quoted above represent the maximum available in respect of a depopulation. Pro rata deductions or increases will be made if the rest period specified after depopulation is less than or more than 4 months.

HARDSHIP GRANT

The Hardship Grant is designed to assist restricted herdowners where animals have to be retained and fed while restricted. **The eligible period is between 1 November and 30 April.** This grant is payable, once eligibility is accepted as long as the herd continues to be restricted subject to a maximum of four months. The grant is intended to facilitate the purchase of fodder. The grant can provide herdowners with up to €253.94 per month.

CESSATION OF PAYMENT
Payment will cease in any of the following circumstances:

- De-restriction of herd.
- Supply of any milk for sale.
- Receipt of any off farm income.
- Animals, other than a replacement bull or a bull in a newly established suitable enterprise, being purchased or moved into a restricted holding with the permission of the District Veterinary Office.
- The herdowner fails to cooperate with Veterinary Inspectors or other authorised officers.
- Depopulation of the herd being deemed appropriate by the Department of Agriculture and Food.

APPLICATION PROCEDURE
The onus is on the herdowner to apply for the hardship grant. the completed application form should be submitted to the District Veterinary Office. Payment will only apply for the eligible period after receipt of the application form.

BSE COMPENSATION

Herds depopulated as a result of a BSE outbreak are assessed for compensation by Department of Agriculture and Food Inspectors. It is the inspectors brief to ensure that a fair compensation is paid to the herdowner for the depopulated stock. This will be based on the market value of the animals at the time of depopulation. The Department of Agriculture and Food valuers will inspect the stock individually and experience to date has indicated that reasonable and fair values are placed on the stock. It should be noted that this is the only form of compensation that the affected herdowner will receive.

Herd owners are allowed to restock 30 days after the animals are removed and after the housing and handling facilities have been thoroughly disinfected.

Note: Where compensation under any of the disease eradication measures exceeds €6,500 a tax clearance certificate is required.

SCRAPIE COMPENSATION

The current policy in Ireland where Scrapie is diagnosed on a farm is to slaughter the entire flock and to prohibit re-stocking of the farm for a period of two years after depopulation.

COMPENSATION FOR LOSS OF SHEEP FLOCK

Compensation for depopulation will be based on live valuations. Table 3.14 provides current guideline prices, however these guidelines are not absolute and the actual valuation will depend on the quality of the animals and the prevailing market conditions.

Table 3.14 Guideline Scrapie Compensation Prices

CATEGORY	€/head
Replacement Ewe Lambs	115
Ewe Hoggetts	133
2 year old Ewes	135
Mature Ewes	125
Stock Rams	381

At the time of depopulation, lambs on the farm will be valued regardless of their age and weight on a 20kg. carcass weight basis taking account of the appropriate lamb price for the year of depopulation which will be based on an average of the two previous years.

COMPENSATION FOR LOSS OF PROFITS

Compensation will be provided for loss of profits that will occur during the depopulation period. This will take account of loss of lamb sales, wool sales and premium payments with an adjustment being made for costs that would have been incurred. This compensation will be paid for the two year depopulation period and also a third year if the farmer, by the end of the third year, has restocked to a level of at least 70% of the number of eligible ewes depopulated. Compensation will also be provided in respect of amendments to a REPS plan required as result of the depopulation and restocking, subject to a maximum of €317.43 for each amendment. If a flock owner leases or sells his quota the income support payments will cease.

THE FALLEN ANIMAL COLLECTION SCHEME

This scheme was introduced in 2001 and provides for the subsidised collection and destruction of fallen ruminant animals. Animal collectors offering this service to farmers must hold a fallen animal license. The charges payable by farmers are as follows:

- €12.50 plus VAT per tagged calf (i.e. animals up to six months)
- €15.90 plus VAT per tagged young adult bovine (i.e. Animals between six months and two years).
- €31.74 plus VAT per tagged adult bovine (i.e. Animals over two years).

QUALITY ASSURANCE AND TRACEABILITY

BOVINE HERD REGISTER

All farmers will now be familiar with the herd register of all bovine animals held on the farm. This register must be kept up to date at all times. The following information must be recorded:

- all bovine animals that are currently on the farm
- all calves that are born on the holding
- all bovines that are moved onto or off the farm
- all bovine animals that die on the farm

Farmers may be required to produce the register at any time for inspection and should retain the herd register for a period of seven years from the date of last entry.

TAGGING & REGISTRATION

The tagging system requires the application of two identically numbered yellow plastic eartags to all calves born on the holding within 21 days of birth. Upon application of the ear tags herdowners are required to complete a corresponding and identically numbered registration form which is supplied with the tags. Herdowners are then required to return the registration form, within seven days, to the registration agency appointed by the Department. On receipt of the completed registration form the agency issues a passport for the animal in question. The passport must accompany the animal each time it is moved from a holding and all movement of the animal throughout its life must be recorded on the passport.

NATIONAL SHEEP IDENTIFICATION SYSTEM

The National Sheep Identification System (NSIS) came into operation on 21 June 2001. Under the system all sheep must be tagged and all sheep movements on and off the farm must be recorded. Processors are required to attach a label indicating the country of origin, the flock number and the individual identifier to the finished carcass.

DISPATCH/MOVEMENT DOCUMENTS

All sheep moving off the farm must be accompanied by a Dispatch/Movement Document completed by the owner, indicating the number of sheep being moved, the individual tag number of each sheep being moved, the flock number of the farm from which the sheep have most recently come and the name and address of the owner of the sheep.

FLOCK REGISTER

Under the NSIS it is a legal requirement that persons who hold or keep sheep on a registered holding maintain records of the individual animal identification number attached to the animals. It is also a legal requirement to keep a written record of the movement of animals onto or off the registered holding. To facilitate the recording of this information Flock Registers were issued to all sheep flock owners.

TAGS AND TAG SUPPLIERS

A number of different tags have been approved for use under the NSIS. Tags are available from approved suppliers only by post. Both long and short term tags have been approved but short term tags can only be used for lambs going directly for slaughter. Long term tags can be used in all circumstances.

NATIONAL PIG IDENTIFICATION AND TRACING SYSTEM

A National Pig Identification and Tracing System (NPITS) came into operation in July 2002. In broad term the system will involve the identification of all pigs that are moved off farm by either ear tags or slap marks and the identification of breeding stock with an individual number. All pig herd owners should have now been issued with a new registration number and only persons with a valid number are allowed to trade in pigs.

NATIONAL BEEF ASSURANCE SCHEME

The aim of the scheme is to guarantee the safety of beef products by:-

- operation of an effective animal identification and tracing system.
- developing high standards of production and processing.
- enforcing these standards through a registration and approval system.

The system of identification and tracing is underpinned by the CMMS computer system which records details of all movements of animals throughout the year. The information is then used to verify the origin, identity and life history of cattle entering the food chain.

FARM STANDARDS
Farm standards will cover such matters as animal identification, animal health and welfare, animal remedies and animal feed.

MEAT PROCESSORS STANDARDS
Standards for meat processors will cover sourcing of cattle supplies, identification and traceability, care of animals, hygiene control, sampling and testing regimes, clean cattle policies and special BSE related matters.

MART STANDARDS

Standards for marts will cover animal identification, equipment, facilities, animal health and welfare.

LABELING OF BEEF

Since September 2000 beef must be labeled to provide consumers with information permitting the identification of the animal or group of animals from which the animal was derived and the approval number and country of the slaughterhouse. From 2002 the regulations require the additional compulsory indication of the Member State or third country where the animal was born, fattened and slaughtered.

The assistance of Michael Brady, Agricultural Consultant, Corran, Waterfall, Cork, in preparing the Livestock & Arable Subsidies section is gratefully acknowledged.

Part 4 – Gross Margins & Budgets

GROSS MARGIN ANALYSIS

This section is intended to give a guideline of gross margins in the main animal and crop production enterprises. Within each sector wide variations of profitability prevail therefore costs, returns and efficiencies should be modified where necessary to reflect individual circumstances. Gross Margin analyses based on the previous year's performance are of limited value in planning for the future. If one were to plan on the basis of the return earned in any given year the result could be misleading. For this reason we have again decided to present the Gross Margin analysis for the various enterprises on the basis on what can be reasonably predicted for 2003 assuming average weather conditions. However predictions by their very nature can be unreliable especially in the context of farm incomes and they should be regarded purely as a guideline for planning purposes.

It should be noted that the Extensification Premium or Disadvantaged Areas payments are only included in the calculations where specified. In the case of crops it is assumed that a contractor is employed for sowing and harvesting and that the farmer uses owned machinery for all other tillage operations.

Crop Gross Margins are presented on an acreage basis as most farmers have not made the transition to the hectare measurement in planning their cropping programmes.

In order to clearly understand what Gross Margin is we set out hereunder an explanation of how Gross Margin is arrived at.

GROSS OUTPUT

This term relates to all of the income earned by a particular enterprise. It includes direct sales income as well as subsidies.

VARIABLE COSTS

This term refers to direct input costs such as feed, fertiliser, seeds & sprays, contractors, veterinary etc., In other words it refers to costs that are specific to that enterprise and does not include overhead or fixed costs which may relate to the entire farm

GROSS MARGIN

The term Gross Margin is simply the difference between Gross Output and Variable Costs as outlined above.

LIQUID MILK

Table 4.1: Liquid milk - gross margin per cow

	Gallons per Cow		
	900	1,150	1,300
Gross Output	€	€	€
Milk price[1] - 140 cents/gal.	1,260	1,610	1,820
Calf @ €155(5% mortality)	147	147	147
Cull cow sales	85	85	85
Total Output	1,492	1,842	2,052
Variable Costs per Cow			
Concentrates	124	171	211
Fodder costs	187	187	187
Veterinary & breeding	67	83	93
Replacement cost	165	171	180
Miscellaneous	25	25	25
Total Variable Costs - /cow	568	637	696
- /gal.	€0.62	€0.56	€0.53
Gross Margin per Cow	924	1,205	1,356
Stocking rate (acres/cow)	1.2	1.1	1
GROSS MARGIN PER ACRE	770	1,095	1,356

[1] The milk price quoted is inclusive of VAT and net of levies & transport

Table 4.2: Liquid milk - sensitivity factors

Factor	Effect on Gross Margin / Cow
Milk price + or - 6 cents/ gal.	€57- €82
Yield per cow + or - 50 gals.	€70

CREAMERY MILK

Table 4.3: Creamery milk - gross margin per cow

	Gallons per Cow		
	800	1,000	1,200
Gross Output	€	€	€
Milk price[1] - 126 cents/gal.	1,008	1,260	1,512
Calf @ €140 (5% mortality)	133	133	133
Cull cows	85	85	85
Total Output	1,226	1,478	1,730
Variable Costs per Cow			
Concentrates	80	120	148
Fodder costs	176	184	192
Veterinary & breeding	63	76	90
Replacement cost	165	171	180
Miscellaneous	25	25	25
Total Variable Costs -/cow	509	576	635
-/gal.	0.64	0.58	0.53
Gross Margin per Cow	717	902	1,095
Stocking rate (ac/cow)	1.2	1.1	1
GROSS MARGIN PER ACRE	598	820	1,095

[1] The milk price quoted is inclusive of VAT and net of levies & transport

Table 4.4: Creamery milk - sensitivity factors

Factor	Effect on Gross Margin / Cow
Milk price + or - 6 cents / gal.	€51- €76
Yield per cow + or - 50 gals.	€63

SINGLE SUCKLING

**Table 4.5:Gross margin analysis for single suckling
selling 1½ yr. olds in Oct/Nov from March/April-born calves**

Assumptions			
Calving rate	90%	95%	95%
Steer weight kg.	450	485	520
Sale price (€/100 kg.)	155	155	155
Heifer weight kg.	400	430	460
Price (€/100 kg.)	133	133	133
Output per Suckling Unit			
Sales per cow	553	629	673
Cull cow sales	70	70	70
Suckler cow subsidy	224	224	224
Special beef premium €150x 0.45)	67	67	67
National Envelope (Replacement Heifers)	11	11	11
Less mortality at 3% of output	-18	-19	-20
Less cow replacement costs	-108	-108	-108
Gross Output per Suckling Unit	799	874	917
Variable Costs per Suckling Unit			
Concentrates	45	45	45
Fodder costs	218	233	248
Straw	67	67	67
Veterinary & breeding	55	55	55
Miscellaneous	21	21	21
Total Variable Costs	406	421	436
Gross Margin Per Suckling Unit	393	453	481
Stocking rate - acres/unit	2	2	2
GROSS MARGIN PER ACRE	203	211	218

Table 4.6: Single suckling - sensitivity factors

Factor	Effect on Gross Margin / Suckler
Selling price + or - 6 cents / kg.	€24 - €29
Selling weight + or - 5 kg.	€6
Plus high rate extensification	€116

SINGLE SUCKLING

Table 4.7: Selling weanlings in Oct/Nov from March/April-born calves

Assumptions			
Calving rate	90%	95%	95%
Steer weight kg.	265	280	300
Sale price steers (€/100kg.)	216	216	216
Heifer weight kg.	245	260	280
Sale price heifers (€/100kg.)	190	190	190
Output per Suckling Unit			
Sales per cow	467	522	561
Cull cow sales	70	70	70
Suckler cow subsidy	223	223	223
National envelope (replacement heifers)	11	11	11
Less mortality at 3% of output	-14	-15	-16
Less cow replacement costs	-108	-108	-108
Gross Output per Suckling Unit	649	703	741
Variable Costs per Suckling Unit			
Concentrates	9	9	9
Fodder costs	116	125	135
Straw	42	42	42
Veterinary & breeding	35	35	35
Miscellaneous	11	11	11
Total Variable Costs	213	222	232
Gross Margin Per Suckling Unit	436	481	509
Stocking rate - acres/unit	1.5	1.5	1.5
GROSS MARGIN PER ACRE	291	240	254

Table 4.8: Single suckling - sensitivity factors

Factor	Effect on Gross Margin / Suckler
Selling price + or - 6 cents / kg.	€15 - €18
Selling weight + or - 5 kg.	€9
Plus high rate extensification	€80

DOUBLE SUCKLING
Selling yearlings in March/April from March/April-born calves

Table 4.9: Double suckling gross margin analysis

Assumptions			
Calving rate (%)	90%	95%	95%
Steer weight kg.	330	350	370
Sale price steers (€/100kg.)	155	155	155
Heifer weight kg.	280	310	335
Sale price heifers (€/100kg.)	133	133	133
Output per Suckling Unit			
Sales per cow	909	996	1,058
Cull cow sales	70	70	70
Suckler cow subsidy + Nat Envelope	234	234	234
Special beef premium	225	225	225
Less calf purchase	-254	-279	-305
Less mortality (3% of output)	-28	-30	-33
Less replacement costs	-68	-108	-108
Gross Output per Suckling Unit	1,088	1,108	1,141
Variable Costs per Suckling Unit			
Concentrates	102	96	85
Fodder costs	274	291	303
Veterinary & breeding	59	59	59
Straw	63	63	63
Miscellaneous	25	25	25
Variable Costs per Suckling Unit	523	534	535
Stocking rate (acres/ unit.)	3	3	3
GROSS MARGIN PER SUCKLER	565	574	606
GROSS MARGIN PER ACRE	257	261	275

Table 4.10: Double suckling - sensitivity factors

Factor	Effect on Gross Margin / Suckler
Selling price + or - 6 cents / kg.	€38- €44
Selling weight + or - 5 kg.	£11.00
Plus high rate extensification	€200

STORES TO FINISH AUTUMN PURCHASE AND SALE OF CONTINENTAL X FRIESIAN BULLOCKS

Over wintered on silage and finished on grass

Table 4.11: Gross margin for stores to finished beef

Assumptions	
Purchase weight kg.	450
Purchase price per 100 kg. Euros (€)	133
Output per Animal	
Weight at sale kg.	600
Sale price per kg. (cents/kg)	230
Sale price per animal (k.o. 54%)	745
2nd. special beef premium.	150
Slaughter Premium	80
Less cost of animal	-599
Mortality @ 2%	-15
Gross Output per Head	361
Variable Costs	
Fodder	154
Veterinary	11
Interest	33
Miscellaneous	38
Total Variable Costs	236
Gross Margin Per Head	125
Stocking rate (acres/animal)	1.3
GROSS MARGIN PER ACRE	96

Table 4.12: Store to finish - sensitivity factors

Factor	Effect on Gross Margin / Head
Selling price + or - 6 cents/ kg.	€42
Purchase price+ or - €0.06 / kg.	€29
Plus high rate extensification	€80

97

SUMMER GRAZING BULLOCKS
March / April purchase of Continental x Friesian
for sale in November

Table 4.13: Gross margin for stores to finished beef

Assumptions	
Purchase weight kg.	475
Purchase price €/100 kg	120
Output per Animal	
Weight at sale kg.	600
Sale price per animal (230cents/kg) 54%	734
Less cost of animal	-570
Mortality allowance of 2%	-18
Special beef premium	150
Slaughter premium	80
Gross Output per Head	376
Variable Costs	
Grazing costs	45
Veterinary	6
Interest	27
Transport & miscellaneous	44
Total Variable Costs	122
Gross Margin Per Head	254
Stocking rate (animals /acre)	1.4
GROSS MARGIN PER ACRE	355.6

Table 4.14: Summer grazing - sensitivity factors

Factor	Effect on Gross Margin / Head
Selling price +/- 5 cent/kg. carcass wt.	€16.20
Purchase price + or - €1 per 100kg.	€6
Plus high rate extensification	€80

CALF TO 2 YRS. - BUCKET REARING CHAROLAIS X FRIESIAN STEERS

Table 4.15: Calf to 2-yr-old beef gross margin

Assumptions		
Weight at sale kg.	600	640
Sale price cents / kg.	230	230
Output		
Sales value assuming 54% k.o.	745	795
Special Beef Premium x 2	300	300
Less cost of calf	-254	-279
Slaughter premium	80	80
Allowance for mortality	-11	-11
Gross Output	860	885
Variable Costs		
Milk powder	41	41
Concentrates	114	123
Fodder costs	205	219
Veterinary	27	27
Transport & levies	30	30
Interest	44	44
Miscellaneous	21	21
Total Variable Costs	482	505
Gross Margin / Unit	378	380
Stocking rate (acres per unit)	1.3	1.3
GROSS MARGIN/ACRE	291	292

Table 4.16: Calf to 2 years - sensitivity factors

Factor	Effect on Gross Margin / Unit
Selling price + /- 6 cents / kg.	€38 - €41
Selling weight + or - 5 kg.	€6.93- €7.08
Plus high rate extensification	€160

MID-SEASON FAT LAMB

Table 4.17: Gross margin per ewe for mid-season lamb

Output			
Lambs sold per ewe put to ram	1.2	1.35	1.5
Lambs (19 kg. @ 380 cents/kg)	87	97	108
Wool	2	2	2
Ewe premium	21	21	21
Less replacement costs	-11	-11	-11
Gross Output	99	109	120
Variable Costs			
Concentrates	6	7	9
Fodder costs	16	17	19
Veterinary dipping & dosing	8	8	8
Transport & commission	2	2	2
Total Variable Costs	32	34	38
Gross Margin Per Ewe	67	75	82
Stocking rate (ewes/acre)	3.5/acre	4.0/acre	5.0/acre
GROSS MARGIN PER ACRE	235	300	410

Note: In disadvantaged areas the Rural World Premium will increase the Gross Margin per ewe by a further €7.

Table 4.18: Mid season fat lamb - sensitivity factors

Factor	Effect on Gross Margin / Ewe
Selling price + or - 10 cents / kg.	€2.28 - €2.85
Lambs sold per ewe + or - 0.1%	€5.71

EARLY FAT LAMB

Table 4.19: Gross margin for early fat lamb

Output			
Lambs sold per ewe put to ram	1.2	1.4	1.6
Lambs (18 kg @ 470 cents / kg)	101	118	135
Wool	2	2	2
Ewe premium	21	21	21
Less replacement costs	-11	-11	-11
Gross Output	113	130	147
Variable Costs			
Concentrates	19	22	25
Forage costs	20	21	22
Veterinary, dipping & dosing	8	8	8
Transport & commission	2	2	2
Total Variable Costs	49	53	57
Gross Margin Per Ewe	64	77	90
Stocking rate (ewes/acre)	3.5/acre	4.0/acre	5.0/acre
GROSS MARGIN PER ACRE	224	308	450

Note: In disadvantaged areas the Rural World Premium will increase the Gross Margin per ewe by a further €7.

Table 4.20: Early fat lamb - sensitivity factors

Factor	Effect on Gross Margin / Ewe
Selling price + or -10 cents / kg.	€2.16 - €8.88
Lambs sold per ewe + or - 0.1%	€6

WEANER PIG PRODUCTION

Table 4.21: Rearing weaners to 32 kgs.

	No. weaners sold / sow / vr.		
	20	22	24
Gross Output			
Sales @ €42/weaner	840	924	1,008
Variable Costs			
Sow & boar replacement	25	25	25
Sow meal @ €197 per tonne	216	216	216
Creep feed @ €267 per tonne	37	41	44
Weaner diet @ €273 per tonne	218	240	262
Vet. medicines & heating	89	90	92
Miscellaneous	26	26	26
Total Variable Costs	611	638	665
Gross Margin per sow	229	286	343

OPTIMUM PRODUCTION TARGETS

Litters per sow per year	**2.4**
Average weaning age (days)	**25**
Bonhams born alive per litter	**11.25**
Number weaned per litter	**10.1**
Pre weaning mortality rate	**9 %**
Weaner mortality rate	**1.5%**
Sow mortality rate	**3%**
Sow culling rate	**34%**

FEED TARGETS

Feed per sow per year	**1.10 tonnes**
Creep feed per weaner	**7 kgs**
Weaner feed per weaner	**40 kgs**
Weight of weaner at sale / transfer	**32 kgs**

Table 4.22: Weaner pig production - sensitivity factors

Factor	Effect on Gross Margin / Sow
Selling price + or - 1 / weaner.	€25.00 - €30.50
Pigs sold per Sow + or - 1	20

FATTENING PIG PRODUCTION

Table 4.23: Finishing bacon pigs 32 kg to 82 kg (all-concentrate diet)

Feed Conversion Efficiencv	(3.0)	(2.8)	(2.6)
Gross Output			
Fatness @ €1.30/kg deadweight	80	80	80
Less: cost of weaner	42	42	42
Variable Costs Euros (€)			
Cost of meal @ €203/tonne	36.58	34.04	31.7
Vet. medicine & electricitv	3.56	3.56	3.56
Less mortalitv	1.27	1.08	1.02
Total Variable Costs	41.41	38.68	36.28
Gross Margin per pig	0.59	3.32	5.72

OPTIMUM PRODUCTION TARGETS

Finisher mortality rate	1.0 %
Average dead weight (75% k.o.)	70 kgs
Feed per finisher	130 kgs
Daily feed intake per finisher	1.83 kgs
Finisher average daily gain	0.7 kgs
Finisher food conversion efficiency (kgs feed / kg wt. Gain)	2.6

Table 4.24: Fattening pigs - sensitivity factors

Factor	Effect on Gross Margin / Pig
Selling price + or - 6 cents / kg.	€4
Food Conversion + or - 0.1	€1.20 - €1.30

PIG PRODUCTION - BREEDING & FINISHING

Table 4.25: Pigs - Integrated Herd

	Number of pigs sold per sow per annum (62kg. dead wt.)		
	20	22	24
Gross Output	€	€	€
Fatners @ €1.30/kg deadweight	1,612	1,773	1,934
Variable Costs (F.C.E = 2.6)			
Sow and boar replacement	25	25	25
Sow meal @ €197 per tonne	216	216	216
Creep feed @ €267per tonne	37	41	44
Weaner diet @ €273 per tonne	218	240	262
Finisher diet @ €203 per tonne	528	580	634
Vet & medicines & heating	152	160	165
Miscellaneous	24	24	24
Total Variable Costs	1,200	1,286	1,370
Variable Costs per Pig	60	58.45	57.08
Gross margin per sow	412	487	564

Table 4.26: Pig integrated herd - sensitivity factors

Factor	Effect on Gross Margin / Sow
Selling price + or - 6 cents / kg.	€74.00 - €89.00
Food conversion + or - 0.1	€35.60 - €39.40

SPRING FEEDING BARLEY

Table 4.27: Spring feeding barley gross margin

Output	€	€	€
Yield (tonnes/ac.)	2.0	2.5	3.0
Grain - €95 per tonne	190	237	285
Straw	35	35	35
EU area-aid	155	155	155
Total Output	380	427	475
Variable Costs			
Seed & sowing	65	65	65
Fertiliser & lime	53	57	60
Spray materials	50	59	69
Harvesting & transport	57	60	63
Interest	9	9	9
Total Variable Costs	234	250	266
GROSS MARGIN PER ACRE	146	177	209

Table 4.28: Spring feeding barley - sensitivity factors

Factor	Effect on G.M./Acre
Price per tonne + or - €5	€12.70 - €19.00
Yield per acre + or - 0.25 tonnes	€23

Note: A two tonne crop will return a negative margin if based on conacre at current prices. A two and a half tonne crop may yield a modest return which does not justify the effort and risk.

MALTING BARLEY

Table 4.29: Malting barley

Output	€	€	€
Yield (tonnes/acre)	2.0	2.4	2.8
Grain - €110 per tonne	220	264	308
Straw	35	35	35
EU area-aid	155	155	155
Total Output	410	454	498
Variable Costs			
Seed & sowing	58	58	58
Fertiliser & lime	53	58	58
Spray materials	51	60	70
Harvesting & transport	58	60	63
Interest	9	9	9
Total Variable Costs	229	245	258
GROSS MARGIN PER ACRE	181	209	240

Table 4.30: Malting barley - sensitivity factors

Factor	Effect on Gross Margin
Price per tonne + or - 4	€12.70 - €17.80
Yield per acre + or - 0.25 tonnes	€28

106

WINTER FEEDING BARLEY

Table 4.31: Winter feeding barley gross margin

Output	€	€	€
Yield (tonnes/ac.)	2.4	2.8	3.2
Sales - €95 per tonne	228	266	304
Straw	32	32	32
EU area-aid	155	155	155
Total Output	415	453	491
Variable Costs			
Seed & sowing	63	63	63
Fertiliser & lime	59	66	69
Spray materials	89	99	107
Harvesting & transport	59	60	63
Interest	9	9	9
Total Variable Costs	279	297	311
GROSS MARGIN PER ACRE	136	156	180

Table 4.32: Winter feeding barley - sensitivity factors

Factor	Effect on Gross Margin
Price per tonne + or - €5	€15 - €20
Yield per acre + or - 0.25 tonnes	€24

Note: A two and a half tonne crop will return a negative margin if based on conacre at current prices. A three tonne crop may yield a modest return which does not justify the effort and risk.

WINTER WHEAT (FEEDING)

Table 4.33: Winter wheat (feeding) gross margin

Output	€	€	€
Yield (tonnes/ac)	2.5	3.25	4.0
Grain - €94 per tonne	235	305	376
Straw	25	25	25
EU area-aid	155	155	155
Total Output	**415**	**485**	**556**
Variable Costs			
Seed & sowing	65	65	65
Fertiliser & lime	72	84	91
Spray materials	99	113	119
Harvesting & transport	60	62	64
Interest	10	10	10
Total Variable Costs	**306**	**334**	**349**
GROSS MARGIN PER ACRE	**109**	**151**	**207**

Table 4.34: Winter wheat (feeding) - sensitivity factors

Factor	Effect on Gross Margin
Price per tonne + or - 45	€15.80 - €25.40
Yield per acre + or - 0.25 tonnes	€24

Note: A three and a quarter tonne crop will return a negative margin if based on conacre at current prices. Planning on a higher yield in a conacre situation is unrealistic.

SPRING WHEAT (MILLING)

Table 4.35: Spring wheat (milling) gross margin

Output	€	€	€
Yield (tonnes/ac)	2.0	2.5	3.0
Grain - €102 per tonne	204	255	306
Straw	25	25	25
EU area-aid	155	155	155
Total Output	384	435	486
Variable Costs			
Seed & sowing	65	65	65
Fertiliser & lime	66	66	77
Spray materials	96	96	108
Harvesting & transport	63	63	63
Interest	10	10	10
Total Variable Costs	300	300	323
GROSS MARGIN PER ACRE	84	135	163

Table 4.36: Spring wheat (milling) - sensitivity factors

Factor	Effect on Gross Margin
Price per tonne + or - €5	€15.90 - €25.40
Yield per acre + or - 0.25 tonnes	€25.40

Note: The returns from spring wheat would not support the renting of conacre at current prices.

WINTER OATS (FEEDING)

Table 4.37: Winter oats (feeding) gross margin

Output	€	€	€
Yield (tonnes/ac)	2.5	2.8	3.2
Grain - €100 per tonne	250	280	320
Straw	38	38	38
EU area-aid	155	155	155
Total Output	**443**	**473**	**513**
Variable Costs			
Seed & sowing	60	60	60
Fertiliser & lime	55	65	69
Spray materials	61	72	82
Harvesting & transport	57	58	61
Interest	9	9	9
Total Variable Costs	**242**	**264**	**281**
GROSS MARGIN PER ACRE	**201**	**209**	**232**

Table 4.38: Winter oats (feeding) - sensitivity factors

Factor	Effect on Gross Margin
Price per tonne + or - €5	€15.90 - €20.30
Yield per acre + or - 0.25 tonnes	€25.40

SPRING OATS (FEEDING)

Table 4.39: Spring oats (feeding) gross margin

Output	€	€	€
Yield (tonnes/ac)	1.75	2.0	2.5
Grain - €100 per tonne	175	200	250
Straw	38	38	38
EU area-aid	155	155	155
Total Output	**368**	**393**	**443**
Variable Costs			
Seed & sowing	60	60	60
Fertiliser & lime	61	56	63
Spray materials	56	60	69
Harvesting & transport	55	56	59
Interest	5	5	5
Total Variable Costs	**237**	**237**	**256**
GROSS MARGIN PER ACRE	**131**	**156**	**187**

Table 4.40: Spring oats (feeding) - sensitivity factors

Factor	Effect on Gross Margin
Price per tonne + or - €5	€11.10 - €15.90
Yield per acre + or - 0.25 tonnes	€25.40

Note: A two tonne crop will return a negative margin if based on conacre at current prices. Planning on a higher yield in a conacre situation is unrealistic..

SUGAR BEET

Table 4.41: Sugar beet gross margin

Output			
Net yield (tonnes/acre)	16	19	22
Value @ €47/tonne (@15% sugar)	752	893	134
Variable Costs			
Seed	41	41	41
Fertiliser & lime	170	170	170
Spray materials	110	110	110
Harvesting & drilling	130	130	130
Transport	80	95	110
Interest & misc.	12	12	12
Total Variable Costs	543	558	573
GROSS MARGIN PER ACRE	209	335	-439

PHYSICAL DATA

Seed: 1.9 lbs. per acre

Fertiliser : 500 kg Beet Compound @ €260 / tonne
100 kg CAN @ €190/ tonne

Herbicide : €80 / acre

Fungicide : €16 / acre

Insecticide : Slug Pellets €19/acre. Leatherjackets €8 / acre

Machinery : Harvesting €99/ac, Sowing €22

Transport : €5 per tonne

Interest : Seed, fertilisers & half of sprays for
6 months @ 8.5%

Table 4.42: Sugar beet - sensitivity factors

Factor	Effect on Gross Margin
Price per tonne + or - €1	€20- €28
Yield per acre + or - 1.0 tonnes	€44

SPRING OILSEED RAPE

Table 4.43: Spring oilseed rape gross margin

Output			
Yield (tonnes/acre)	0.7	1.0	1.3
Output @ €170/tonne	119	170	221
EU area-aid	155	155	155
Total Output	**274**	**325**	**376**
Variable Costs (€)			
Seed & sowing	48	48	48
Fertiliser & lime	80	80	80
Sprays & chemicals	31	31	31
Harvesting	49	49	49
Transport	4	5	6
Interest & misc.	9	9	9
Total Variable Costs	**221**	**222**	**223**
GROSS MARGIN PER ACRE	**53**	**103**	**153**

PHYSICAL DATA

Seed : 5.5 - 7.0 lbs. per acre @ €2 per lb.
Fertiliser : 200 kg 10.10.20 @ €250 / tonne
150-200 kg CAN / acre @ €190 / tonne
Herbicide : €9 / acre
Fungicide : None
Insecticide : Slug pellets @ €10 / acre. Insecticide spray @ €6-9 / acre.
Transport : €5 per tonne
Interest : Seed, fertilisers & half of sprays & contractor charges for 7 months @ 9%

Table 4.44: Spring oil seed rape - sensitivity factors

Factor	Effect on Gross Margin
Price per tonne + or - €6	€4 - €8
Yield per acre + or - 0.25 tonnes	€34

WINTER OILSEED RAPE

Table 4.45: Winter oilseed rape gross margin

Output			
Yield (tonnes/acre)	1.0	1.4	1.7
Output @ €170/tonne	170	238	289
EU area-aid	155	155	155
Gross Output	325	393	444
Variable Costs			
Seed & sowing	51	51	51
Fertiliser & lime	98	98	98
Sprays & chemicals	82	82	82
Harvesting	48	48	48
Transport	5	8	9
Interest	9	9	9
Total Variable Costs	293	296	297
GROSS MARGIN PER ACRE	32	97	147

PHYSICAL DATA

Seed: 7.0 lbs. per acre @ €2 per lb

Fertiliser :   150 kg 10.10.20 @ €250 / tonne
      200-250 kg urea / acre @ €235 / tonne

Herbicide :   €20 / acre

Fungicide :   €22-28 / acre

Insecticide :   Slug pellets @ €10/ acre

Desiccant: €19/acre

Machinery :   Contractor charges per acre: ploughing €25, tilling €20,
      rolling €5, sowing €16, fertiliser spreading €6,
      spraying €6, combining €48

Transport :   €5 per tonne

Table 4.46: Winter oil seed rape - sensitivity factors

Factor	Effect on Gross Margin
Price per tonne + or - €6	€6 - £11
Yield per acre + or - 0.25 tonnes	€34

SPRING FIELD BEANS

Table 4.47: Spring field beans gross margin

Output			
Yield (tonnes/acre)	1.5	1.8	2.2
Output @ €130/tonne	195	234	286
EU area-aid	178	178	178
Total Output	373	412	464
Variable Costs			
Seed & sowing	67	67	67
Fertiliser	29	29	29
Spray materials	57	57	57
Harvesting & transport	59	59	59
Interest	10	10	10
Total Variable Costs	222	222	222
GROSS MARGIN PER ACRE	151	190	242

PHYSICAL DATA

Seed : 15 - 17 stone per acre @ €508 per tonne. Rate depends on Thousand Grain Weight

Fertiliser : 150 -200 kg 0.10.20 or 0.7.30 per acre @ €210 / tonne

Herbicide : €26 / acre

Fungicide : €28 / acre

Insecticide : €2 / acre

Transport : €5 per tonne

Interest : Seed, fertilisers & half of sprays & contractor charges for 8 months @ 8.5%

Table 4.48: Spring field beans - sensitivity factors

Factor	Effect on Gross Margin
Price per tonne + or - €6	€9 - €14
Yield per acre + or - 0.25 tonnes	€29

WINTER FIELD BEANS

Table 4.49: Winter field beans gross margin

Output			
Yield (tonnes/acre)	1.5	2.0	2.5
Output @ €130/tonne	195	260	325
EU area-aid	178	178	178
Total Output	373	438	503
Variable Costs			
Seed & sowing	67	67	67
Fertiliser	29	29	29
Spray materials	43	43	43
Harvesting & transport	54	57	59
Interest	11	11	11
Total Variable Costs	204	207	209
GROSS MARGIN PER ACRE	169	231	294

PHYSICAL DATA

Seed :   15 - 17 stone per acre @ €508 per tonne. Rate depends on Thousand Grain Weight

Fertiliser :   150 -200 kg 0.10.20 or 0.7.30 per acre @ €210 / tonne

Herbicide :   €9 / acre

Fungicide :   €25 / acre

Insecticide :   €6 / acre

Transport :   €5 per tonne

Interest :   Seed, fertilisers & half of sprays & contractor charges for 10 months @ 9%

Table 4.50: Winter field beans - sensitivity factors

Factor	Effect on Gross Margin
Price per tonne + or - €6	**€9 - €16**
Yield per acre + or - 0.25 tonnes	**€29**

LINSEED

Table 4.51: Linseed gross margin

Output			
Yield (tonnes/acre)	0.5	1.0	1.5
Output @ €114/tonne	57	114	171
EU area-aid	155	155	155
Total Output	**212**	**269**	**326**
Variable Costs			
Seed	22	22	22
Fertiliser	29	29	29
Spray materials	26	26	26
Harvesting sowing & transport	58	60	63
Interest	8	8	8
Total Variable Costs	**143**	**145**	**148**
GROSS MARGIN PER ACRE	**69**	**124**	**178**

PHYSICAL DATA

Seed :	25 kg per acre @ €1 per kg
Fertiliser :	125 kg 18.6.12 per acre @ €230 / tonne
Herbicide :	€22 / acre
Growth Reg.	€4 / acre
Transport:	€5 per tonne
Interest:	Seed, fertilisers & half of sprays & contractor charges for 6 months @ 9.5%

Table 4.52: Linseed - sensitivity factors

Factor	Effect on Gross Margin
Price per tonne + or - €6	€3 - €9
Yield per acre + or - 0.25 tonnes	€27

PROTEIN PEAS

Table 4.53: Protein peas gross margin

Output			
Yield (tonnes/acre)	1.0	1.5	2.0
Output @ €137 / tonne	137	206	274
EU area-aid (for protein crops)	178	178	178
Total Output	315	384	452
Variable Costs			
Seed	57	57	57
Fertiliser	32	32	32
Spray materials	49	49	49
Harvesting & sowing transport	75	77	80
Interest	10	10	10
Total Variable Costs	223	225	228
GROSS MARGIN PER ACRE	92	159	224

PHYSICAL DATA
Fertiliser : 150 kg 0.10.20 per acre @ €210 / tonne
Herbicide : €21 / acre
Fungicide : €25 / acre
Insecticide : €2 / acre
Transport : €5 per tonne
Interest : Seed, fertilisers & half of sprays & contractor charges for 6 months @ 8.5%

Table 4.54: Protein peas - sensitivity factors

Factor	Effect on Gross Margin
Price per tonne + or - €6	€6 - €13
Yield per acre + or - 0.25 tonnes	€34

MAINCROP POTATOES

Table 4.55: Maincrop potatoes (kerrs pink/records) gross margin

Output			
Saleable yield (tonnes /ac.)	10	12	14
Price/tonne ex-farmyard	165	165	165
Gross Output	**1,651**	**1,981**	**2,311**
Variable Costs			
Seed 1.0 tonne @ €250 / tonne	250	250	250
Fertilisers	160	160	160
Sprays	167	167	167
Slug pellets	29	29	29
Scutch control	14	14	14
Planting & de-stoning	100	100	100
Harvesting in bulk	168	168	168
Transport to store @ €4 / t	44	53	62
Grading @ €18 / t	180	216	252
Bags @ €12.5/ t	127	152	178
Interest	44	44	44
Total Variable Costs	**1,283**	**1,353**	**1,424**
GROSS MARGIN PER ACRE	**368**	**628**	**887**

PHYSICAL DATA

Fertiliser :   600 kg 7.6.17 per acre @ €265 / tonne

Sprays :   Herbicide €28 / acre, fungicides €130 / acre and desiccant €26 / acre

Note: It is assumed that 50% of seed is home produced and valued at €170 per tonne. The remainder is purchased at €330 per tonne.

RETURNS FROM POULTRY, FRUIT AND VEG.

Table 4.56: Guideline net margins from a range of enterprises

Poultry	€
Free range egg production - per 1000 birds	3810-5080
Broilers - per 1000 birds	1651-2032
Turkey fattening - per 1000 birds	1905-2540
Fresh turkeys - per 1000 birds	4445-5715
Broiler breeders - per 1000 birds	1905-2540
Vegetables	
Carrots - per acre	508-1270
Onions - per acre	317-762
Parsnips - per acre	1143-2540
Cabbage (spring) - per acre	38-508
Swedes - per acre	508-889
Celery - per acre	3810-6985
Green broccoli - per acre	190-508
Lettuce - per acre	3175-4826
Mushrooms - per house	4445-6350
Brussels sprouts - per acre	889-2540
Fruit	
Strawberries - per acre	1270-1905
Blackcurrants - per acre	635-1270
Apples - per acre	127-635
Raspberries - per acre	1016-1905

Caution: The returns as set out above are purely a guideline and the wide spread in returns is indicative of annual price fluctuations.

SAMPLE FARM BUDGETS

COMPLETE FARM BUDGET FOR A DAIRY FARM

The following budget is based on a dairy enterprise producing a 70,000 gallon quota from a 70 cow spring calving herd in 2002. All calves are sold with the exception of those kept for replacements. The farm carries a total debt of €40,000.

Table 4.57: Complete budget for a dairy farm 2002

Total Gross Margin (€)	57,400
Overhead Costs	
Bank interest & charges	3,048
Light & heat	2,195
General farm repairs	2,852
Machinery running costs	3,683
Telephone	720
Motor	3,830
Casual wages / farm relief	1,850
Accountancy	1,325
Insurance	1,930
Depreciation / machinery replacement provision	5,019
Sundries	480
Total	**26,932**
NET PROFIT[2]	**30,468**

[1] See gross margin analysis for creamery milk production, page ....

[1] Assuming the total net value of farm assets is € 635,000 the net return on investment is 4.82%

COMPLETE FARM BUDGET FOR A TILLAGE FARM

The following budget is based on a tillage farm of 120 acres in 2001, producing 380 tonnes of Sugar Beet from 20 acres, 100 tonnes of Spring Barley from 40 acres, 146 tonnes of Winter Wheat from 45 acres and 15 acres of set-side. Total farm debt including leased equipment is €44,450.

Table 4.59: Complete budget for a tillage farm year 2002

Gross Margins[1]	€
Sugar beet	6,700
Winter wheat	11,655
Spring barley	7,080
Set-aside	2,325
Total Income	**27,760**
Overhead Costs	
Bank interest & charges	3,365
Light & heat	843
General farm repairs	2,707
Machinery running costs	7,032
Telephone	713
Motor	3,830
Casual wages / farm relief	1,849
Accountancy	1,060
Insurance	1,600
Depreciation / machinery replacement provision	7,800
Sundries	460
Total	**31,259**
NET PROFIT[1]	**-3,499**

[1] Assuming the total net value of farm assets is €762,000 the net return on investment is -4.6%..

COMPLETE FARM BUDGET FOR A 40 COW SINGLE SUCKLING FARM

The following budget is based on a 80 acre farm in a less severely disadvantaged area with 40 suckler cows selling the progeny as weanlings in October/November. The farm has €31,750 total debt, is very efficient and is participating in REPS.

Table 4.60: Complete budget for a single suckling farm 2001

Gross Margin	20,360
Disadvantaged area payment (€76.20 / ha.)	2,466
REPS	4,888
TOTAL INCOME	**27,714**
Overhead Costs	
Bank interest & charges	2,254
Light & heat	792
General farm repairs	2,588
Machinery running costs	3,240
Telephone	712
Motor	3,830
Casual wages / farm relief	750
Accountancy	1,060
Insurance	1,700
Depreciation / machinery replacement provision	3,830
Sundries	580
Total	**20,756**
NET PROFIT[1]	**6,958**

[1] Assuming the total net value of farm assets is € 570,000 the net return on investment is 1.23%.

COMPLETE FARM BUDGET BASED ON CALF TO BEEF PRODUCTION

The following budget is based on a 100 acre farm engaged in a 70 livestock unit calf to 2 year old beef system. The farm has €31,750 total debt, is very efficient and is participating in REPS.

Table 4.61: Complete budget for a drystock farm 2001 (Euros)

Gross Margin	26,660
REPS	5,499
TOTAL INCOME	**32,159**
Overhead Costs	
Bank interest & charges	2,603
Light & heat	792
General farm repairs	2,970
Machinery running costs	2,359
Telephone	720
Motor	3,830
Casual wages / farm relief	700
Accountancy	1,060
Insurance	1,700
Depreciation / machinery replacement provision	3,830
Sundries	444
Total	**21,008**
NET PROFIT[1]	**11,151**

[1] Assuming the total net value of farm assets is €508,000 the net return on investment is 2.2%

COMPLETE FARM BUDGET FOR A SHEEP FARM

The farm consists of 100 acres in a less severely disadvantaged area with a 400 ewe flock producing 1.5 lambs per ewe. The farm has a debt of €19,050, is efficiently run and is participating in REPS.

Table 4.62: Complete budget for a sheep farm in year 2001 (Euros)

Gross margin	**32,800**
REPS	**6,100**
Disadvantaged area payment + rural world premium	**5,882**
Total Income	**44,782**
Overhead Costs	
Bank interest & charges	**1,932**
Light & heat	**792**
General farm repairs	**2,997**
Machinery running costs	**2,486**
Telephone	**710**
Motor	**3,830**
Casual wages / farm relief	**1,600**
Accountancy	**1,060**
Insurance	**1,500**
Depreciation / machinery replacement provision	**3,830**
Sundries	**444**
Total	**21,181**
NET PROFIT	**23,601**

[1] Assuming the total net value of farm assets is €635,000 the net return on investment is 3.7%.

COMPLETE BUDGET FOR 300 SOW PIG UNIT

The unit is selling 22 pigs per sow @ €1.30 / kg. dead wt per annum It is assumed that €254,000 is borrowed and that the unit is owner run.

Table 4.63: Complete budget for a 300 Sow integrated pig unit 2001

Gross Margin	146,100
Bank Interest & Charges	20,495
General Repairs	17,602
Machinery Running Costs	7,366
Telephone	720
Motor	3,830
Wages/Farm Relief	24,500
Accountancy	1,778
Insurance	1,860
Depreciation / Machinery replacement provision	12,446
Sundries	3,300
Total	**93,897**
NET PROFIT[1]	**52,203**

[1] Assuming the total investment cost €1,016,000 the net return on investment is 5.14%.

Farm Management Data

GUIDE TO AGRICULTURAL CONTRACTOR CHARGES

Table 5.0 Agricultural Contractor Charges

SERVICE	€ (incl. V.A.T.)
Silage Harvesting	80-95/acre
Slurry Spreading 1.200 gls	33/hour
Slurry Spreading 1.500 gls	40/hour
Slurry Agitation	38/hour
Hay Cutting	18-20/acre
Hay Tedding	10/acre
Baling -small square (incl. twine)	38-40//bale
Big bale	3.60-4/bale
Big Bale Silage (wrapped)	9/bale
Fertiliser Spreading - bulk	16-20/tonne
Fertiliser Spreading - bags	26-30/tonne
Ploughing	27-32/acre
De-stoning	105/acre
Harrowing (3 runs)	42/acre
Discing (1 run)	16/acre
Rolling	9/acre
Cereal Combine Drilling	16-20/acre
One Pass System Combined	36/acre
Maize Precision Sowing	26/acre
Spraying	6-8/acre
Cereal Combining	47-52/acre
Maize Harvesting	110-120/acre
Power Harrowing	45-50/hour
Sugar Beet - precision sowing	18-20/acre
Sugar Beet - steering hoeing	10-12/acre
Sugar Beet - band spraying	10-12/acre
Sugar Beet Harvesting	85-90/acre
Hedgecutting - flail type	33/hour
Mechanical digging - wheeled	26-28/hour
- tracked	42-48/hour
Tractor Hire (90-120HP)	30/hour

RELATIVE VALUE OF FEEDSTUFFS

Table 5.1: Relative values based on soya @ €250 & barley @ €116/tonne

	Dry Matter %	M.E.	Crude Protein	Value /tonne
Barley	86	12.8	12	116
Barley Straw	86	6.5	4	41
Brewers Grains	25	10	25	35
Distillers Grains	88	12.2	27	166
Fodder Beet	18	12.1	8	18
Hay (good)	86	9.2	9	58
Hay (average)	85	8.6	8	66
Kale	16	12.1	16	22
Maize	86	13.8	10	128
Molassed Beet Pulp	88	12.5	10	110
Molasses (Beet)	73	11.2	9	86
Oats	85	12	11	115
Potatoes	21	13.3	8	18
Silage (good)	27	10.8	12	20
Silage (average)	24	10.2	14	18
Soya Bean	88	13.4	48	250
Sugar Beet Tops	16	9.9	12.5	17
Superpressed Beet pulp	20	11.8	12	25
Swedes	10.5	14	11	13
Wheat	86	13.8	12	132

FARM BUILDINGS

CROP STORAGE REQUIREMENTS

Table 5.2: Crop storage requirements

Crop	Average Space Required for 1 tonne.	
	Cubic Feet	**Cubic Metres**
Silage	50 ft.³	1.46 M.³
Hay	330 ft.³	9.63 M.³
Barley	50 ft.³	1.46 M.³
Wheat	45 ft.³	1.31 M.³
Oats	70 ft.³	2.04 M.³
Died molassed pulp	116 ft.³	3.38 M.³
Swedes	65 ft.³	1.90 M.³
Potatoes	54 ft.³	1.58 M.³
Maize silage	49 ft.³	1.43 M.³
Fodder beet	64 ft.³	1.8 M.³

Table 5.3: Storage capacity of settled silage

Width in metres	Approx. Capacities of Settled Silage in tonnes per metre of length at depths of:			
	1.5 m	**1.8 m.**	**2.1 m.**	**2.4 m.**
7 metres	7.0	9.0	10.5	12.0
8 metres	8.5	10.2	12.0	13.7
9 metres	9.6	11.5	13.5	15.4

HOW TO MEASURE CROP STORAGE REQUIREMENTS

The measurement of feedstuffs in store can be calculated using the above figures. The first step is to measure the volume of feedstuffs in store. If the feedstuff is stored in a square or rectangular store or silage pit the volume is calculated by multiplying the length by the width and by the average height in metres and dividing by 1.4.

If the store is cylindrical, as with many meal bins, then the volume is calculated using the formula $3.14 \times r^2h$, where, r = radius and h = average height. Once the volume is known it can be divided by the relevant figure in Table 4.72 to give a measurement in tonnes.

Example 1

A pit full of silage measures 20 m. long by 10 m. wide by 2.1 m. high.

Tonnes of silage in pit:

$$= \quad \frac{20 \times 10 \times 2.1}{1.4} \quad = \quad 300 \text{ tonnes.}$$

Example 2

A circular grain bin is 3 metres in diameter i.e. 1.5 m. in radius and contains wheat to a height of 4 metres.

Tonnes of wheat in bin:

$$= \quad \frac{3.14 \times (1.5 \times 1.5) \times 4}{1.31} \quad = \quad 21.57 \text{ tonnes.}$$

ANIMAL HOUSING - SPACE REQUIREMENTS

Table 5.4: Animal housing - space requirements

	Housing System	Space Requirement
Suckler Cows	Slatted with calf creeps (with passage)	4.5 - 5.2 m²
	Straw bed with calf creeps (with passage)	7.4 - 8.3 m²
Cattle	Slatted incl. passage - weanlings	2.2 - 2.8m² / hd.
	- stores / finishers	2.8 - 3.2 m² / hd
Calves	Individual pens up to 4 weeks	1.12m² / calf
	Individual pens up to 8 weeks	1.8m² / calf
	group pens up to 8 weeks	1.10m² / calf
	group up to 12 weeks	1.50m² / calf
Sheep	Ewe housing - slatted	0.9 - 1.2 m² / ewe
	Ewe housing - straw bedded	1.1 - 1.4m² / ewe
Slurry	Dairy Cows - slatted tank	1.5m³/month
	- uncovered tank	1.8m³/month
	Cattle 450 kg. - slatted tank	1.2m³/month
	- uncovered tank	1.4m³/month
	Cattle 250 kg. - slatted tank	0.6m³/month
	- uncovered tank	0.8m³/month
	Suckler Cow - slatted tank	1.3m³/month
	- uncovered tank	1.6m³/month
	Sows - dry	0.14m³/month
	- suckling	0.56m³/month
	Weaners	0.09m³/month
	Finishers - dry fed	0.14m³/month
	- liquid	0.17m³/month
	Poultry - layers	0.43m³/100/month
	- broilers	0.26m³/100/month
	Sheep - ewes	0.17m³/month

GUIDE TO COST OF FARM BUILDINGS

Table 5.5: Guide to cost of farm buildings

	Euros (€)
Cattle & Cow Housing	
Dairy Cows - Slatted Easy Feed	1600 - 1860/cow
Calving boxes	1860 - 2130/hd
Weanlings - Slatted house	530 - 660/hd.
Stores - Slatted house	800 - 930/hd.
Weanlings - Loose shed	330 - 400/hd.
Stores - Loose Shed	460 - 530/hd.
Calf Housing	330 - 460/calf
Suckler Cows - Straw bed & Slatted passage	830 -900/suckler
Suckler Cows - Purpose built slatted	1,060 - 1,200 /suckler
Sheep Housing	
Straw bedded	100 115/ewe
Slatted	190 - 220/ewe
Pig Housing	
Sows - rearing to weaner	1,400- 1,500/sow
Fattening	170 - 190/pig
Fowl	
Broiler - Breeding	30/bird
Broiler - Commercial	6/bird
Layers - Commercial	16/bird
Layers - Free range	20/bird
Turkey Fattening	14/bird
Farm Roadways (compacted hardcore)	5.7 -6.35/m²
Concrete Areas (concrete on hardcore)	23 - 25/m²
Sheep Fencing (5 wire)	1.90/m
Paddock Fencing	1/m
Timber Post & Rail Fencing (3 rail)	14/m
Mushroom Unit -5 house	152,400- 165,100

PLANNING PERMISSION REQUIREMENTS

The construction of all farm buildings with a floor area in excess of 300 sq. metres requires planning permission. However works consisting of roofed or open structures that are less than 300 sq. metres in area, while exempt, must meet certain conditions:

- No structure shall be used for any non-agricultural purpose.
- The total area of such structures for pigs, cattle, sheep, poultry, deer or rabbits, including roofless structures and open yards situated within the farmyard complex or within 100 metres of that complex shall not exceed 450 sq. metres (900 sq. metres if no animal housing present) area in aggregate. The total area of the individual structure shall not exceed 300 sq. metres.
- A roofed structure for horses and ponies shall not exceed 100 sq. metres and the total area of all such structures within the farmyard complex shall not exceed 150 sq. metres.
- A roofed structure for greyhounds shall not exceed 50 sq. metres and the total area of all such structures within the farmyard complex shall not exceed 75 sq. metres.
- A roofless hard surfaced yard or enclosed area in connection with the keeping of horses, ponies or greyhounds shall not exceed 100 sq. metres and the total area of all such structures within the farmyard complex shall not exceed 150 sq. metres.

However these exemptions are subject to the following conditions:

- The structures concerned must be used for agricultural purposes only and shall not be situated within 10 metres of any public road.
- No such structure within 100 metres of any public road shall exceed 8 metres in height above ground level.
- No such structure shall be situated, or no effluent from such structures shall be stored, within 100 metres of any dwelling house, school, church or building used for public assembly, save with the consent of the owner and occupier thereof..
- Effluent storage facilities adequate to serve the structure having regard to its size, use, location and the need to avoid water pollution shall be provided. This condition does not apply to buildings where effluents do not arise.

ENVIRONMENTAL IMPACT ASSESSMENT (EIA)

The following agricultural and forestry developments must be subjected to EIA as part of the planning process. An application for planning permission, including an Environmental Impact Statement (EIS), must be submitted in such cases:

- The use of uncultivated land or semi-natural areas for intensive agricultural purposes, where the area involved would be greater than 100 hectares.
- Water management projects for agriculture:
  - where the catchment area involved would be greater than 1,000 ha
  - where more than 50 hectares of wetlands would be affected
- Afforestation where the area on its own, or together with areas planted within the previous three years, would be over 70 hectares; or replacement of broadleaf forest by conifers, where the area would be over 10 hectares.
  Land reclamation for the purposes of conversion to another type of land use, where the area involved would be greater than 100 hectares.
- Peat extraction which would involve a new or extended area of 50 hecatres or more.
- Poultry rearing installations where the capacity would exceed 1,000 units and where units have the following equivalents; 1 broiler =1 unit, 1 layer, turkey or other fowl = 2 units.
- Pig rearing installations where the capacity would exceed 1,000 units on gley soils or 3,000 units on other soils and where units have the following equivalents; 1 pig =1 unit, 1 sow = 10 units.

EIA will be required for projects in the case of pig and poultry installations even where the listed thresholds are not exceeded, if the planning authority considers that there may be significant effects on the environment.

PLANNING CHARGES

The following scale of charges currently apply:
- Farm buildings other than for keeping horses, ponies or greyhounds, are charged at €0.95 for each square metre of gross floor area in excess of 300 square metres subject to a minimum fee of €73 and a maximum charge of €276.
- Buildings for keeping horses, ponies or greyhounds are charged at €0.95 for each square metre of gross floor area in excess of 100 square metres per sq. metre subject to a minimum fee of €73 and a maximum charge of €276.
- The use of uncultivated land or semi-natural areas for intensive agricultural production is charged at €276.

135

- Initial afforestation is charged at €4.60 per hectare of site area. The replacement of broadleaf high forests by conifer species is €73 or €4.60 per hectare of site sown which ever is greater.
- Peat extraction is charged at €4.60 for each hectare of site area.
- The use of land for a golf or pitch and put course costs €46.20 for each hectare..
- Erection of a dwelling €59.
- Alteration of a dwelling €30.

NUTRIENT VALUE OF SLURRY

The cost of agitating and spreading slurry with a vacuum tanker varies widely depending on the water content of the slurry and the distance from the point of spreading. Nevertheless, a guideline of €8 per 1,000 gallons is a useful indication of the likely cost from a contractor.

The nutrient value of slurry depends on the type of slurry and the method of storage. As an example the nutrient value of slurry from a covered slatted tank is estimated as follows:

Table 5.6: The nutrient of slurry from a covered slatted tank

	Units per 1,000 gallons			Approx. value
	N	P	K	
Cattle Slurry	40	6	40	€16
Pig Slurry	37	12	18	€15

STANDARD LABOUR REQUIREMENTS

Table 5.7 sets out the standard labour requirements for the main farming enterprises expressed in Standard Man Days (S.M.D's) which is the equivalent of an eight work day carried out by an adult worker. A Man Work Unit is comprised of 225 Standard Man Days. The figures are based on Teagasc research and are generally regarded as the definitive reference in measuring the labour requirement of a farming operation.

Table 5.7 Standard Labour Requirements

Enterprise S.M.D's	Good Layout	Poor Layout
Dairying per cow	5	10
Single Suckling per cow (calf to 6 months)	2.5	3.5
Double Suckling per cow (calf to 6 months)	3.5	5.5
Multiple Suckling per cow (calf to 6 months)	5.5	12.0
Cattle (0-6 mts) per head	1.0	1.5
Cattle (6-12 mts) per head	0.6	1.0
Cattle (12-18 mts) per head	0.3	0.4
Cattle (18-24 mts) per head	0.6	1.1
Early Fat Lamb per Ewe	0.7	1.0
Mid Season & Store Lamb per Ewe	0.7	1.0
Mountain & Hill per Ewe	0.6	0.6
Hoggetts for six months per head	0.2	0.3
Lambs finishing on slats per head	0.075	-
Sows producing weaners per sow	3.6	4.0
Sows producing finished pigs per sow	4.0	0.1
Fattening pigs per head	0.05	6.0
Mare	10	-
Mare and foal	12	-
Mare + Foal + Yearling	16	-
Mare + Foal	20	-
Potatoes	14.0	17.0
Cereals per acre (all machinery owned)	1.5	-
Cereals per acre (main work done by contractor)	2.0	-
Sugar Beet (main work done by contractor)	7.0	-
Sugar Beet (main work by contractor)	5.5	-

THE COST OF FORAGE

GRASS SILAGE PRODUCTION COSTS

Table 5.8: The cost of grass silage per acre (Euros)

	Bulk	Baled
Yield (tonnes) or bales @ 667 kgs	10	15
Fertilisers		
130 kgs urea 46%N (120 units N / acre)	31	31
150 kgs 0.10.20 per acre @ €210 / tonne	32	32
Lime		
2 tonnes / acre every 4 years @ €19 / tonne.	10	10
Contractor		
Total cost for bulk silage (precision chop)	90	
Cutting		22
Baling (including plastic) @ €9 / bale		135
Transport @ €1 / bale		15
Polythene cover	10	
Additive	14	
Cost per acre	187	245
Cost per tonne	19	25
Cost per bale	-	12

HAY PRODUCTION COSTS

Table 5.9: The cost per acre of making hay

	ROUND	SQUARE
Yield bales per acre	14	140
Fertilisers		
100 kgs CAN 27.5%N @ €190 / t (55 units N)	€19	€19
100 kgs 0.10.20 per acre @€210 / tonne	€21	€21
Lime		
2 tonnes / acre every 4 years @ €19 / tonne.	€9	€9
Contractor		
Cutting	€22	€22
Baling	€54	€56
Cost per acre	€125	€123
Cost per bale	€8.92	€0.87

GRAZING GRASS

Table 5.10: The cost of grazed grass at varying levels of inputs

	€
Very High Fertiliser Inputs	
Fertilisers	
545 kgs CAN 27.5%N (300 units N / acre)	104
150 kgs 0.10.20 per acre @ €210/ tonne	32
Lime 2 tonnes / acre every 4 years @ €19 / tonne	10
Cost per acre	146
High Fertiliser Inputs	
Fertilisers	
364 kgs CAN 27.5%N (200 units N / acre)	69
100 kgs 0.10.20 per acre @ €210 / tonne	21
Lime 2 tonnes / acre every 4 years @ €19 / tonne	10
Cost per acre	100
Moderate Fertiliser Inputs	
Fertilisers	
273 kgs CAN 27.5%N (150 units N / acre)	52
75 kgs 0.10.20 per acre @€210 / tonne	16
Lime 2 tonnes / acre every 6 years @ €19 / tonne	6
Cost per acre	74
Low Fertiliser Inputs	
Fertilisers	
150 kgs CAN 27.5%N (82 units N / acre)	28
50 kgs 0.10.20 per acre @€210/ tonne	11
Lime 2 tonnes / acre every 6 years @ €19 / tonne	6
Cost per acre	45

MAIZE SILAGE PRODUCTION COSTS

Table 5.11: Maize silage production costs (Euros €)

	Production Level		
Yield (tonnes / acre)	16	18	20
Yield (dry matter / acre)	4	4.7	5.25
Variable Costs			
Seed	76	76	76
Fertiliser	88	88	88
Spray materials & spraying	43	43	43
Plough, till & sow	75	75	75
Harvesting & covering	125	125	125
Interest	13	13	13
Total Variable Costs	407	407	407
Less EU area-aid	-148	-148	-148
Cost per acre	259	259	259
Cost per tonne dry matter	64	54	49

INPUT DATA - MAIZE SILAGE

Seed :	€72 per acre pack (45,000 seeds per acre)
Fertiliser:	150 kgs CAN @ €190 / t & 200 kgs 0.7.30 @ €1210 / t and 3,000 cattle slurry / acre @ €6 / 1,000 depending on soil fertility
Herbicide:	€14 / acre
Insecticide:	€14 / acre
Machinery :	Contractor charges per acre: ploughing €27, tilling €21 sowing €25, spraying €15
Note:	Arable aid is payable on maize grown on eligible land only and will be dependent on the National Base Area.

FODDER BEET PRODUCTION COSTS

Table 5.12: Fodder beet production costs per acre (Euros €)

	Production Level		
Yield (tonnes / acre)	30	33	35
Yield (dry Matter / acre)	4.2	4.6	4.9
Variable Costs			
Seed	56	56	56
Fertiliser & spreading	153	153	153
Spray materials & spraying	140	140	140
Plough, till & sow	66	66	66
Harvesting & covering	108	108	108
Interest	13	13	13
Cost per acre	536	536	536
Cost per tonne dry matter	128	116	109

INPUT DATA

Seed: €48 per acre pack

Fertiliser: 500 kgs beet compound @ €260 / tonne & 50 kgs CAN @ €190 / tonne

Herbicide : €76 / acre

Fungicide : €15 / acre

Machinery : Contractor charges per acre : ploughing €27, tilling €21, sowing €18, fertiliser spreading €7, spraying €6, harvesting and covering €102

OTHER FORAGE AND ROOT CROPS

Table 5.13: Other forage & root crops - cost per acre Euros (€)

	Swedes	Rape	Kale	Stubble Turnips
Yield (tonnes / acre)	30	17	15	10
Yield (Dry Matter / acre)	2.1	1.4	1.5	1
Variable Costs				
Seed	23	15	30	14
Fertilisers & spreading	79	58	62	57
Spray materials & spraying	83	-	-	-
Plough, till & sow	63	63	63	63
Total Cost per acre	248	136	155	134
Cost per tonne dry matter	118	97	103	134

Part 6 - Planning for Retirement and Succession

WILL'S & ENTITLEMENTS

No farmer is too young or old to make a will. A will is a highly important document and should if at all possible be prepared by a solicitor. Making a will ensures that your assets pass to the person of your choice and much unnecessary expense and administration will be avoided after your death.

The other main advantage of making a will is that the whole question of inheritance tax will have been addressed. If there is a potential problem, you will at least be afforded the opportunity to put measures in place to avoid leaving a substantial inheritance tax bill to your nominated successor.

In the event of your being unable or not wanting to consult a solicitor you should at least ensure that:

- You have made a written will. A verbal will is of no use regardless of how many people witness your making it.
- You must state your name and address.
- You must revoke all former wills.
- You must appoint at least one and preferably two executors.
- Your will must be signed by you and your signature witnessed by two persons, neither of whom can benefit under the will.
- You must be of sound mind.
- You must date the will.

A witness to a will or his/her spouse cannot benefit under that will.

ENTITLEMENTS OF SPOUSE WHERE A WILL IS PRESENT
Where a will is made and the testator is survived by his or her spouse the surviving spouse may elect to take the following.

- Their entitlement under the will
         or
- One third of the estate where there are children
- One half of the estate where there are no children

ENTITLEMENTS OF SPOUSE WHERE NO WILL IS PRESENT
Where a person dies without a will (intestate) the following are the entitlements of the relatives:

144

- Where there is a spouse with no children the spouse is entitled to everything.
- Where there is a spouse with children, regardless of age, the spouse is entitled to two thirds and the children to one third in equal shares.
- Where there are surviving children and no spouse the estate is divided between the children. If one of the children is no longer living his or her share passes to his or her children.
- Where a son or daughter dies without a will, their estate passes in its entirety to the parent or parents. If the parents are dead the estate passes to the brothers and sisters or the children of deceased brothers or sisters.

A will should be reappraised at regular intervals, as circumstances can change or tax legislation alter. A will remains in force until it is replaced by a new will. However, a will is revoked on marriage unless that will has been clearly drawn up with the marriage in mind.

ALTERING A WILL

Any alterations made to a will after signing will be invalid. Where one wishes to alter the content of a will it is essential that the family solicitor is consulted.

REVOKING A WILL

This refers to cancelling a will, whether for good or with a view to changing its contents. Making a new will and mentioning in it that all former wills are revoked is the most effective method of revocation. Destroying a will may also be an effective means of revocation but not to be recommended unless a new will has been made which revokes all previous wills. A photocopy of a will, in the absence of an original, may be sufficient to take out probate providing the person who made the copy can swear to its authenticity.

It should be noted that a will is automatically revoked upon the marriage of the person who made the will, unless it is specified in the will that it was made with the intention of getting married.

CAUTION:- In all possible cases, wills should be drawn up by the family solicitor as wills that are not professionally drawn up may cause serious difficulties after the death of the testator. Secondly, it is vital that you inform some reliable person or institution, such as your bank, of the whereabouts of your will.

GRANT OF PROBATE

A Grant of Probate is authorisation from the courts to carry out the provisions of the will. Various documents setting out the assets and liabilities of the deceased persons estate are sent to the Probate Office, Four Courts, Dublin or to the District Probate Registry at your nearest Circuit Court Office. While in theory it is possible for the lay person to take out probate it is really a matter for a solicitor to deal with. Where there is no will a Grant of Administration is taken out. In this case an administrator must be agreed by the beneficiaries to the estate and he or she will then perform a similar role to an executor.

TRANSFERRING, LEASING OR SELLING THE FAMILY FARM

Transferring, leasing or selling the family farm will require consideration of a number of matters not least the tax implications, pension considerations and the actual cost associated with transferring, selling or leasing.

INCOME TAX IMPLICATIONS OF TRANSFERRING OR SELLING

Transferring or selling the entire farm will generally mean a cessation of trading. This may have a number of consequences from a tax point of view. If, for example, tax is being assessed on the basis of 'income averaging' there may be an additional liability to income tax where averaging resulted in a substantial saving in the year immediately prior to ceasing. Furthermore, where the transferee was already farming there may be a paper profit on the transfer of livestock, particularly where the stock was valued at a low rate. Where the farm tax return was being made by way of farm profile the entire proceeds arising from the disposal of stock will be taxable.

INCOME TAX IMPLICATIONS OF LEASING

Where one is ceasing to farm altogether the same situation applies as for transferring. However, one of the obvious differences between leasing and transferring is the fact that the leased lands will attract rental income. Depending on one's circumstances rental income may be subject to income tax. However, for farmers of 55 years or over with leases for seven year or longer leases to unconnected persons, the first €7,620 in rent receipts is tax free. For leases of between five and seven years the relief is €5,080.

This concession is also available to farmers younger than 55 years who are permanently incapacitated by mental or physical infirmity from carrying on farming.

Leasing of land to family members does not attract any tax concessions and the lessor will be liable for tax on the rent specified in the lease regardless of whether or not it is paid.

Before you approach your solicitor advice should be sought from your tax advisor as to the income tax implications of ceasing and in particular the timing of the cessation.

GIFT TAX IMPLICATIONS

In the vast majority of transfers to sons or daughters or favourite nieces or nephews there are no gift tax implications as land and agricultural assets are valued at only one tenth of their market value for this purpose. However the recipient must be a farmer by definition, in other words 80% of their gross asset value, after receiving the gift, must comprise agricultural property, livestock, bloodstock or machinery. Take for example a farmers son who has a house worth €190,500 (irrespective of the size of mortgage) and receives land and stock worth €635,000 from his father. In this case the agricultural assets do not comprise 80% or more of his total asset value after receiving the gift, in which case he is not entitled to 'agricultural relief' (see taxation section) and the gift is valued at market value. If the gift were received in the tax year 2002 there would be a liability to gift tax of €45,270 assuming the son had received no previous gifts or inheritances. In such circumstances the liability could have been avoided if the investments could have been converted to agricultural assets prior to the transfer. If the recipient is the owner of a house which could not be classed as agricultural property it would be important to have the house valued to ensure that he or she fits the definition of a farmer as set out above before proceeding with a transfer.

CAPITAL GAINS TAX IMPLICATIONS

Capital gains tax will rarely be a problem associated with family transfers however, there are certain circumstances which can give rise to capital gains tax. Such circumstances might arise if the period of ownership was not very long or the farmer transferring was under 55 years. However where a farm is being transferred within the family, by a farmer who is over 55 years, to a qualifying son, daughter or favourite niece or nephew, no capital gains tax will arise provided the farm was owned for a period of 10 years or more and was used for farming purposes and that the transferee does not dispose of it within six years. Transfers between husbands and wives are not liable to capital gains tax.

Selling the farm can in many cases give rise to capital gains tax but this will depend on a number of factors such as the age of the farmer, the length of ownership and the sale proceeds. For more detailed information on selling all or part of the farm refer to the taxation section of this handbook.

STAMP DUTY

Stamp duty is not a concern for the person disposing of property, so in the case of a sale it is the purchaser who pays it. However in the case of family transfers it will be a concern if the transferee is not eligible for the zero rate (see taxation section). The rate of duty will generally amount to 3% of the value of the land and buildings transferred. If a milk quota attaches to the lands, the value of this is also subject to stamp duty.

For stamp duty purposes the farm will be valued at current market value. The value of farm buildings will be considered but it is true to say that farm buildings are generally not separately valued but rather, are reflected in the overall farm valuation. Milk quota should be valued as if it were being sold as a going concern with the land. The value of farm machinery and livestock is not subject to stamp duty, but in the case of transfers of relatively low value, may have a bearing on the rate of duty. For example if land valued at €57,150 was being transferred to a son, the rate of duty would be 2%. However, if livestock and machinery valued at €31,750 were also being transferred the rate would be 3%, as the value of all the assets being transferred would be over €76,200 but only the land would be subject to stamp duty.

Table 6.1 sets out the liability to stamp duty on a range of values in a case where the son or daughter is not entitled to the special 'relief for young trained farmers'.

Table 6.1 Stamp duty rates - normal rate

Land Value €	Other Assets €	Stamp Duty €
40.000	25.000	1.000
120.000	40.000	3.600
180.000	70.000	5.400
250.000	85.000	7.500
400.000	100.000	12.000
600.000	120.000	18.000
800.000	140.000	24.000

Stamp duty on leases amounts to 1% of the average annual lease premium. However, where the specified rent is below the commercial letting value of the land, the Revenue Commissioners treat the amount by which the consideration is below the commercial letting value as a gift. In this case the full market letting value is multiplied by the term of the lease in years and stamp duty at the full rate is applied to the gift portion. This situation can often apply to family leases where the rent does not reflect the full commercial letting value of the lands.

Example:

John leases his 100 acre farm to his son Michael for a rent of €4,000 per year for 10 years. The Revenue Commissioners consider this to be €7,000 per year below a commercial rent value. In this case the son will be deemed to be receiving an annual gift of €7,000 for each of ten years, or in other words €70,000 in total. Stamp duty at a rate of 6% will be chargeable amounting to €4,200. This will also have an implication for any future gifts as the combined value of all gifts received since 5 December 1991 is used to determine a liability to gift tax. (See Taxation Section).

It is important therefore, that leases reflect an annual rent that is not far removed from the average commercial letting value for the particular area and that the annual rent is actually paid over as the Revenue Commissioners will take the view that the lessor is taxable on the stated annual rent regardless of whether he receives it or not.

LEGAL FEES

In general it can be expected that legal fees will amount to approx. 1% to 1.5% of the value of the assets being transferred. However this may vary depending on the complexity of the particular case. The cost of preparing a lease will generally be in the range €500 to €600.

Never has the climate been more conducive to transferring the family farm, with the availability of the Early Farm Retirement Scheme, Stamp Duty exemption, Stock Relief for young trained farmers and Installation Aid.

SOURCES OF INCOME IN RETIREMENT

Up until recent years one of the greatest obstacles to handing on the family farm was the prospect of a meagre income thereafter. Generally this income was provided by the state in the form of a non contributory pension which was means tested and was reduced if the recipient had any other income or savings of any consequence. Thankfully the position has improved considerably with the introduction of the contributory old age pension and the Scheme of Early Retirement from Farming.

CONTRIBUTORY STATE PENSION

In order to qualify for a contributory pension you will have to have made certain PRSI contributions and met certain conditions. The PRSI scheme for the self-employed which came into effect in 1988 should entitle persons to a pension on reaching their 66th. birthday providing they have made the necessary PRSI contributions.

CONDITIONS FOR A FULL PENSION

To qualify for a full pension the following conditions must be met:

- You must have started paying PRSI before you were 56 years of age.
- You must have at least 260 weeks (if you were 66 since 6 April 2002) of insurable employment in which the appropriate contributions were made

and

- a yearly average of at least 48 weeks PRSI paid or credited for the period from 5 April 1979 to the end of the tax year before you reach pension age

or

- a yearly average of at least 10 weeks PRSI paid or credited from 1953 (or the time you started insurable employment, if later) to the end of the tax year before you reached age 66. A yearly average of 10 will entitle you to a minimum rate pension while an average of 48 are required for a maximum pension.

Note: An annual contribution is equivalent to 52 weeks contributions.

RATES OF CONTRIBUTORY OLD AGE PENSION

The following rates are effective since 4 January 2002:

Personal rate	€147.30
Person with adult dependent under 66	€245.40
Person with adult dependent over 66	€261.11

A contributory pension is not means tested therefore assets such as property, investments and savings can be retained without affecting the pension.
Note: For rate changes announced in Budget 2002 see page 12.

APPLYING FOR THE PENSION

You may apply any time from five months of reaching your 66th. birthday The form is simple to complete and can be had from Old Age Contributory Section, Pension Services Office, College Road, Sligo. (071)69800. The application must be accompanied by your birth certificate and if you are married your spouse's birth certificate and your marriage certificate.

NON-CONTRIBUTORY OLD AGE PENSION

Any person having attained the age of 66 is entitled to the non-contributory pension provided they satisfy a means test. Eligible spouses may apply separately for the pension. Farmers who continue to own their farms after the age of 66 may have the estimated value of the farm, excluding the family home, assessed against them.

Farmers who sign over their farms in order to qualify for non-contributory pensions should bear in mind that any obligation imposed on the recipient in respect of maintenance or care of the donor may result in a reduction of the pension. Generally, the phrase 'by virtue of natural love and affection' is included in the deed of transfer so that no such obligation can be imputed.

MEANS TEST

Your means will be determined by calculating a notional income based on savings, investments or property of which you are in possession (your home is excluded). The actual income from investments and money in a savings account is not taken as means. Instead the values of the savings, investments and property you possess are added together and a formula is used to work out your means as follows:

- First €12,697 not counted (€25,394 for couples)
- Where capital is between €12,697 - €25,394 (€25,394 - €50,788 for couples) weekly income is determined at €1 per each €1,000.
- Where capital is between €25,394 - €38,092 (€50,788 - €76,184 for couples) weekly income is determined at €2 per each €1,000.
- Where capital is over €38,092 (€76,184 for couples) weekly income is determined at €4 per each €1,000..

Example:
John is 66 years old, widowed and has €37,000 in savings. How will this affect his application for a non-contributory old age pension ?

John would be entitled to €134 per week if not for the existence of his savings. Unfortunately his pension will be reduced by the amount of notional income arising on the €37,000 savings, which is calculated as follows:

- First €12,697 not counted
- €12.70 per week on the next €12,697..
- €23.21 per week on the remaining €11,606..

The pension will therefore be reduced by €35.91 on a weekly basis, leaving him with an old age pension of only €98.09 per week.

RATES
The rates of non contributory pension are (effective from 4 January 2002):

Personal rate	€134
Person with adult dependent under 66	€225.5

Note: For rate changes announced in Budget 2002 see page 12.

PRIVATELY FUNDED PENSIONS

A farmer who has handed over the farm and ceases to farm may not be able to continue to contribute to his existing personal pension policy. Under current legislation a person can only pay into a personal pension policy if he has an income which can be defined as 'relevant earnings' i.e. income from self employment or non pensionable earnings. So when a farmer ceases to have 'relevant earnings' the fund will grow and mature in the normal way but no additional contributions to the fund can be made.

The type of situation outlined where people with inadequate pension funds are prevented from making contributions has been acknowledged by the Government and a new type of privately funded pension scheme is due to be launched in 2003. This new scheme will enable any person with or without 'relevant earnings' to contribute. This new type of pension fund is called a **Personal Retirement Savings Account or PRSA** and is covered in more detail on page 201

EARLY FARM RETIREMENT SCHEME

The Scheme of Early Retirement from Farming 2000 (EC 1750/1999) became operational 27 November 2000 having replaced the original scheme introduced in 1993. It is expected that approximately 7,250 farmers will avail of the new scheme which runs until 2006. The scheme is aimed at reducing the age profile of farmers and to increase farm size. The need for these changes is reflected by the fact that, in Ireland, average farm size is 64 acres and approximately 40% of farmers are 55 years or older while only 18,000 are under 35 years of age.

ELIGIBLE LANDS FOR PAYMENT UNDER THE EARLY RETIREMENT SCHEME

From 1 April 2001 only U.A.A. (utilisable agricultural area) lands owned or leased which were subject to an area-aid application at the time of signing the transfer/lease documents are eligible. Exceptions to this rule may be allowed under Force Majeure with the prior approval of the Minister, e.g. in situations where it was necessary to let the land for a short period prior to retirement because of illness or where an applicant is medically certified of having been incapable of making an area aid application..

Lands transferred/leased to eligible transferees or reassigned to non-agricultural use on or after 1 January 2000 are eligible for inclusion under the scheme. Lands where legal documents were signed prior to 1 January 2000 but not stamped and/or brought to dealing number stage may also be eligible.

UTILISABLE AGRICULTURAL AREA

For the purposes of determining Utilisable Agricultural Area (U.A.A.) under the scheme, the following should not be included:

* The dwelling house including associated buildings and amenity grounds not used for agriculture.
* Farm buildings including glasshouses, polythene tunnels, associated farmyards and waste areas.
* Roads, including public road area if any and the area under internal farm roads.
* Commercial forestry which does not include shelter belts.
* Area under water excluding drains.
* Land held in fee simple subject to turbary or grazing rights.
* Grazing rights on lands where the fee simple is owned by another.
* Land retained by a transferor, which must not exceed 1 ha.
* Pension lands under the previous Early Retirement Scheme (1992 - 1999) are

ineligible for inclusion until after the expiry date of that pension.

TRANSFERS BETWEEN SPOUSES

Transfers/leases of lands between transferor's and their spouses/partners after 1 January 2000 (unless as eligible transferee's under the scheme) cannot be used by the transferor to avoid compliance with the terms and conditions of the scheme. The owners of such lands as at 1 January 2000 will be regarded as being in joint management with the applicant and will have to comply with the terms and conditions of the scheme.

MINIMUM SIZE OF HOLDING

Agricultural holdings to be transferred or reassigned must comprise a minimum of 5 ha. of UAA.

LANDS THAT CAN BE RETAINED

The applicant may retain the dwelling house and a maximum of 10% but not more than 1 hectare of U.A.A. of the holding, provided a minimum of 5 ha. of UAA is transferred or reassigned. The area retained may not be used for commercial farming by the transferor

ELIGIBILITY FOR THE SCHEME - THE TRANSFEROR

In order to become a transferor, the applicant must on the date the completed application is received in the Department's Office:

- Have ceased commercial farming
- Have the lands subject to the pension transferred/leased with the relevant buildings and quota rights to eligible farming transferees
- Have his/her herd or flock/cereal reference number cancelled, transferred or made dormant
- To between his/her 55th and 66th birthday on the date a completed application is received by the Department.
- Provide a Personal Public Services Number (PPSN), previously called an RSI number.
- Have farmed an area of not less that 5 hectares of eligible lands, as owner/joint

owner, leaseholder/joint leaseholder and/or tenant in common at the time of signing the transfer/lease documents.

- Have practised farming for the 10 calendar years prior to the signing of the transfer/lease documents and **have derived not less that 25% of his/her total income units from farming at the time the transfer documents are signed.**
- To be admitted to the scheme the transferor must undertake to cease all commercial farming activity definitively. He/she may, however, continue non-commercial farming activity on the retained area and retain the use of the buildings for non-farming purposes.
- Once a completed application has been received by the Department, an applicant must continue to abide by the terms and conditions for the full period for which he/she is eligible for the pension and is prohibited from returning to farming at any date in the future.

THE ELIGIBILITY TEST FOR TRANSFERORS

The transferor must have total income from farming and non-farm sources of not more that 200 income units at the time of signing the transfer documents (except in the case of a free and definitive transfer of all the agriculture holding to a family member, where no income limit will apply). Where lands are owned/ jointly owned/ jointly leased by a transferor's spouse/partner, only the non-farm income of the applicant is taken into account. Income units are calculated by reference to the values as set below.

Table 6.2 : Calculation of Income units

Enterprise	Units	Enterprise	Units
Cattle 6-24 months	0.6	Milk Quota 400 gals.	1
Cattle over 24 months	1	Tillage crops per ha.	1
Suckler Cows	1	Intensive crops/ha.	2
Ewes	0.15	Off-farm income / €254	1
Deer sitka/fallow	0.1	Glasshouse /ha.	125
Red deer	0.3	Sows -breeding only	0.8
Horse	1	Sows-breeding & finishing	1.1
Broilers/1000 places	3	Hay/Silage for sale /ha.	1
Broiler breeders /1000	8	Forestry	1
Layers /1000 birds	3	Rabbits /100	1
Turkey fattening /1000	3	Milking Goats/goat	0.3
Free range layers /100	1.5		

Income units from forestry, agri-tourism and crafts will not qualify for inclusion in the calculation of the 20 income unit minimum threshold from farming owned/leased

155

land. However it can be included in the calculation of the 50 income unit total, at the rate of 1.0 units per hectare of forestry, and per €254 of gross taxable income from agri-tourism and crafts. The gross taxable income will be calculated on the basis of output less production costs.

ELIGIBLE SPOUSE
There are a number of differing circumstance that will determine which spouse should apply:

- Where one spouse is over age 66 and the other is under age 66 and over age 55 the younger spouse may apply if he/she has been working full-time on the farm or has acted in a joint managerial role on the farm for the previous ten years. Furthermore, the land does not have to be in the name of the younger spouse.
- Where both spouses are between 55 and 66 the younger spouse can apply, thus maximising the pension period.
- Where one spouse is over 56 and the other is under 56 the older spouse may apply providing he/she has been working full-time on the farm or has acted in a joint managerial role on the farm for the previous ten years. Furthermore, the land does not have to be in the name of the applicant spouse. An example of such a situation might be where the wife is over 55 and the husband is under age 55. However both parties have to undertake to permanently cease farming.
- If both spouses have lands registered in their individual names and have farmed them independently both may be entitled to the pension providing they satisfy all of the other conditions for eligibility. Farming independently would mean having separate herd numbers, making separate tax returns and generally satisfying the Department that both farms were operated separately.

JOINT MANAGEMENT
Where an applicant is not the owner/leaseholder of the agricultural holding involved, he/she will only be admitted to the scheme if they are in actual joint management of the holding with the owner/leaseholder/tenant in common, in the calendar year prior to application. In the case of joint owners, joint lease holders and joint management, each party must undertake to cease all commercial farming definitively. Spouses can be considered to be in joint management. In such cases evidence of entitlement must be supplied such as a marriage certificate.

JOINT ENTERPRISES

Where an agricultural holding is managed as a joint enterprise with another agricultural holding, a maximum of one pension only is payable. For the purpose of the scheme, agricultural holdings will be adjudged to be managed as a joint enterprise if they share any of the following:

- common herd numbers
- a common application for Area Aid
- common handling facilities for livestock
- common farm accounts/farm profile/receipts
- livestock intermixing and/or adjoining boundaries not stock proof.

Where the land is owned by more than one person but farmed as a joint enterprise, either party (but not both) can apply for the pension based on their own area of ownership provided that:

- If the person remaining in farming does not sign a waiver for the pension, then the person applying for the Early Retirement pension will only be entitled to a pension calculated on a pro rata basis of the entire holding.
- Where lands are jointly owned/leased by two or more individuals, only one party can apply for the pension on the total area.

ELIGIBILITY FOR THE SCHEME - TRANSFEREE

A 'farming transferee' must on the date the completed application is received in the Department's Office be between their 18th and 45th birthday . The upper age limit will be reduced, by one year at a time, to 40 as in the following table.

Table 6.3 : Transferee upper age limit

Application lodged in year ending;	Upper age limit
Year ending 31 December 2002	44
Year ending 31 December 2003	43
Year ending 31 December 2004	42
Year ending 31 December 2005	41
After 31 December 2005	40

The transferee must also on the date the completed application is received in the

Department's Office be:

- If born on or after 1/1/75, have a minimum of three years farming experience and satisfactorily completed a course of training in agriculture or horticulture of a least 180 hours duration.
- If born before 1/1/75, have been engaged in farming for at least 5 years or is otherwise in the opinion of the Minister deemed to have acceptable farming experience or ability.
- Succeed the transferor(s) as a head of an agricultural holding which must be at least 5 hectares of UAA.
- Have a herd/flock/cereal number.
- Provide a Personal Public Services Number (PPSN)
- Undertake to practice farming/forestry/agri-tourism on all the pension lands for a period of five years or for as long as the pension is granted. Provided that prior Departmental approval is given, however, an exception may be allowed to the obligation to farm all the pension lands for the period of the pension where either the transferor or the transferee wishes to dispose of a small area of land of up to and including two hectares for non-farming use provided that the pension lands are not reduced below the minimum 5 hectares level. There will be a consequent pro-rata reduction in the pension dating back to the date of receipt of a completed application.
- Farm the pension lands for a period of 5 years or for as long as the pension is granted to the transferor, whichever is the greater. However, where it is not possible to farm the pension lands for the full period, the lease(s) can be reassigned to another eligible transferee for the remaining period of the pension. Prior written approval from the Department is necessary if a transferee wishes to sell/dispose/reassign the land to another eligible transferee. In such cased, the pension may continue to be paid.
- Undertake to follow Good Farming Practice. A farming transferee who has been recorded as being in breach of Good Farming Practice or found to be in non-compliance with the relevant legislation, will be subject to penalties.
- Reside within 70 miles (122 kilometres) of the holding on a permanent basis.

Where the land is owned/leased by separate individuals or as a joint owner/leaseholder and farmed as one agricultural holding, either party can be deemed an eligible transferee based on the total area, provided that the transferee owned or jointly owned or jointly owned land as a tenant-in-common and had sufficient land to meet the minimum 20 unit threshold in their own right, and that the herd/flock/cereal number was in the joint names, or in the name of the transferee prior to the application for the pension. An application will not be accepted until the farming transferee(s) has met all the conditions of the scheme. Prior to the transfer of the lands, where a transferee is not already at the minimum viability threshold and does not take over sufficient land and quota(s) to allow him to reach the minimum, then an application will not be accepted until such time as the transferee can establish that he has reached the minimum level required. In such cases an Area Aid application/IACS declaration will be necessary.

THE ELIGIBILITY TEST FOR TRANSFEREE'S
The eligible transferee must meet the following conditions:
- Meet a viability threshold of at least 50 income units of which at least 20 Income Units must be derived from farming owned/leased land and rented land cannot be used for the purpose of making up the 20 units. Lands leased with an unexpired term can be used for the purpose of calculating the 20 income unit minimum threshold provided that these lands or an equivalent or greater area are held for the period of the pension.
- Where the pension land fails to generate the minimum 20 income unit threshold, then additional lands (owned/leased) will be required to achieve the 20 income unit threshold for the duration of the pension.
- Be subject to an upper non-farm income limit of not more than 100 (€25,400) units in the tax year prior to receipt of the application. Where lands, required to generate the minimum 20 income units from farming, are held in joint ownership/lease by a transferee's spouse or where the transferee had lands transferred/leased to him/her by their spouse after 1 January 2000, the non-farm income of both must be aggregated and cannot exceed 100 income units in the tax year prior to the application.

With the prior approval of the Department, a transferee may enter into a partnership arrangement with another head of holding.

NON -FARMING TRANSFEREE
Where an eligible farming transferee cannot be found for all or part of the agricultural holding, all or part of it may be transferred to one or more non-farming transferees for non-agricultural purposes. A non-farming transferee, including a corporate body (Limited Company), must on the date the application is lodged in the Department's office take over all or part of the pension lands for non agriculture purposes, forestry or the creation of ecological reserves for a period of five years or for as long as the pension is granted to the transferor, whichever is the greater.

The transferor will not qualify for payments under the scheme until the non-farming transferee(s) has met all the conditions of the scheme.

DETAILS OF THE PENSION

RATE OF PENSION PAYABLE

The pension consists of a basic payment of €5,403 plus €338 per hectare, i.e. €136.70 acre, up to a maximum of 24 hectares (59.3 acres). Thus the maximum pension payable is therefore €13,518. Payment is made on a monthly basis by direct post or to a bank account.

ELIGIBLE AREA FOR PAYMENT

Payment will be based on the lesser of the area as per the legal documents or the gross area declared in the Area Aid application/IACS declaration.

COMMENCEMENT OF PENSION

The pension is payable from the date of lodgement of a valid application. Thus, if it takes three months for the Department to process a valid application the retiring farmer will be entitled to three months' arrears of pension at that time.

DURATION OF PENSION

The pension will be paid for not more than 10 years from the date on which a fully validated application is received for the Scheme but in any event will not be paid beyond the age of 68 for those transferors entering the Scheme in the year ending 31 December 2002. The maximum age for payment will be reduced for those entering the Scheme in each succeeding year, as per the following table.

Table 6.4: Duration of pension

Application lodged in year ending	Pension paid to age
Year ending 31 December 2002	68th. birthday
Year ending 31 December 2003	67th. birthday
Y/E 31 December 2004 onwards	66th. birthday

DEATH OF PENSIONER

Where the pensioner dies within the pension period, entitlement to the pension for the balance of the period may be transferable to the spouse and/or dependent relatives subject to the following;

- the conditions regarding transferee and pension lands continue to be met.
- the resulting total annual income does not exceed the sum of the pension and the average industrial wage as determined by the Central Statistics Office.

ERS GENERAL POINTS

SELLING A SITE DURING PARTICIPATION IN THE SCHEME

Provided that written notification is given to the Department of Agriculture, Food and Rural Development an exception may be allowed to the obligation to farm all the pension lands for the period of the pension where either the transferor or the transferee wishes to dispose of a small area of land of up to and including two hectares for non-farming use, e.g. sale of sites, provided that the pension lands are not reduced below the minimum 5 hectares level. Such disposals will result in a reduction in the pension dating back to the commencement of the pension at a rate of €338 per year of pension for each hectare disposed of. In the case of the transferee disposing of land no reduction will apply if an equal or greater amount of land is replaced within four months.

GET OUT CLAUSE

If, after 5 years or more, all or part of the lands are disposed of with the transferor's agreement to a party who is not another eligible farming transferee, the pension will cease but payments already made may be retained. If all or part of the lands are disposed of without the transferor's agreement, then an appropriate penalty will be applied to the transferee.

NON MEANS TESTED

The pension is not means tested so an applicant may be in receipt of other income such as lease income from the retirement lands while receiving the Farm Retirement Pension.

NATIONAL RETIREMENT PENSIONS- APPLICANT

Where a person is receiving or becomes entitled to a National Retirement Pension the ERS pension will be reduced by the amount of the National Retirement Pension regardless to the age of the applicant. The only exception to this rule is recipients of the contributory widows pension who are be eligible to receive both pensions until age 66. The following types of pensions are National Retirement Pensions:

- Survivors Non-contributory Pension
- Retirement Pension
- Invalidity Pension
- Blind Person's Pension

Where the 'joint management' system has been used to qualify the participant the pension will be reduced if either party is in receipt of a National Retirement Pension.

NATIONAL RETIREMENT PENSIONS - SPOUSE

Where the participant leased or transferred in excess of 24 hectares of their own land, including their share of lands jointly owned, to qualify for the maximum pension, then any National Retirement Pension payable to the spouse/partner will not be deducted from the pension. However where the participant has used his or hers spouse's/partners land to qualify for a higher pension than that based on his or her own land, the pension shall be reduced by the amount of National Retirement Pension paid to both the participant and his or her spouse/partner in joint management.

Participants must apply for the Contributory Old Age Pension when they reach 66 years. Furthermore, in the event of them not being eligible for a contributory pension they must make a request to the Department of Social, Community and Family Affairs to be considered for a Non-contributory Pension.

ACTIVITIES THAT A RETIRED FARMER CANNOT PURSUE

A retiring farmer must cease all commercial farming. If the retiring farmer has an agricultural contracting business he may not continue this as it is considered to be farming. An eligible transferor may not buy or sell livestock as an agent or dealer. A retiring farmer or their spouse in joint management cannot earn an income from any work that would form part of the normal business of the farm. For example the eligible transferee cannot pay the retired person or their spouse in joint management a wage in respect of the maintenance of farm records.

DISPOSING OF LANDS OUTSIDE THE TERMS OF THE SCHEME

Land may only be disposed outside the scheme prior to entry by sale or definitive transfer. Such disposals are subject to an upper limit of 20% of all lands farmed which are owned or held on long term lease on 1 January 2000. The sale or transfer of such lands must be at least brought to dealing number stage before the application is submitted. In addition the land parcel numbers must be updated to reflect this change before an application is made under the scheme. However, where this disposal will result in bringing the income units below 200, it cannot be used to qualify an applicant in relation to this condition. Where agriculture holdings are jointly managed, a similar restriction will apply. It should be noted that this condition differs from the old scheme where there was no restriction on disposals of land by lease, sale or transfer to ineligible transferees prior to entry to the scheme. It should also be noted that this 20% limit does not apply for land afforested prior to entry into the scheme.

METHODS OF TRANSFER
The land can be transferred by way of sale, gift or lease to either a related or unrelated person.

JOINT OWNERSHIP
Where lands are jointly owned/leased by two or more individuals, either party (but not both) may apply for the pension on the total area.

TENANTS IN COMMON
Where the land is held as tenants-in-common, a Deed of Partition must be completed to enable either party to apply for the pension based on their own area of ownership, unless:
- the lands are declared as commonage for area aid purposes.
- all the lands in the tenancy are transferred/conveyed/leased to the transferee and,
- they are not required to meet the minimum 20 income unit threshold.

MINIMUM LEASE PERIOD
The land must be leased for a period of at least five years or the maximum pension period. This means that if the pension is for ten years than the lease must also be for a period of not less than ten years from the date of acceptance. However a lease may contain a clause providing for the termination of the lease by either party on or after the expiration of five years from the commencement of the pension.

EARLY RETIREMENT AND FORESTRY
It is permitted to afforest land prior to entering the scheme and receive the full forest premium. It should be noted however that each hectare of forestry counts as 1 income unit in determining whether you satisfy the 200 income unit ceiling for eligibility.

FARM WORKERS

Under the scheme farm workers who lose their employment as a result of the farmer's early retirement may also be eligible for a pension of €3,501 (£2,756.47) per year until they reach 65 years of age, subject to a maximum of two workers per holding. This pension is available for both paid farm workers and family helpers. In all cases they must be registered employees in order to receive the pension.

The worker must fulfil certain conditions on the date that the legal transfer documents are signed, transferring the holding from the transferor to the transferee as follows:

- be aged between 55 and 65 years of age
- have devoted at least half of his working time as a family helper or farm worker to farm work during the preceding 5 years.
- have worked on the transferor's agricultural holding for at least the equivalent of two years full-time during the four-year period preceding the early retirement of the transferor
- undertake to stop farm work completely and definitively and have paid PRSI contributions since 1st January 1998.

Not more than two workers per agricultural holding may qualify under the scheme.

APPLICATION PROCEDURE

Application forms are available on request from local Farm Development Service Offices. **Due to the complex nature of the scheme the Department requires that intending participants only engage the services of appropriately indemnified/insured agricultural advisors/consultants/solicitors.**

An application is not deemed to be complete until all the transfer documents and the undertakings have been signed and lodged, accompanied by the relevant supporting documents, with the Department of Agriculture Food and Rural Development, Johnstown Castle Estate, Co.Wexford.

DOCUMENTATION REQUIRED
The application form must be accompanied by some or all of the following documents:

- Stamped Deed of Transfer or Lease Agreement of lands being transferred.
- Up to date Folio(s) and folio map(s) of lands transferred.
- Lease agreements, Stamped Deed of Transfer and folios of transferee's lands
- Applicant's birth cert
- Marriage cert if joint management application.
- Transferee's birth cert
- Land Commission Consent to all leases
- Confirmation of cancellation/transfer of applicant's herd number
- Evidence of transferee's herd no./flock no./cereal no.
- Evidence of non farm income of both transferor and transferee in year prior to application in the form of a P60 or, in the case of earnings from self employment, a long tax assessment, or a certified copy of the income tax computation from your accountant.
- Both parties PPSN numbers.
- Confirmation of Milk Quota where appropriate
- Income Units calculation by Agricultural Advisor/Consultant
- Certificate of 10 years farming by Agricultural Advisor/Consultant
- Confirmation of transferee's farming qualifications by Agricultural Advisor/Consultant
- Completed application forms

COMPLIANCE PROCEDURES

PENSION DECLARATION FORM

A form described as a Pension Declaration Form setting out the terms and conditions under which the person entered the scheme will issue each year from the Department. Participants will have to sign the form confirming that they continue to observe the terms of the scheme and their signature must be witnessed by any of the following; a medical doctor, accountant, bank manager, teacher, minister of religion, commissioner for oaths, solicitor or a Garda. This form should be dealt with and returned immediately.

RIGHT OF ENTRY

The Department is required to carry out inspections under the terms of the Early Retirement (ERS 2) 2000 and is obliged to inspect land, premises, plant, equipment, livestock and records of both participants and transferees to ensure compliance with the terms and conditions of the Scheme. A percentage of applications will be subject to a prepayment compliance inspection to confirm eligibility with the terms and conditions of the Scheme. Further compliance inspections will be carried out on an annual basis in respect of approved applications. Cases will be selected on both a random and a risk- selected basis to ensure compliance with the terms and conditions of the Scheme.

RESPONSIBILITY OF APPLICANTS

The approval or payment of aid under the scheme is conditional on the applicant's compliance with the terms and conditions of the Scheme at all times. It will also be the responsibility of the applicant to notify the Department in writing of any material changes in the circumstances relating to his and the transferee (s) participation.

PENALTIES

Failure to comply with the terms and conditions of the Scheme will result in an appropriate monetary penalty proportionate to the breach. In addition, more serious breaches of the terms and conditions may lead to the participant being suspended or excluded from the Scheme for a period commensurate with the seriousness of the breach and the refund of moneys paid. Where monetary penalties are not paid within the period requested, the Department will take whatever action is necessary for their recovery. Where a farmer is found to be engaged in farming activity at the time of a visit by a Department inspector he/she will lose 20% of the annual pension for the first offence. A second offence will result in the loss of 50% of the annual pension and a third offence will mean expulsion from the scheme.

In cases where penalties are applied, participants have ten days from the date of formal notification of the penalty to submit an appeal to the Early Retirement Section stating out the grounds for their appeal. They will be notified of the outcome in writing.

RETIREMENT SCHEME – POINTS TO NOTE

TIMING OF APPLICATION

The date which determines whether an applicant or a transferee has met the upper age limit for the scheme is the date that the application is lodged with the Department and **not** the date the transfer or lease was signed as was the case with the previous scheme. Accordingly cases where either the applicant or the transferee are nearing the upper age limit will be highly time sensitive in terms of having the application prepared. Furthermore 31 December is a crucial deadline for those applicants who do not have ten years to run on entering the scheme. Lodging the application before 31 December will extends the payment period by up to twelve months depending on one's birthday.

VOLUNTARY PRSI CONTRIBUTIONS

Where an applicant is of an age that, had he remained self employed, he would have been entitled to a contributory pension on reaching 66 years, it is essential that an application is made to register as a voluntary contributor to PRSI. To be eligible to become a voluntary contributor a person must have at least three years paid under the compulsory scheme of PRSI and apply within twelve months of the year in which the last compulsory payment was made. The amount of voluntary contribution is based on a flat rate of €273 per annum.

PERSONAL PENSIONS

Participants may not be able to continue to contribute to a personal pension policy. Under current legislation a person can only contribute to a personal pension policy if he has an income which can be defined as 'relevant earnings'. The retirement pension or income from leasing are not deemed to be relevant earnings. However a new type of privately funded pension scheme is due to be launched in 2003. This new scheme will enable any person with or without 'relevant earnings' to contribute. This new type of pension fund is called a **Personal Retirement Savings Account or PRSA** and is covered in more detail on page 201.

FORESTRY

A transferor who has land planted before retiring from farming and is entitled to a forestry premium may retain that land and continue to receive the premium. If this forest land is transferred with the holding the transferee who obtains it can apply for the premium. A farming transferee may use the land received for forestry provided that he/she practices farming as a main occupation on the enlarged holding.

Where it has not been possible to locate an eligible transferee, land may be reassigned to forestry, by a non-farming transferee (e.g. Coillte) providing the Department can be satisfied that all reasonable effort was made to locate an eligible transferee. However, while forest planting grants and maintenance grants will be payable, the forest premium will not be paid on that land as long as the transferor is in receipt of the Early Farm Retirement Pension. When the retirement pension ceases the retired farmer will be entitled to receive the forest premium thereafter but will only be entitled to the non farmer rate of premium .

COST OF PREPARING AN APPLICATION

The cost of preparing an application will very much depend on the amount of work involved. You will require the services of a solicitor to prepare a lease or transfer. In general leases will cost €450-€550 to have drawn up and transfers will cost 1-1.5% of the value of the land. Apart from the transfer or lease the greater portion of the application requires the services of an agricultural advisor or consultant to make the actual application. As the volume of work involved in the application is very substantial intending participants can expect the actual application fee to fall somewhere between €1,400 and €2,000.

Example 1: Transferring a farm worth €380,000 to a son or daughter and applying for the E.R.S. It is assumed that the transferee is eligible for the stamp duty exemption.

	€
Legal Fees	**4,800**
Registration fees, folios etc.	**380**
Preparing application	**1,900**
Telephone & outlay	**55**
V.A.T	**1,416**
Total	**8,551**

Example 2: Leasing a farm worth €12,000 per year and applying for the E.R.S.

	€
Cost of preparing lease	**570**
Search fees, folios etc.	**40**
Stamp Duty	**120**
Preparing application	**1,900**
Telephone & outlay	**55**
V.A.T	**537**
Total	**3,222**

Important: Seek out a professional who is known to have experience in this area as the scheme is very complex and bad advice could cost you the pension.

EARLY RETIREMENT SCHEME – TAXATION ASPECTS

Availing of the Early Retirement Scheme requires serious consideration of a number of matters, not least taxation. The question of income tax arises regardless of whether the farm is being transferred or leased. However in the event of the farm being transferred, gift tax may also be a consideration, as will stamp duty and legal fees.

Under the scheme a farmer must cease farming. This will result in triggering special income tax rules which apply when a trade ceases and which in some cases may increase the tax liability for the final year. On the other hand there may be an opportunity to carry back a loss which occurs in the final tax year against profits of the three preceding tax years.

GIFT TAX, CAPITAL GAINS TAX AND STAMP DUTY
See section on Selling. Leasing or Transferring the family farm, page 146.

INCOME TAX
The pension is taxable in the same way as any other form of income. The full range of personal tax credits and allowances is available, such as the marriage allowance, single/widowed allowance, PAYE allowance and age allowance. A married person currently in receipt of the maximum pension, who has no other income and is under 65, will pay no tax. However a single person in similar circumstances will pay €43 per month. Income received from a lease agreement drawn up for the purposes of the retirement scheme is taxable in the same way as any other income. If, however, the parties to the lease were unconnected, the first €7,620 is tax free in the case of a lease of seven or more years' duration. If the lease is greater than five and less than seven years this allowance is €5,080. This is a very valuable relief as €7,620 income exempt from tax could be worth up to €3,200 in tax savings.

Part 7 - Farm Performance Analysis and Opportunities

APPRAISING YOUR FARMING OPERATION

For most farmers there has been a gradual decline in disposable incomes over the past ten years. While CAP reform may have gone some way towards compensating for falling commodity prices the reality is that farmers' incomes, on average, have fallen well behind their industrial counterparts. Many farmers have had no choice but seek off farm income while others have struggled on annual incomes that are scarcely above the poverty line. It is probably fair to say that practically all farmers apart from the larger dairy producers are finding it increasingly difficult to make ends meet. Many are at a cross roads and options such as the Early Retirement Scheme are tempting, despite the fact that ceasing to farm is not the preferred option.

For many farmers additional annual income of five to ten thousand Euro per year could make all the difference. It is essential that you thoroughly investigate all the possible options open to you in terms of generating additional income or cutting certain costs. There are few situations where that five to ten thousand Euro cannot be found if you stand back and objectively appraise your position. Seeking advice from a good agricultural consultant or advisor might be the best money you will ever spend.

A FARM BUSINESS HEALTH CHECK

It is essential to establish the health of your farming operation in terms of whether you are gaining or loosing ground. In some cases you may mot be actually losing ground but because of a bad cash flow situation you appear to be. Solving this problem can often be as simple as restructuring your repayments. However in many instances the farm is gradually loosing ground which, if not checked will eventually culminate in a crisis. The question is how does one check the health of one's farm financial position ?. The answer in the first instance is simple enough if you have an accountant doing your accounts. You simply ask him to examine your net worth position over the past five years and ascertain if you are worth more or less than you were five years ago, not taking into account increases in property values or once off windfalls such as income from sale of a site. If you are worth more, or the position has not changed, you can be reasonably happy and just concentrate on finding way of improving your income, and perhaps your cash flow along the lines set out further on in this section.

If it is established that your net worth is declining you need to take immediate action as there is unquestionably trouble up ahead. The best action is to talk to a good consultant or advisor.

INCOME OPTIONS TO CONSIDER

Some of the following options may appear obvious but have you seriously considered all of them ?. **Warning:** you may have to shed some silly hangups !.

- **REPS** - less than half of all farmers are participating in REPS which makes no sense in the current farming climate. Have you seriously considered the reasons for not joining. Don't dismiss the medium to long term gain if the short term gain is not so attractive. Some of the apparent constraints that REPS places on you may apply in any event when the Nitrates Directive is implemented.
- **Forestry** - many farms have a certain proportion of land that is marginally productive and that would not be missed if taken out of production. The tax free return is very attractive.
- **Subsidies** - subsidy maximisation should not be left to chance. Talk to a consultant or advisor about subsidy planning. A small adjustment could make a big difference.
- **Starting a small intensive enterprise** - there a re many possibilities that might be compatible with your existing farming operation. A range of options are set out in this section.
- **Farm Assist** - it is now considerably easier to qualify (see page 189). Many farmers are not aware that they are eligible for payment and are missing out on their entitlements. Maximum payment for a husband and wife is €197 per week. Payments can be made directly to your bank account so there is no question of you having to attend at your local Employment Exchange or Post Office in order to receive payment.
- **Farm Relief Work** - what work are you best qualified for ?. The answer is obvious. Ten hours per week could make the repayment on the car or the tractor. The Farm Relief Service is constantly looking for operatives.

COST SAVINGS TO CONSIDER

While commodity prices continue to fall, costs continue to rise. There is little you can do about price increases but there may be a lot you can do about curtailing wastage and unnecessary expenditure.

- **Bank charges and interest** - are your loans at the best available rates. The bank wont automatically grant you their best rates, you'll have to bargain. Bank overdrafts are generally the most expensive form of credit so use seasonal loans instead.
- **Co-op/Merchant credit** - this is by far the most expensive credit that farmers avail of. Not alone is the rate of interest charged well above bank rate but you

are being doubly penalised in that you are also paying a credit price as compared to a cash price. Always ask for their best price, it could be worth a lot over a twelve month period.

- **Input purchases** - shop around for oil, feed and fertiliser purchases. Loyalty to your local merchant or co-op often goes unrewarded.
- **Fertiliser usage** - only use what the land needs. Unnecessary use of fertiliser is one of the greatest areas of waste on Irish farms. A soil test may be well worth the money. Talk to your advisor/consultant.
- **Tax bills** - ensure that your accountant is claiming all of the possible legitimate expenses that you are entitled to. See taxation section.

SUPPLEMENTARY FARM ENTERPRISES

If you are thinking of setting up a supplementary enterprise or an additional income generating activity then you have to take your own unique circumstances into consideration. . There is plenty of help from a variety of sources out there who will be glad to assist. In most instances Teagasc or your agricultural consultant should be your first port of call. The following is a list of enterprises for consideration:

Equine Activities
- Sport horse production
- Livery services
- Riding school
- Trekking/Trail riding

Poultry enterprises
- Free range eggs
- Farm Fresh Turkeys
- Free range geese
- Free range chickens

Agri Tourism Enterprises
- Angling holidays
- Pheasant shoots
- Theme farms

Organic enterprises
- Free range organic pork
- Organic beef & lamb
- Organic free range chicken
- Organic potatoes
- Organic vegetables

Food Preparation
- Home style Chutneys & Marinades
- Home style Ice Cream
- Farm yard Cheeses
- Home made Chocolate
- Home made Soups
- Home made Yoghurts
- Home style cooked hams

Information on many of the enterprises listed above can be found on the Teagasc website www.teagasc.ie

GREEN ENERGY FARM PROJECTS

For those people interested in jumping in at the deep end and investing in large infra structural projects there are two particular areas which are generating considerable interest at present. These are wind farming and anaerobic digesters. These projects require large capital investment and much investigation and research will be required before even considering if they have anything to offer in your particular situation.

ANAEROBIC DIGESTERS

Anaerobic digesters are environmentally friendly waste treatment plants that have the added benefit of producing green energy in the form of biogas. This gas which is mainly methane can be used to generate electricity. The gas produced from the slurry of 100 cows is sufficient to power the farm and ten average homes so there is huge potential for a unit serving a number of farms which could sell electricity on to the national grid . They also produce a compost that is ideal for gardening purposes as well as a liquid residue that has worthwhile fertiliser properties and is far more flexible than slurry and less harmfull for spreading on land. Digesters are capable of handling not alone animal slurry's but also many types of domestic and commercial waste products. Given the current problem of disposing of domestic and commercial waste and the looming problem of farm slurry disposal, digesters offer huge potential into the future. A small number of digesters are currently operating successfully in this country. In mainland Europe and the U.S. it is generally accepted that they offer the most viable solution to disposing of farm wastes and the popularity of the system is growing at a rapid pace. In Ireland local pollution by-laws restricting the spreading of slurry and the forthcoming Nitrates Directive will certainly bring digesters to the fore front of waste management.

THE PROCESS

The process is naturally occurring and does not involve the use of any chemicals. The steps are as follows:

- The waste material is pumped into tanks where naturally occurring bacteria commence the decomposition process. The process is speeded up by heating the tanks. The heat can be produced from the biogas generated by the system .
- The decomposition process generates biogas (methane and carbon dioxide) which can be used to create electricity.
- The by products of the process are an odourless compost and a liquid manure which has only a slight odour and is far more environmentally friendly than slurry.

ADVANTAGES
- Reduces the problems associated with slurry storage and spreading.
- Produces useable/slaeable biogas.
- Produces saleable compost.
- Eliminates smells from slurry spreading and storage.
- Eliminates weed seeds and pathogens from slurry.
- Reduces Greenhouse gasses.
- Income potential from disposal of commercial waste.

COST AND RETURNS
The cost of establishing a unit is quiet significant. However developments in this area are progressing rapidly and capital costs are reducing. The cost of establishing a unit to service a farm of 70 cows, along with a certain amount of commercial waste, will be in the region of €300,000. Such a unit will only be of marginal profitability and will be dependant on acquiring electricity sales and also payment for taking in commercial waste. Given the average farm enterprise size in Ireland it would appear the real potential for digesters is where a unit is set up to service a number of farmers within an area who agree to supply their slurry.. This would provide economy of scale and would be a considerably more attractive proposition to a purchaser of electricity.

WIND FARMING

Wind farming has emerged as a possible viable alternative income source for farmers who have land in suitable locations. In recent times the deregulation of the electricity market and Ireland's obligations to reduce greenhouse gas emissions under the UN

Kyoto Protocol has increased both the interest level and the urgency of developing wind farming.

A TYPICAL WIND FARM

A typical wind farm in Ireland is around 5 Mega Watt (MW) capacity. This size of wind farm will typically have seven turbines and will generate up to 15 million units of electricity per year which is enough power for up to 3,000 homes. The turbines will be at least 250 metres apart and this size of unit could prevent emissions of 12,000 tonnes of CO_2.

OPTIONS FOR THE LANDOWNER

There are a number of options open to landowners who are not interested in developing their own wind farming project but who have a suitable site:

- For people who would like to have some involvement but would prefer not to go it alone there is the option of a partnership with a commercial wind farming company.
- Renting the land to a commercial wind farming company.
- For people who own a suitable site which might otherwise be generating little income there is the option of selling to a commercial wind farming company. In such cases it would be advisable to have the energy generating capacity of the site established independently as this will have a major bearing on its value.

DEVELOPMENT COSTS AND RETURNS

The initial cost of testing the suitability of the site will be in the region of €9,000 -€19,000. In the event of the project not going ahead some of the equipment may be saleable thereby reducing the cost. The actual installation cost will be in the region of €1,000,000 - €1,200,000 per Mega Watt so a 5 MW wind farm with seven turbines will cost up to €6m.

The gross return from a 5 MW unit is currently in the region of €500,000 - €700,000 per annum. However, as the demand for green energy, i.e. non-fossil fuel based, increases the price for energy will increase. The net return from a 5 MW unit will depend on the amount borrowed and the maintenance charge for the turbines.

RENTING A WIND FARM SITE

Renting a good site to a developer can be quiet lucrative. Rents generally amount to 2.5% of electricity sales which can range from €2,500 to €4,,000 per turbine. Where the renting option is availed of the farmer should in all cases consult his own solicitor to ensure that a suitable rental agreement is entered into.

FURTHER INFORMATION

The Irish Wind Energy Association (IWEA) is the association for the promotion of wind energy in Ireland. They can be contacted at 078-46072. Meitheal na Gaoithe the Irish Wind Farmers Co-operative Society Ltd can be contacted at 056 52111. The ESB are actively seeking suitable sites and can be contacted at 01 7027724.

OFF FARM INVESTMENTS

The poor rate of return from farming in term of return on investment, generally less the 1%, has prompted some farmers to look beyond the farm gate for alternative opportunities.

Table 7.1 Returns on various investments made in 2002

Rented residential accom. - Ireland	4 - 6%
Rented residential accom - U.K.	6 - 8%
Rented commercial property - Ireland	5 -7%
Bank/Building Society deposits	0.5-3%
Credit Union Savings	4 - 5%
Farmland - non dairying	0.5 -1%
Farmland - dairying	1 - 6%

Note: Rented accommodation and farmland returns do not include asset appreciation

BUYING RESIDENTIAL PROPERTY TO RENT

Many farmers have considered the idea of purchasing residential property as an alternative to on farm investment. Indeed many have done so and have made a handsome return on their investment.

TAXATION TREATMENT OF RENTED RESIDENTIAL PROPERTY

In arriving at the taxable rent from residential premises a person may claim a deduction from gross rent in respect of such items as:

*   ground rent
*   rates
*   the actual cost of maintenance, repairs, insurance and management fees
*   wear and tear on furniture and fitting
*   Mortgage/loan interest.

For more detailed information on the taxation treatment of various types of rented residential accommodation refer to the taxation section of this handbook.

COSTS AND RETURNS OF RENTING A HOUSE

The return on investment is currently at its lowest for many years as rents have not matched house price increases in the past six years. In 1996 the typical return on investment before appreciation was closer to 7%. The current rate of return is such that there is little or no prospect of the property generating sufficient income to cover costs plus a mortgage repayment for at least five to eight years. However just because the property may not be paying for itself does not mean that it is not a good investment as it will almost certainly increase in value over the period.

As an indication of the costs involved in renting a house table 7.2 deals with a new house bought for the purpose of renting and costing €177,000. Assuming that the monthly rent attained is €760 and that on average the house is occupied for 95% of any given year, the costs and returns as set out provide a reasonable basis for what to expect.

Table 7.2 Cost and returns from Renting a house (Euro €)

Cost of House	177,000
Stamp Duty	5,310
Legal Fees	2,032
Fit Out Costs	
Painting Contractor	2,500
Furniture & Floor Covering	8,200
Tiling	1,400
Curtains	1,800
Equipment	1,900
Total Cost	200,142
Annual Rent	8,664
Return on Investment excluding appreciation	4.32%

If we assume that 85% of the cost of the house including fit out is borrowed at 4.75% interest, table 7.3 sets out the cash flow shortfall that will arise

Table 7.3 Calculation of net annual shortfall (Euro €)

Annual Rental Income	8,664
Mortgage protection	-250
Annual maintenance	-600
	-1,000
Mortgage Repayment (20 yr. loan)	-13,270
Net income available for mortgage payment.	6,456
Annual shortfall	6,814

No tax arises as allowable outgoings exceed income

MAXIMISING RENTAL INCOME

While rents have increased dramatically in recent years they have not increased at the same rate as property prices. However, there are a number of options which can be taken in order to ensure that the optimum rent is received.

- Furnish the property to a high standard. The quality of furnishing demanded today is significantly higher than previously. While a good fit out may be more expensive initially it is essential if trying to secure higher rents and regular tenancy.
- Offer extras such as television (it is the tenants responsibility to pay the licence), video, dishwasher.
- Install an alarm system.
- Secure parking is an added attraction especially for city centre apartments

DEVELOPING YOUR BUSINESS IDEA

A new business cannot be developed without research, planning, technical and management ability and capital. The feasibility of the proposal must be fully examined before embarking on the new business.

THE FEASIBILITY STUDY

Before undertaking the project the feasibility study looks at all aspects of the proposed business to assess if it is a worthwhile venture. Both financial and technical assistance may be available from Leader or the County or Local Enterprise Boards in preparing a feasibility study. If the feasibility study indicates that there is a demand for your product or service the next step is to prepare a business plan.

PREPARING A BUSINESS PLAN

A business plan is not simply a document that you have prepared professionally and that you present to the bank manager or funding agency. Rather it should be the fruits of a thorough investigation into all aspects of the proposed business. Ideally it is something into which you should have a major input, and if possible done mainly by you with minimal professional assistance. A good business plan should be approached in an honest and realistic fashion with the primary purpose of ascertaining whether the project is a good one and that it is likely to provide you with a worthwhile return. Planning ones future generally requires a certain amount of optimism but in the case of business plans that optimism must be tempered with realism. In other words you cannot assume that you are going to sell large quantities of your product or service if you have not ascertained that clearly a demand exists.

As we have already stated preparing a business plan should be largely done by yourself and there is no great reason why that should not be possible. A business plan contains a logical sequence of checks and investigations that embrace all of the fundamental aspects of business. The following is a list of the essential elements of the plan;

INTRODUCTION

Give a brief description of the business along with name(s) and address(es) of the promoter(s), accountant, solicitor and bankers. The introduction should be preceded by a table of contents for the entire business plan.

SUMMARY

Summarise the key elements of the plan so that the reader can get a quick overview of the project.

MAIN BODY OF PLAN

The main body of the plan should comprise the following,

- **Project Description** - describe the project in some detail, the goals set and the strategies for achieving them.
- **Management** - give details of relevant training, expertise and experience.
- **Products or Services** - give a detailed account of the products or services to include technical approvals where appropriate and any research and development carried out.
- **Market Analysis** - give details of any market research carried out, market size and current competition.
- **Marketing and Sales Strategies** - give details of how you propose to market and sell your product or service.
- **Manufacturing or Operations** - give details of how and where you propose to manufacture the product or perform the service.
- **Financial Projections** - include budgets, projected profit & loss accounts, cash flow statements for the first three years.

181

- **Financial Package** - indicate the extent of your own financial input, the type and amount of loan finance required, the amount of grant assistance required if appropriate and details of funding from any other source.
- **Conclusion** - highlight the strengths and opportunities and also the weaknesses and threats. Provide a reasoned case why a banker, grant awarding agency or external investor should commit funds to the business.

FUNDING AND ASSISTANCE

There are a number of agencies out there which can assist you in starting a new farm enterprise or start a small business whether it be by providing advice or actual financial grant assistance. The important thing to remember is that these organisations are there to help you and will be delighted to hear from you. The following pages contain details of some but not all sources of funding, however if you talk to any of the organisations listed they will point you in the right direction.

LEADER FUNDING

There are a number of Leader Companies around the country. A central part of each Leader Company's role is the allocation and administration of grant aid under two separate rural development programmes. These programmes are LEADER +, which is funded wholly through the European Union and the National Rural Development Progarmme (NRDP), of which the majority of funding comes from the Irish exchequer. NRDP funding is largely reserved for rural tourism projects. Both programmes are administered nationally by the Department of Agriculture, Food and Rural Development. Whatever the project type, interested potential applicants should note that both programmes require any project to be innovative in its concept or approach in benefiting the quality of life of the rural dwellers of the region, in economic. social, environmental or cultural terms. Leader will not grant-aid any projects or parts of projects retrospectively. The range of projects eligible for aid under Leader are as follows::

- Innovative business, crafts and services
- Small scale projects which involve new technology
- Community and group tourism schemes
- Food development and processing
- Alternative agricultural enterprises
- Environment enhancement programmes

GRANT APPLICATION

LEADER + grant-aid is available to small enterprises, individuals with a business project and to community groups with either a business or a community beneficial project, if they meet the programmes criteria. All grant-aid applications to the Leader Groups for either the LEADER + or the National Rural Development Programmes are processed in an identical manner. Both programmes provide part-funding so applicants are expected to fund a percentage of any project themselves.

PRE APPLICATION CONTACT

Persons or groups successful in their application for grant-aid are known as 'project promoters'. In the first instance of a potential promoter contacting the company to inquire as to the possibility of aid, that contact is passed to the appropriate development officer who, either in person or in writing will inform the applicant of their opinion of the project idea being eligible for grant-aid. If it is agreed to be suitable, the development officer will supply the appropriate inquiry/application form to the applicant. The promoter is likely to be asked for supporting documentation as it is relevant to the project, such as two separate quotes for capital or other works, proof of ownership of property, details of the company's or community group's structure.

AREA BASED PARTNERSHIP COMPANIES

These companies operate in 38 disadvantaged areas around the country. Their aim is to tackle unemployment, underemployment and social exclusion through a range of locally targeted and focused programmes and services. Some of these companies also operate the Leader programmes.

For further information on partnership companies in your area and the specific services they offer contact: Area Development Management (ADM), Holbrook House, Holles Street, Dublin 2.

THE AGRICULTURAL CONSULTANTS ASSOCIATION

Most private agricultural consultants offer assistance and advice in appraising new projects and making submissions for funding. Members offices are spread throughout the country. See page 23.

TEAGASC

Teagasc provides advice and training for those considering supplementary farm and rural enterprises. Contact your local Teagasc office and talk to the Rural Enterprise Adviser. You can also get in touch with the Teagasc Rural Development Centre, Athenry, Co. Galway (091) 845200 or refer to page 364 of this handbook for local offices.

Part 8 - Family & Education Matters

HEALTH AND WELFARE ENTITLEMENTS

The main welfare entitlements that may concern farmers are:

- Widow's/widowers contributory pension
- Carer's Allowance
- Free Schemes to people over 75
- Farm Assist
- Family income supplement
- Medical cards
- Child benefit

Note: Contributory and Non Contributory Old Age Pensions are dealt with in the section dealing with retirement and succession pages 150 and 151.

WIDOW'S/WIDOWER'S CONTRIBUTORY PENSION

Widow's/Widowers Contributory Pension is available to widows and widowers provided the necessary employed or self employed PRSI contributions have been made..

HOW TO QUALIFY

The pension may be based on either your own or your late spouse's PRSI contributions which must amount to a minimum of three years.

RATES

See page 12 for rates effective from January 2003. The rats effective from January 2002 are:

	Weekly rate
Personal rate age under 66	€123.30
Personal rate aged over 66	€144.80
Additional for each dependent child	€ 21.60
Living alone allowance (66 or over)	€ 7.70

CARER'S ALLOWANCE

The Carer's Allowance is a payment for carers on low incomes who live with and look after certain people who need full-time care and attention. Carers who are providing care to more than one person may be entitled to up to 50% extra of the maximum rate of Carer's Allowance each week, depending on the weekly means assessed. It is not unusual in a family farm situation to have an elderly family member in residence who would qualify the person looking after them for this allowance assuming they satisfy the means test.

HOW TO QUALIFY
* are aged 18 or over
* satisfy a means test
* live with the person(s) you are looking after
* are caring for the person(s) on a full-time basis
* are not employed or self-employed outside the home
* are living in the State
* are not living in a hospital, convalescent home or other similar institution and the person(s) you are caring for is/are:
* so disabled as to need full-time care and attention (medical certification is required)
* not normally living in a hospital, home or other similar institution
* age 66 or over

or

* under age 66 and getting a Blind Person's Pension, Invalidity Pension or Disability Allowance (formerly DPMA) from the Department of Social, Community and Family Affairs or an equivalent payment from a country covered by EU Regulations or a country with which Ireland has a Bilateral Social Security Agreement.

Note: Where the care of one person is shared only one person gets the allowance.

MEANING OF 'FULL-TIME CARE AND ATTENTION'
The person(s) being cared for must be so disabled or invalided as to require:

* continuous supervision and frequent assistance throughout the day in connection with his/her normal personal needs, for example, help to walk and

187

get about, eat or drink, wash, bathe, dress etc.
or
- continuous supervision in order to avoid danger to themselves, and
- so incapacitated as to be likely to require full-time care and attention for at least 12 months.

Note: The person being cared for may attend a non-residential course of rehabilitation training or a non-residential day care centre approved by the Minister for Health and Children.

WHAT THE CARER MAY DO
- Attend an educational or training course to take up voluntary or community work for up to 10 hours per week
- Work part-time as a Home Help for a Health Board for around 10 hours per week
- Engage in limited self-employment in your home. (Any income earned will be assessed as means.)
- During your absence, adequate care for the person requiring full-time care and attention must be arranged.

The requirement to provide full-time care and attention will be assessed on an individual basis. It is not intended, nor is it desirable, that a carer would be expected to provide care on a twenty four hour basis. In this regard, the above arrangements will be applied in a flexible manner, having due regard to both the needs of the carer and the person requiring care.

DETERMINATION OF MEANS
Your means are any income you or your spouse/partner have or property (except your home) or an asset which could bring in money or provide you with an income. The means test is similar to that operating under the Farm Assist in regard to savings and investments. However the first €191 income of a single carer will not be assessed as means or the first €382 combined earnings in the case of a couple.

RATE OF PAYMENT
Full rate caring for one person   €122.60
Full rate caring for more than one person   €183.90

188

Additional for each child dependant - full rate   € 16.80
Additional for each child dependant - half rate   € 8.40

Carers aged 66 or over receive an additional €15.20.
Where your assessed means are greater than €7.60 per week the rate is reduced by €2.50 for every €2.50 of assessed means.

FARM ASSIST

Farm Assist is a weekly means-tested payment for low income farmers. Farmers who have income from another source (such as other self-employment, insurable employment, capital etc.) may still qualify for a payment under the Farm Assist Scheme.

ELIGIBLE FARMERS

Farmers between 18 and 66 years who farm land within the state may be eligible. It is not necessary for you to own the land you farm to be eligible however if you rent or lease your land to another person you are not eligible.

MEANS TEST

To qualify for this scheme your means as determined by Social Welfare must be below a certain level. Your means include any income or property (excluding your home) you may have and any other assets that may provide you with an income. On completion of form Farm 1, a Social Welfare Inspector will visit your home and examine all of your farm income and expenditure documentation. It is important that you have as much documentation as possible available in order to provide the Inspector with adequate information to determine your eligibility. Failure to provide sufficient information, or withholding information, may give the inspector no choice but to turn down your application or at least postpone a decision until such information as he or she deems necessary is available.

DEPARTMENT OF SOCIAL, & FAMILY AFFAIRS

IS FARM ASSIST FOR YOU?

The Department of Social and Family Affairs wishes to remind farmers that it is now easier to qualify for FARM ASSIST.

WHAT IS FARM ASSIST?

FARM ASSIST is a weekly means-tested payment for farmers on low income.

HOW DO I QUALIFY?

You will qualify if you:

- are engaged in farming

- are aged between 18 and 66

- satisfy a means test

HOW MUCH CAN I GET?

Your payment is made up of a personal rate for yourself with extra amounts for your adult and child dependants, less your weekly means assesment.

HOW TO APPLY

Information leaflet SW27 and application form are available from your Social Welfare Local Office or from the Department's Information Services, Tel: 01 704 3000. Alternatively, you may download the leaflet and application form from the Department's Website at: **www.welfare.ie**

CALCULATION OF MEANS

Means can arise from a number of sources and are treated as follows:

Means from Self Employment Including Farming: Income from self employment is treated on a factual basis, that is gross income less any expenses incurred in earning that income. However if you have a child dependant the first €254 of net income is disregarded for each of the first two children, and €381 is disregarded for each subsequent child. You are then assessed on 70% of the remaining income from self employment.

Means from REPS and SACS: Income from these schemes is assessed separately from other farm income in that €2,540 is deducted from your annual payment and half of the balance remaining after deduction of expenses incurred is taken as means.

Means from Insurable Employment: If you have dependant children, 60% of your average net weekly earnings is assessed as weekly means and if you have no dependant children €12.70 per day worked is deducted from your net weekly earnings and 60% of the remaining earning is assessed as weekly means.

Seasonal Work: If you have seasonal work you are assessed with your earnings only during the period while you were actually working

Means from Investments and Savings: The actual income from such savings or investments is not taken but rather a notional income is arrived at as follows:

- First €12,697 not counted
- €12,698 to €25,395 is assessed at €1 per €1,000
- €25,396 to €38,092 is assessed at €2 per €1,000
- Over €38,093 is assessed at €4 per €1,000.

Means from Spouse's/Partner's Earnings: If this income arises from insurable employment and they work 1, 2 or 3 days per week, €38.10 is deducted from their earnings. If they work 4 or more days the deduction is €88.90.. Additionally an extra allowance may be made for travel expenses. If the spouse's/partner's income is from self employment the calculation is the same as that set out above for the principal earner.

RATE OF FARM ASSIST

The maximum personal rate is €118.80 from January 2002. The additional payment for a dependant spouse/partner is €78.80 and €16.76 for a dependant child. The amount actually paid is the difference between your assessed means and the maximum rate of payment that you could be entitled to. For example, if your assessed means are €70 per week and you are married with three dependant children you should receive €177.88 i.e. €247.88 - €70.

It should be noted that if you qualify for a full allowance for your spouse or partner you will get the full rate child dependant allowance, otherwise you will get half the child dependant allowance.

EXTRA BENEFITS
If you are getting Farm Assist you are entitled to butter vouchers, fuel allowance (subject to certain conditions) and Christmas bonus.

TAXATION
Generally where an individual or family is receipt of farm assist they are below the tax exemption limit. However farm assist is not a tax free source of income and must be included as part of your total income.

WHEN AND HOW TO APPLY
You can get a form Farm 1 from your local Social Welfare Office and complete and return same to that office.

FREE SCHEMES TO PEOPLE OVER 75

All people who are over 75 since October 2000 and who currently are not entitled to any of the free schemes are now entitled to the following:

Free electricity/natural gas
Covers standing charges and 1,500 units of electricity or the equivalent in natural or bottled gas.

Free TV licence
When renewing your licence bring along notification that you have been awarded an Electricity or Gas Allowance.

Free telephone allowance
Provides for a contribution towards your telephone bill and covers rental charges and up to €2.41 worth of calls in each two monthly billing period.

The benefits listed are available regardless of income or household composition and no means test applies

FAMILY INCOME SUPPLEMENT

This is a weekly cash allowance to help families on low incomes. Many farmers are not eligible because a condition of the scheme is that it applies to people who earn income in the services of an employer and are employed for at least 19 hours per week. However, technically, a farmer might be eligible where his or her spouse is working and the combined family income is below certain limits.

Farmers who are employers should take note of FIS, as it may be relevant to farm workers who are married with families. The availability of such a payment might have the effect of making it relatively more attractive for that person to remain in your employment. The scheme is applicable only where the employee has dependent children. It is up to the employee to apply under the scheme, although the claim form must be countersigned by the farmer.

The limits currently applying are set out in Table 8.1 below. Payment is made on the basis of 60% of the difference between the actual gross income and the relevant income limit.

Table 8.1: Family income supplement income limits

No. of Children	1	2	3	4	5	6	7	8
Income Limit (€)	362	388	413	438	470	496	517	539

EXAMPLE
Joe works for a farmer and is paid €380 per week before deduction of tax and PRSI. He is married with six children. The FIS payable is 60% of the difference between €496 and €380, i.e. €69.60 per week.

Applications are made at the local social welfare services office or to the Social Welfare Services Office, Family Income Supplement Section, 157/164 Townsend Street, Dublin 2.

CHILD BENEFIT

Child benefit or children's allowance, as it is more commonly known, is paid to each qualifying child living with or being supported by a parent or guardian. It is not means-tested and is payable up to age 16. Dependants who are physically or mentally handicapped or who are in full-time education qualify for child benefit up to the age of 19.

RATES
The rates effective from April 2002 are as follows:

Table 8.2: Monthly child benefit payments

No of children	Monthly Payment Rate €
1	117.60
2	235.20
3	382.50
4	529.80
5	677.10
6	824.40
7	971.70
8	1119.00

Twins - Child benefit will be payable at one and a half times the normal monthly rate for each child.

HOSPITAL CHARGES

The daily in-patient charge for a public ward in a public hospital is €36, subject to a maximum of €360 in a twelve month period. The outpatient charge is €40 per visit which will only apply to the first visit of any episode of care. Where a patient has a written referral from a doctor no outpatient fee is charged. Certain people are exempt, notably those with medical cards and all babies up to 6 weeks old.

ACCOMMODATION CHARGES IN PUBLIC HOSPITALS

A person may opt for private or semiprivate accommodation in any of the state run hospitals. The following table sets the daily charges (additional to the €36 daily charge) for private and semiprivate accommodation in a public hospital.

Table 8.3: Daily charges in public hospitals

	Private room	Semi-private	Day-care
Regional Hospitals	€302	€236	€217
County Hospitals	€251	€160	€180
District Hospitals	€156	€133	€116

DRUGS PAYMENT SCHEME

This scheme covers the cost of drugs over €65 per month for the entire family.

Registering for the Scheme: It is important that all families or individuals living on their own register for the scheme as the manner in which it operates is that once you become registered you receive a card which your chemist will use each time you require a prescription to record your purchase. Once your expenditure exceeds £65 in any month you will not be required to pay for any further prescribed drugs.

Application Forms: All families should have received registration forms in the post. However many people were not aware of the necessity of completing and returning these forms and hence many are not yet registered. The form is simple to complete but does require all of the family members RSI numbers. Your own RSI number can be found on any income tax bill or assessment but to acquire your children's numbers you may need to telephone (01) 7043281 or for family members who were on the DCSS the number is (01) 8343644.

MEDICAL CARDS

Medical cards are available to individuals or families where the health board is satisfied that the income level is below a certain limit. Persons in receipt of a medical card are entitled to the following services free of charge:

- General practitioner services
- Prescribed drugs and medicines
- All in-patient services in a public hospital
- All outpatient public hospital services
- Dental, ophthalmic and aural services and appliances
- Maternity and infant care service

ELIGIBILITY

Eligibility is determined by a means test. Your income as determined for tax purposes will be a major determining criterion but the criterion of income alone may not ensure eligibility and the final decision lies with the health board. It should be noted that savings and investments are considered only insofar as the income they generate. In other words the notional calculation of income from savings or investments used in assessing eligibility for Non Contributory Old Age Pensions or Farm Assist does not apply in this case. In certain cases of serious conditions requiring ongoing expensive treatment, the health board may grant a card to that individual and not to the entire family, where the income limit is exceeded.

The **Income limits** effective from 1 March 2002 are:

Table 8.4: Income limits for medical card eligibility

Category	Aged Under 66 €/week	Aged 66-69 €/week
Married couple	190.50	214.00
Single person (living alone)	132.00	144.00
Single person (living with family)	117.00	124.00
Allowance for child under 16	24.00	24.00
Allowance for other dependants	25.00	25.00

From 1 July 2001 every person over 70 is entitled to a medical card.

SICKNESS AND MEDICAL CARE INSURANCE

In recent times this area of insurance has grown significantly in popularity. There are a number of different types available as follows:

- Permanent health cover
- Serious illness cover
- Permanent and total disablement insurance
- Hospital income plans
- Medical expenses cover.

PERMANENT HEALTH COVER

This type of cover provides you with an income in times of sickness or ill-health. Depending on the terms agreed at the time of setting up the policy, benefit can commence either shortly after the insured becomes ill, or after a delayed period, which will reduce the cost of cover. Benefit will be paid for the duration of your illness or until you reach a specific age. Benefit is restricted to between 66% and 75% of income that was earned in the previous tax year and is subject to income tax.

Permanent health policy contributions are allowable against tax, subject to the restriction that the amount allowable cannot exceed 10% of your income for that tax year.

Table: 8.5: Guide costs of Permanent Health Cover

Age	Sum Insured	Monthly Premium
25 years	€10,000 p.a.	€45
35 years	€10,000 p.a.	€58
45 years	€10,000 p.a.	€80

SERIOUS ILLNESS COVER

In simple terms this is life insurance that is paid out without the insured person dying. The policy will cover a specific range of serious illnesses such as cancer, stroke, heart attack or most heart complaints needing surgery. It will also cover kidney failure, blindness, benign brain tumour and a number of other serious illness.

Serious illness claims will be paid only if the person affected by the illness survives for a predetermined period, usually 14 days.

The proceeds of a serious illness claim are not taxable and premium payments are not allowable against tax. If the policy provides life assurance and serious illness protection, the life cover will (optionally) continue without penalties, even after a serious illness claim has been made.

Table 8.6: Guide costs of Serious Illness Cover

Age	Sum Insured	Monthly Premium
25 years	€100,000	€39
35 years	€100,000	€57
45 years	€100,000	€190

HOSPITAL INCOME PLANS

A number of companies are now offering insurance which pays a weekly sum while the policyholder is hospitalised.

The cost of this type of insurance can be small in relation to the potential benefits and may have particular appeal to farmers, as a small monthly premium will provide benefit that would adequately cover the cost of farm relief wages. The benefit could be up to €120 per day tax free income, while the injured person is hospitalised.

MEDICAL EXPENSES COVER

Every citizen in the state is entitled to free hospital care and consultant treatment. However the reality is that significant delay can be experienced when the need arises for treatment of certain life-threatening conditions. Health insurance will cover the cost of private treatment, which in most cases is readily available.

VHI OR BUPA

A member of either scheme can choose varying levels of cover depending on how much they are prepared to spend. It is worth spending some time comparing what each scheme has to offer as there are certain services offered by one that may not be covered by the other and your particular needs may dictate which company to choose. Both companies offer reductions for group scheme members. Generally your Co-op or accountant will operate a group scheme.

Level of Cover: The level of cover provided is determined by the particular plan or scheme you enter. The VHI plans range from A to E with plan A providing semiprivate and day care cover in a public hospital and also from 35 - 100% of the cost of certain types of heart surgery in the Mater Private and Blackrock Clinics. As you progress up the scale, the level of cover rises to full cover in the costliest private hospitals under plan E.

BUPA has three levels of cover. The Essential Scheme is the basic scheme which is broadly similar to VHI plan A but does provide private room cover in a number of hospitals and also full cover for certain forms of heart surgery at the Mater Private and Blackrock Clinics. The middle level scheme called the Essential Plus Scheme is broadly similar to the VHI Plan B. The top level cover which is described as the Essential Gold Scheme is broadly equivalent to VHI plan E.

COST: From 1 April 2001 fees charged by VHI and BUPA have a built in tax credit. In other words tax relief is reflected in the charge and it will no longer be necessary to claim tax relief in your annual tax return. Table 8.7 sets out VHI and BUPA charges for adults, students and children in a group scheme as follows.

(1) Basic cover schemes i.e. VHI Plan A Option and BUPA Essentials Scheme
(2) Mid- range cover i.e. VHI Plan B Option and BUPA Essentials Plus Scheme
(3) Top range cover i.e. VHI Plan E Option and BUPA Essential Gold Scheme

Table 8.7: Annual costs of various VHI & BUPA policies (net of income tax)

	VHI (€)			BUPA (€)		
	Adult	Child	Student	Adult	Child	Student
(1)	330.3	113.94	138.99	238.11	76.89	76.89
(2)	478.41	175.41	200.47	329.57	114.87	114.87
(3)	1,315.91	530.05	554.34	1180.75	384.29	384.29

Note: Table 8.7 compares schemes that are broadly but not exactly similar. There will be some variation in cover for certain procedures between VHI and BUPA. There will also be variation in the limits of cover and excesses over which cover will apply.

Both companies have excellent web sites, www.vhihealthcare.com and www.bupaireland.ie which will enable you to decide which offers you best value for money.

PERSONAL PENSIONS

Since people are generally living longer (the average male retiring at 65 lives to age 79 whilst the average female lives to 83), if you were to retire tomorrow could you see yourself 'enjoying' a healthy and active retirement on the state pension of €147 (single) or €261 (married) per week. Instead you would prefer to maintain your current standard of living and with this in mind perhaps you should organise additional retirement benefits through a personal pension..

START IN TIME

The reality is, you are never too young to start saving for your retirement. Remember, your retirement is likely to be the longest holiday of your life, so the earlier you start saving the better. Starting 5 years later than planned reduces the ultimate income at retirement by approximately 35%. Table 8.8 sets out the likely pension and lump receivable at age 65 for a person paying €127 per month and increasing by 3% every year after that.

Table 8.8: Likely pension and lump sum at various starting ages

Present Age	Pension €	Lump Sum €
35 years	6,460	27,277
45 years	3,127	13,285
55 years	1,495	4,827
Growth rate of 6% and final annuity rate of 7.9% assumed		

SELECTING YOUR BENEFITS

At retirement a pension fund will be available to you and you can take 25% of this fund as a tax free lump sum. Traditionally the balance of your fund was used to purchase an annuity. This ensures a guaranteed regular income is paid to you, generally on a monthly basis for the rest of your life. The actual size of your monthly annuity will depend on the size of the fund, your age, when you retire and prevailing annuity rates. Rates are currently in the region of 6% for individuals retiring at 65.

New retirement options were introduced in the 1999 Finance Act whereby at retirement you are no longer obliged to purchase an annuity, though if you need regular income it might be the most suitable option Instead you can transfer your retirement fund into another investment type described as an ARF or an AMRF.

APPROVED RETIREMENT FUND (ARF)

If your fund exceeds €63,500 and you have a guaranteed income of €12,700 per annum, you can invest in an ARF. From this you draw income as required, including a lump sum. As such you have full access to your fund and can pass it to your dependants on your death. However payments are subject to tax and the fund may run out.

APPROVED MINIMUM RETIREMENT FUND (AMRF)

If your fund is less than €63,500, or you don't have other guaranteed income, you can invest your fund in an AMRF. Before you reach age 75 you can only draw interest from the fund to ensure it does not run out. At age 75 you can withdraw income from the fund but as with the ARF withdrawals are subject to tax.

If you invest in an ARF or AMRF you can at any stage use your fund to purchase an annuity.

PERSONAL RETIREMENT SAVINGS ACCOUNT

Personal Retirement Savings Account or PRSA is a new type of savings plan which the Government plans to introduce sometime early in 2003. It will be suitable for people who want to save for their retirement and everyone will be eligible to take out a PRSA. It will be possible to contribute to a PRSA even if you have no earned income. PRSA's can be taken out with banks, life assurance companies and other regulated investment firms. The following are the main attractions of a PRSA

- You will be able to contribute as little as €300p.a. to your PRSA.
- An employer can contribute to your PRSA, but is not legally obliged to do so.
- Contributions, within certain limits, are allowable against tax on any income you may have from a self-employed trade or profession or a non-pensionable job.
- Relief is also available against PRSI and the Health Levy.
- If you happen to be in employment your PRSA can move with you if you change jobs.
- You can normally draw on your PRSA fund at any time between ages 60 and 75.
- There are no limits on PRSA benefits. When you draw on your PRSA, 25% of the accumulated fund can be taken tax free, with the balance being used to purchase a taxable pension for life or invested in an Approved Retirement Fund which you can draw on during retirement.
- PRSAs will not be subject to substantial initial commissions and charges in the way that normal personal pension premiums can. Charges cannot exceed 5% of each contribution in the case of a standard PRSA in addition to an annual fund charge of no more than 1% pa.

The generous assistance of Brendan Lee, FBD Life & Pensions Ltd., in preparing this article is gratefully acknowledged.

SEPARATION AND DIVORCE

Marriage breakdown leading to separation and divorce is now a feature of Irish life. Information from the 2002 census is not yet available but there is ample evidence that legal separations and divorce are rapidly gaining momentum. In Northern Ireland for example the incidence of divorce in 1971 was 400 annually but by 200 this figure had risen to 2,400. There is no reason to believe that we wont follow the same pattern and while the incidence among farm families is below the average, marriage breakdown certainly exists and legal separations are certainly on the increase

When a marriage breaks down the problems build up. Knowing one's options and entitlements is vitally important as many people have preconceived ideas about their rights that may be grossly inaccurate and may only serve to aggravate their problems. Where marriages break down there are a number of possible option as follows.

SEPARATION

MEDIATED AGREEMENTS
Mediated agreements are drawn up through mediation. Mediation is a process whereby separating couples are helped to resolve any disputes they may have in relation to children, financial support and other issues, and then reach agreement on how they will manage these when they separate. The mediator encourages the separating couple to co-operate with each other in working out a separation arrangement to which both agree. Both parties are required to attend the mediation sessions A mediation service is not a legal service and under the Judicial Separation and Family Law Reform Act 1989 if you consult a solicitor he is required to highlight the desirability and availability of counselling and mediation services and give the persons concerned a list of names and addresses of people qualified to provide help. However persons opting for a Mediated Agreement should seek legal and financial advice so that they know their rights and make informed decisions .

Mediation normally takes up to six sessions. Mediation in the Family Mediation Service is free of charge. Other services may request a nominal contribution.

SEPARATION AGREEMENTS
Where a couple can agree the terms of their Separation Agreement either voluntary or through a solicitor, they can opt for a Deed of Separation without having to involve the courts. This is a legal written contract between both parties to the marriage setting out their future rights and duties to each other. The document is signed by both spouses and witnessed. The Separation Agreement becomes a legal contract at the time specified in the Deed of Separation. Legal separations of this nature may incur

considerable costs if agreement is difficult to reach.

JUDICIAL SEPARATION

Where a marriage has broken down to the extent that all mediation has failed and one or both spouses is not happy simply to be separated, but wishes to copper fasten the separation, an application may be made to the Circuit Family Court for a Decree of Judicial Separation under The Judicial Separation and Family Law Reform Act 1989. On granting a Decree of Judicial Separation the court is empowered to grant maintenance and property orders, some of which can be far reaching. Before hearing an application for a decree of separation the court has the power to grant interim orders concerning such matters as maintenance, barring orders and the protection of the family home.

To acquire a Decree of Judicial Separation the applicant must provide adequate grounds, such as any of the following:

- the other spouse has committed adultery
- the other spouse has acted in such a way that the couple could not reasonably be expected to live together
- the applicant was deserted for a continuous period of at least one year immediately preceding the date of application
- the spouses have lived apart from one another for a continuous period of at least one year immediately preceding the date of the application and both spouses agree to the decree being granted
- the spouses have lived apart for a continuous period of at least three years immediately preceding the date of application, in which case both spouses need not agree to the decree
- the marriage has broken down to the extent that the court is satisfied in all the circumstances that a normal marital relationship has not existed between the spouses for a period of at least one year immediately preceding the date of the application

MAINTENANCE

It must be emphasised that in all cases of separation every effort must be made to agree such matters as maintenance allowances and division of assets if relevant. Failure to do so will result in court action and the associated hefty legal costs. However if recourse to the court is sought, once a decree of separation has been granted, the court is empowered to make three types of maintenance order:

- a periodical payments order
- a secured periodical payments order i.e. the spouse who is ordered to pay maintenance must put up some security e.g. property or investments. If he defaults on the payment, the property must then be sold or the investments cashed to pay the maintenance.
- a lump sum order. This might arise where a spouse requires funds to meet a liability reasonably incurred in maintaining herself or her infant child.
- In determining appropriate levels of maintenance the court will take account of the following:
- the income capacity, property and other financial resources which both spouses have or are likely to have
- the financial needs, obligations and responsibilities which they have or are likely to have
- the standard of living enjoyed by the family before the separation
- the age of each, the length of the marriage and the length of time they lived together
- any physical or mental disability of either
- any contributions which either spouse has made or are likely to make to the welfare of the family, including any financial contribution as well as contributions to looking after the home and caring for the family
- the effect of marital responsibilities on the earning capacity and, in particular, the loss of capacity resulting from staying at home to care for the family
- the conduct of each spouse if the court considers that it would be unjust to disregard it
- the accommodation needs of each spouse.

Maintenance payments for the spouse will be determined by the court on the basis of his or her needs as presented to the court. However the ability of the remaining spouse to pay maintenance will be taken into account. Maintenance payments in respect of children are currently being awarded at approximately €95 per week where ability to pay is established.

MAINTENANCE ORDER

Where a voluntary agreement cannot be reached, an application may be made to the District or Circuit Family Court for a maintenance order under the Family Law (Maintenance of Spouses and Children Act. 1976. In order to get a maintenance order you must show that your spouse has failed to provide such maintenance as is proper in the circumstances. You do not have to be living apart and you need not be intending to separate, but, in practice, most people applying for maintenance are living apart. When deciding on the level of maintenance to be granted the court will consider the income earning capacity, the property and other financial resources of both spouses. It will also consider the dependent children and the financial and other responsibilities of the spouses towards each other and towards the dependent children. Each case will be decided on its merits and it is certain that one or both parties will suffer some loss in living standard. If one spouse is considered to have behaved badly, the court may order that spouse to take a greater loss. A spouse who has deserted may not get a maintenance order unless the court considers it unjust not to make an order. Maintenance orders under this act are weekly or monthly payments and it is not possible to get a lump sum, unlike the situation obtaining under the Judicial Separation Act.

VOLUNTARY MAINTENANCE AGREEMENT

Marital breakdown does not in all cases mean separation; it may simply be about the right of maintenance. There is a considerable body of legislation now in place to protect the rights of spouses, be it in the context of separation or simply the right of maintenance within an existing marriage.

Where a person is faced with marriage breakdown, the exact nature of the circumstances should determine the correct course of action. If you do not wish to seek a judicial separation, then your main concern may well be maintenance and/or a roof over your head. Ideally, agreement should be reached outside court with the assistance of your solicitor.

In general, spouses have an obligation in law to support each other and to support their children. Where this support is not forthcoming it may be possible to avoid the cost and inconvenience of court action by entering into a voluntary agreement about maintenance. As for separation agreements such agreements may be of little use unless they are registered with the court, which means that the enforcement procedures of the court are available to ensure the implementation of the agreement. It should be noted that any clause in such an agreement that prohibits a spouse from subsequently suing for maintenance is void. In other words a person cannot waive their rights to go to court for maintenance. Failure to agree voluntarily will inevitably take both parties into court.

FAILURE TO PAY

In cases where a spouse fails to pay maintenance as instructed by a Court Order an Attachment of Earnings Order can be sought from the court if the person who defaults is in employment, on Social Welfare or on a private pension. The employer or Government Department who pays the spouse will be ordered to deduct the maintenance payments from the individuals earnings.

THE FAMILY HOME

The family home cannot be sold without the consent of either spouse. Normally if the family home is in joint names, both spouses will share equally in the net proceeds in the event of sale. If it is in the sole name of either spouse, the other spouse will have a right to a share in the proceeds only to the extent that he or she can show that they made a financial contribution to the purchase of the house or its mortgage repayments. However, in the case of a judicial separation the court has power to order the transfer of the family home to one or other spouse and/or children regardless of who was the registered owner. In the case of farmers the family home is often an integral part of the farm yard and generally where the husband is carrying on the farming it is unlikely that the wife will wish to remain resident in the farm yard. In such situations alternative accommodation will have to be found and contributed towards by the husband.

FARM PROPERTY

Unless the property is jointly owned, the spouse who is the registered owner will generally retain sole possession of that property unless any of the following circumstances apply, in which case the court is empowered to make a Property Adjustment Order of some or all of the property:

- Where, in determining maintenance, the court made an order for a payment of a lump sum, a periodic payments order or a secured periodic payments order, a spouse may seek a property adjustment order to ensure that the terms of the aforementioned orders are met. A property adjustment order can entail the sale or transfer of property such as land.
- A spouse can claim to have contributed in some way to the value of the land. This contribution could be by way of financial or possibly physical input that contributed to the value of the property. If the court is satisfied that such a claim is valid it will be taken into account in the property adjustment order.
- Where a spouse is departing the family home because it is not practical or reasonable to remain resident there, the court will generally take a sympathetic view towards awarding sufficient proceeds to acquire alternative suitable accommodation, providing that the remaining spouse has sufficient assets or earning capacity to provide for such an award.

The court has wide discretion to transfer property between spouses and to order the sale of property. It has to be said that the Judicial Separation Act does establish a framework for property resolution and as the law evolves in term of judgements handed down it is becoming increasingly apparent that entitlement is not just based on contribution but also on partnership in the context of a marriage being a partnership.. This applies to all property and not just the family home and the transfer of property may be made whether or not one spouse has made a financial contribution to the purchase of the property. Unlike maintenance orders, property adjustment orders are made only once and the court will not make a second order unless it becomes apparent that information was deliberately concealed at the time of making the order. When deciding on property adjustment orders, the court takes into account the same factors as are taken into account when deciding maintenance under the act.

SUCCESSION RIGHTS

On separation it is possible and quite common, as part of a separation agreement, for a spouse to waive their succession rights. While this is not essential, it can remove the prospect of problems for the succeeding generation. The court, on granting a judicial separation, may order that that one or both spouse's succession rights be extinguished.

DIVORCE

A Decree of Divorce dissolves a marriage and allows either or both spouses to remarry. Unlike Judicial Separation divorce means that if the couple resume their relationship after the granting of a divorce they will not be married in the eyes of the law. Generally speaking the same procedures involved in Judicial Separation also apply to Divorce. However the conditions that must be met to acquire a divorce differ from Judicial Separation. The following conditions apply;

- The spouses must have been living apart for a period amounting to four out of the five previous years. If the couple have lived separately and apart in different residences with all matrimonial relations having ceased, the 'living apart' definition is satisfied. Where, because of financial constraints, the couple still live under the same roof but apart, insofar as that is possible, the 'living apart' condition may be satisfied providing they can show that there has been a complete breakdown of the married relationship.

207

- There must be no reasonable prospect of reconciliation.
- Proper arrangements have been made for spouses and any dependant members of the family. The definition of dependants includes the children (adopted or natural) of the marriage and children from a prior marriage or relationship and also children for whom either or both spouses have assumed the role of parent. Dependency generally ceases at age 18 but can continue until 23 where the child is pursuing a full time course in education, and indefinitely where a child is unable to look after themselves due to mental of physical disability. .
- At least one of the spouses must be either domiciled in the State at the date the proceedings were started, or ordinarily resident in the State for at least one year prior to that date.

CHILDREN

Where the couple have agreed arrangements in place the Court will not normally alter these arrangements. However if agreement cannot be reached the courts will decide on all aspects that concern the child's welfare such as custody, access and maintenance. In so doing the court may order that the family be assessed by a relevant professional. It is within the power of the court to declare that a parent is unfit to have custody of a child even after the death of the other spouse.

MAINTENANCE

The courts will apply similar criteria as those outlined for Judicial Separation other than for the fact that conduct within the marriage is not considered unless it was such that it would be considered to offer a pointer to future behaviour in term of meeting certain obligations. There is no rule of thumb applied in determining maintenance but the following matters will be considered;

- the income earning capacity, property and other financial resources which both spouses have or are likely to have in the future.
- the financial needs, obligations and responsibilities which they have or are likely to have including the remarriage of either spouse.
- the standard of living enjoyed by the family before the separation
- the age of each, the length of the marriage and the length of time they lived together
- any physical or mental disability of either spouse.
- any contributions which either spouse has made or are likely to make to the welfare of the family, including any financial contribution as well as contributions to looking after the home and caring for the family

- the effect of marital responsibilities on the earning capacity and, in particular, the loss of capacity resulting from staying at home to care for the family
- the accommodation needs of each spouse.

In determining maintenance of dependants the court will take account of any financial means or resources which they also may possess. The courts will also take account of their present circumstances such as the cost of education courses they are undergoing or are likely to undergo.

Maintenance payments will cease where the spouse receiving the maintenance remarries or dies. Maintenance of children will only cease when they reach 18 or 23 if in full time education or if they cease to be dependant before that. If at any time after the granting of a divorce there is a change in circumstances either party can apply to the court to vary or suspend any order for maintenance.

THE FAMILY HOME

The Divorce Act recognises the accommodation needs of both spouses and their dependants. There a number of options in regard to the family home as follows;

- The family home may be sold and the proceeds divided in what ever proportions the court decides
- The family home may be transferred to one of the spouses. The court may order that the spouse receiving the home make a payment to the other spouse to compensate them for the loss of their interest in the property.
- One spouse may be given the right to reside in the Family Home for life or for a period of time set down by the court. Such a period of time could be until the children were no longer dependant.

FARM PROPERTY

The treatment of land is similar to that obtaining for Judicial Separation. However it should be noted that the Divorce Act permits a divorced spouse in certain circumstances to apply for a property order at any time during the lifetime of either spouse. Therefore it could be said that while divorce brings a permanent end to the relationship it may not in all cases be final.

SUCCESSION

Having been granted a divorce the former spouses have no succession rights. In other words if either spouse dies the other former spouse has no claim on his or her estate.

OBTAINING A SEPARATION OR DIVORCE

Where all attempts at salvaging a marriage have failed you are best advised to seek out a good solicitor who has experience in this area. Obtaining a separation or divorce is a complicated process and should be put in the hands of a competent professional.

COSTS

The costs involved in obtaining a separation or divorce will be directly related to the degree of difficulty involved in arriving at agreement on all issues in question. Every case will be different and it would be impossible to quantify the likely costs involved. However unless the separating spouses are agreed on all matters such as maintenance, child custody and property, legal costs can be substantial reaching to five figure sums in difficult cases.

TAXATION

See taxation section dealing with separated and divorced persons.

EDUCATIONAL COURSES IN AGRICULTURE

Courses relating to agriculture are available through a number of third-level institutions and a number of state and semi-state organisations. Apart from the obvious benefits of education and training, many schemes and certain tax concessions are now conditional on having completed a training course.

AGRICULTURE COURSES

UNIVERSITY DEGREE IN AGRICULTURAL SCIENCE

Course aim: To provide a degree qualification with option to for students yo specialise in one of the following:

• Agribusiness and rural development
• Agricultural and environmental science
• Animal and crop production

- Animal science
- Commercial horticulture
- Engineering technology
- Food science
- Forestry
- Landscape horticulture

Duration: The duration of the course is four years, including a period of in-service experience.

Location: This course is based in UCD.
The syllabus for the first year of study is common to each B.Agr. Sc. Degree programme. The courses for the second, third and fourth years are specific to the individual degree programmes. Each degree programme offers 'required' courses which are compulsory for all participating students and 'elective' courses which afford students an element of choice within their chosen degree programme. On-farm or off-farm professional work experience in approved degree-related areas, to be taken as an integral component of the third year course requirement, is mandatory for each B.Agr. Sc. Degree programme.

Career opportunities: technical, advisory and consultancy work, enterprise management, production in the food industry, research, education and marketing.

UNIVERSITY DIPLOMA IN ENVIRONMENTAL IMPACT ASSESSMENT

Course Aim: The courses is aimed at persons with a professional or personal interest in Environmental Impact Assessment, especially potential developers, planners and those engaged in environmental consultancy.

Location: The course based at UCD Belfield is

Duration: The course runs from January to May on Fridays and Saturdays.

UNIVERSITY DIPLOMA IN RURAL DEVELOPMENT

Course Aim: The course is targeted at people who are involved in rural development in a professional or voluntary leadership capacity. It provides the participants with the

211

knowledge and skills necessary to initiate and manage local rural development

Location: The course based at UCD Belfield.

Duration: This is a two-year, part-time, distance learning diploma for adults.

NATIONAL CERTIFICATE IN AGRICULTURE

Course Aim: The course has been developed to provide the education and training needs of future commercial farmers and skilled workers in the agricultural industry and is accredited to the Higher Education and Training Awards Council (HETAC)..

Course Location: This course is offered jointly by a number of Institutes of Technology and some agricultural colleges

Course Duration: It extends for two years.

Recruitment: Recruitment is through the CAO system.

Entry Requirements: Leaving Certificate subjects, including Mathematics and either English or Irish. If there are more applicants than places the standard points system will be used to rank students.

Career Prospects: As well as a career in farming graduates can look towards Farm Management, Environmental Management & Monitoring, Agri Industry and Sales & Marketing.

Maintenance Grant: VEC (Means Tested).

NATIONAL CERTIFICATE IN AGRICULTURAL SCIENCE

Course Aim: The aim of this two year third level course is to train people for the agri-service industry as field or laboratory technicians or sales personnel

Course Duration:. Two years.

Course Location: This course is offered jointly by Kildalton Agricultural College and Waterford I.T,.

212

Recruitment: Recruitment is through the CAO system.

Entry Requirements: Minimum of five passes in Leaving Certificate subjects at Grade D3 or better ordinary level.

Career Prospects: As well as a career in farming graduates can look towards Farm Management, Environmental Management & Monitoring, Agri Industry and Sales & Marketing.

Maintenance Grant: VEC (Means Tested).

NATIONAL CERTIFICATE IN AGRI-BUSINESS

Course Aim: This HETAC accredited course is aimed at students seeking to work in the Agri Business Sector.

Course Duration:. Two years.

Course Location: This course is offered jointly by Mountbellew Agricultural College and Galway I.T,.

Recruitment: Recruitment is through the CAO system.

Entry Requirements: Minimum of five passes in Leaving Certificate subjects at Grade D3 or better ordinary level.

Career Prospects: Career opportunities exist in agricultural marketing, administration and management.

Maintenance Grant: VEC (Means Tested).

NATIONAL CERTIFICATE IN AGRICULTURAL MECHANISATION

Course Aim: This HETAC accredited course is aimed at providing skilled technicians for the farm machinery industry in Ireland.

Course Duration:. Two years.

Course Location: This course is offered jointly by Pallaskenry Agricultural College and Limerick I.T,.

Recruitment: Recruitment is through the CAO system.

Entry Requirements: Minimum of five passes in Leaving Certificate subjects at Grade D3 or better ordinary level. The subjects must include maths and either English or Irish.

Career Prospects: Career opportunities exist in machinery retailing and the machinery operation and manufacturing sectors.

Maintenance Grant: VEC (Means Tested).

VOCATIONAL CERTIFICATE IN AGRICULTURE

Course Aim: This FETAC accredited course is aimed at people wishing to make a career in farming but who do not wish to attend a third level course.

Course Duration:. Two years in an Agricultural College or three years through a Teagasc Training Centre..

Course Location: Agricultural Colleges and Teagasc Training Centres.

Recruitment: Through the Agricultural Colleges and Teagasc Training Centres.

Entry Requirements: There are no minimum educational requirements.

Maintenance Grant: Teagasc Grant (non means tested)

VOCATIONAL CERTIFICATE IN AGRICULTURE (ADAPTED FOR MATURE STUDENTS)

Course Aim: This FETAC accredited course is aimed at people who have an off farm job and are farming part time.

Course Duration:. Three years part time.

Course Location: Teagasc Training Centres.

Recruitment: Through the Teagasc Training Centres.

Entry Requirements: There are no minimum educational requirements.

ADVANCED CERTIFICATE COURSES

Courses are offered for people who wish to specialise in the following areas:
- Pig Production
- Dairy Herd Management
- Farm Machinery & Arable Crops
- Drystock Management

Course Aim: This FETAC accredited course is aimed to provide young people with the necessary in dept knowledge and skill required for work in the particular specialised area.

Course Duration: Two years in the case of Pig Production and eighteen months in the case of Farm Machinery & Arable Crops and Drystock Management..

Course Location:
Pig Production - Mellows College.
Dairy Herd Management - Clonakilty College
Machinery & Arable Crops - Kildalton College..
Drystock Management - Gurteen College

Recruitment: Direct to College.

Entry Requirements: FETAC Vocational Certificate in Agriculture Level 2.

Maintenance Grant: Teagasc Grant (non means tested)

ADVANCED CERTIFICATE IN FARM MANAGEMENT

Course Aim: This FETAC accredited course run by the Farm Apprenticeship Board, is aimed to provide students with skills in farm management.

Course Duration: Three Years.

Course Location: Master Farms and Mellows College Athenry.

Recruitment: Direct to Farm Apprenticeship Board.

Entry Requirements: FETAC Vocational Certificate in Agriculture Level 2.

Maintenance Grant: Paid Apprenticeship

TEAGASC ADVANCED COURSES

Teagasc offers advanced courses in Dairy Herd Management, Drystock Management, Tillage and Crop Management. These courses are run at the local Teagasc centres and extend to two days per month over eighteen months and entry is a Certificate in Farming in the particular specialty. An advanced course in Business Management is also run at local Teagasc centres for persons who completed the advance course in either dairying, drystock or tillage and runs for two days per month for one year.

TEAGASC RURAL DIVERSIFICATION CERTIFICATE COURSES

Teagasc run FETAC accredited courses leading to a Certificate in Floristry and a Certificate in Irish Home Hospitality. Details from the local Teagssc centre.

TEAGASC SHORT COURSES

The duration of these courses is 10 - 150 hours on average. Topics covered include REPS, rural enterprise, forestry, spraying, food safety and adult courses in Agriculture. Courses run specifically for women cover topics such as farm management, schemes and rural enterprise. Further information can be gained from a local Teagasc Education Officer.

HORTICULTURE COURSES

DEGREE IN HORTICULTURAL SCIENCE

Course aim: The Horticulture industry is worth more than €350 million to the Irish economy each year. Horticultural Science explores the areas of fresh food production, nurseries and garden centres, sports turf management, and the study of the beneficial relationship between humans and plants. Graduates of this programme are equipped to move into any of these interesting and rewarding career areas.

Location: This course is based in UCD.

Duration: The duration of the course is four years, including a period of in-service experience.

Career opportunities: Careers for Horticultural Science graduates include food production management and quality assurance, management of garden centres and plant nurseries, distribution and retail facilities, technical advisory and consultancy, education, research and horticultural therapy.

DEGREE IN LANDSCAPE HORTICULTURE

Course Aim: Landscape Horticulture involves the design, implementation and management of open space in urban and rural areas. This degree programme is the only one of its kind offered in Ireland. The course involves both art and science and aims to give its graduates the creative and technical skills necessary to design quality environments.

Location: UCD

Duration: Four Years including a period of in service training,

Employment
Graduates pursue a variety of careers with many gaining employment in Landscape Architecture offices or in the Parks/Planning sections of Local Government. Other careers include the management and design of sports and leisure facilities, horticultural therapy in rehabilitation and education, or in 'design and build' landscape construction enterprises.

NATIONAL DIPLOMA IN HORTICULTURE

Course Aim: This HETAC accredited course aims to provide students with a firm grounding in technical skills in the areas of landscape design and construction, sport turf management, nursery stock production and food crop production

Course Location: This course is offered jointly by Kildalton College & Waterford I.T., Warrenstown College and Blanchardstown I.T. and The College of Amenity Horticulture Botanic Gardens and Blanchardstown I.T.

Duration: Three years. It is possible to progress from this course to the B.Agr. Sc. degree course at UCD.

Recruitment: Recruitment is through the CAO system.

Entry Requirements: Minimum of five passes in Leaving Certificate subjects at Grade D3 or better ordinary level to include Maths and either Irish or English..

Career Prospects: Career opportunities exist in all aspects of the horticultural industry.

Maintenance Grant: VEC (Means Tested).

VOCATIONAL CERTIFICATE IN HORTICULTURE

Course Aim: This FETAC accredited course is aimed at students who want to make a career in horticulture but who do not wish to complete the third level course.

Course Location: Kildalton College, An Grianan, Warrenstown College and the National Botanic Gardens..

Duration: Two years.

Recruitment: Direct to colleges listed above..

Entry Requirements: No minimum entry requirements.

VOCATIONAL CERTIFICATE IN GREENKEEPING

Course Aim: This FETAC accredited course aims to provide a sound theoretical background and practical skills training in greenkeeping and groundsmanship.

Course Duration: Two block release.

Course Location: College of Amenity Horticulture (National Botanic Gardens) and An Grianan College.

Recruitment: Direct to the Golfing Union of Ireland.

Entry Requirements: minimum of five passes in Leaving Cert. Ordinary subjects.

FORESTRY COURSES

UNIVERSITY DEGREE IN FORESTRY B.Agr.Sc. (Forestry)

Course Aim:
The Forestry degree programme at UCD is the only degree of its kind in Ireland. The programme provides highly qualified professionals for the forest industry chain from nurseries through management to wood processing. With ambitious national targets to increase the percentage forest cover from 9 to 17% by the year 2030, this is definitely a growth sector for suitably qualified graduates.

Location: UCD

Duration: Four Years including a period of in service training,

Employment: A degree in forestry opens up many different career paths for graduates. Forestry graduates find themselves working in all areas of the forest industry, including both the public and private sectors, manufacturing industries, management companies, advisory/consultancy firms, and financial services. Forestry graduates also find employment in areas outside of forestry, such as natural resource management, nature conservation, information technology, and land use planning.

VOCATIONAL CERTIFICATE IN FORESTRY

Course Aim: This FETAC accredited course aims to provide training to students who wish to take up jobs as forest workers or supervisors.

Course Location: Ballyhaise, Co.Cavan

Duration: Two years.

Recruitment: Direct to college.

Entry Requirements: There are no minimum entry requirements.

Career Prospects: Career opportunities exist in all aspects of the horticultural industry.

COURSES IN HORSE PRODUCTION / EQUINE SCIENCE

B.Sc DEGREE IN EQUINE SCIENCE

Course Aim: The course is aimed at students, who wish to follow a professional career in the horse industry with the opportunity to underpin their career aspirations with specialist knowledge and skills.

Course Duration: Four Years

Course Location: Limerick University

Entrance Requirement: Applicants are required to hold at the time of enrolment the Established Leaving Certificate (or an approved equivalent) with at least Grade C3 in two Higher Level subjects and Grade D3 in four Ordinary or Higher Level subjects (including Mathematics; Irish or another language; and English). It is desirable that candidates applying for this programme should have a reasonable level of competency in horse riding and/or have experience of working with horses.

NATIONAL CERTIFICATE IN EQUINE STUDIES

Course Aim: This HETAC accredited course is aimed at providing the student with business studies and equine related knowledge and skills for a range of job opportunities within the equine industry.

Course Duration:. Two years.

Course Location: This course is offered jointly by Gurteen Agricultural College and Athlone I.T,.

Recruitment: Recruitment is through the CAO system.

Entry Requirements: Minimum of five passes in Leaving Certificate subjects at Grade D3 or better ordinary level. The subjects must include maths and either English Irish or other continental language..

Career Prospects: Career opportunities exist in equine and related business.

Maintenance Grant: VEC (Means Tested).

VOCATIONAL CERTIFICATE IN HORSE BREEDING AND TRAINING

Course Aim: This FETAC accredited course aims to provide knowledge and skills, relating to the sport horse and in particular adding value to young horses.

Course Duration: Two Years.

Course Location: Kildalton College.

Entry Requirements: There is no minimum entry requirement.

Employment Prospects: There are good employment opportunities in the industry including, stud farms, training yards and equestrian centres.

FOOD SCIENCE / TECHNOLOGY COURSES

A number of degree courses are available that provide a professional qualification in the areas of food science and technology. These courses include:
- Degree in Agricultural Science- Food Science (UCD)
- Degree in Food Business (UCC)
- Degree in Food Process Engineering (UCC)

- Degree in Food Technology (UCC)
- Degree in Engineering - Agriculture & Food (UCD)

THE FINANCING OF AGRICULTURAL EDUCATION

EDUCATIONAL GRANTS

Educational grants, insofar as they refer to courses already referred to in this section, are available as follows:

- Higher Education Grants Scheme
- Vocational Education Committees Scholarships Scheme
- European Social Fund (ESF)
- Teagasc

The grants referred to above, other than the Teagasc grant, are all governed by similar conditions and offer similar rates of grant. The same application form is used for all three schemes but the Higher Education Grants Scheme is administered by the Local Authorities and the VEC and ESF schemes by the Vocational Educational Committee. These currently operate as three separate schemes. It does not matter whether the application is lodged with a county council, corporation or local VEC; whichever agency receives the application will assess it and refer it to the other agencies, if necessary.

ELIGIBLE PERSONS
The grants are available to students who shall be at least 17 years on 1 January following the date of application, and also to mature students i.e. people who are at least 23 years of age on 1 January of the year of entry to an approved course and living away from home

ACADEMIC ATTAINMENTS
A candidate who, having completed the Leaving Certificate or equivalent and having secured a place to pursue a third level course, will be eligible for grant aid. A mature student who secures a place on an approved course will also be eligible.

VALUE OF GRANTS

The amount of grant payable will be determined by a means test. As fees are no longer payable for many courses the grant now only refers to maintenance. However certain courses do not attract free fees and in such cases the grant may be available to students who already were in receipt of a grant for such a course The amount of grant payable will be determined on the basis of a means test as well as proximity to the particular educational institution i.e. living within 15 miles attracts the 'adjacent rate'.

The following rates apply for the 2002/03 academic year:

Table 8.9: Maintenance grant rate

	Non-Adjacent rate	Adjacent rate
Full Maintenance	€2,510	€1,004
Part Maintenance (50%)	€1,254	€501

MEANS TEST

Qualification for grant assistance is means tested in accordance with the income limits set out on table 8.10. Means are assessed when applying for the first years grant and on a random basis thereafter.

Table 8.10: Income limits for higher education grants based on a full tax year

Number of dependent children	Full maintenance incl. Reg.Fees	Part maintenance (50%)	Registration Fees only	Half Registration Fees only
Less than 4	€29,228	€30,965	€34,872	€36,987
4 - 7	€32,122	€33,858	€37.769	€39,790
8 or more	€34,872	€36,897	€40,660	€42,683

In cases where up to two children are attending full-time education in 2002/2003, the above income limits may be increased by €3,534. For each additional child in full-time education the income limit is increased by €7,067.

To support your claim for a grant the application form, which being the same for all three types of grant, must be accompanied by:

- Copy of farm accounts, i.e. trading/profit and loss account, capital account and balance sheet (for each business) , or
- Copy of farm profile as submitted to Inspector of Taxes

- Letter from Inspector of Taxes exempting a farmer from making a tax return
- Computation of profit/(loss) for tax purposes for the tax year immediately prior to the year of application
- Copy of notice of tax assessment for tax year immediately prior to the year of application

Farm Accounts must include (a) details of lands occupied (b) usage of land occupied (c) livestock numbers reconciliation.

In determining a farmer's income for the purpose of establishing means, certain expenses which would be allowable for tax purposes are disallowed and certain income not chargeable to tax is included in determining eligibility.

The following expenses are not allowable:

- Leasing charges on equipment or vehicles
- Interest on capital expenditure
- Capital allowances as claimable for tax purposes

The following income items are reckonable:

- Payments under the temporary suspension of milk quota
- Part of the proceeds of an endowment assurance policy calculated as follows: (policy proceeds) less (amount of premiums paid in to policy) divided by the number of years the policy was in force

Payments in respect of retirement annuities are deductible insofar as they are allowable for tax purposes.

TEAGASC GRANTS

For the academic year 2002/03 grants of €2254 for residential and €902 for non-residential students are available for people who obtained a place in agricultural college and who are otherwise eligible.

224

Part 9 - Forestry

PRIVATE FORESTRY

OBJECTIVE OF THE AFFORESTATION SCHEMES

Forestry has been recognised by the European Union as having a major role to play, both in the reform of the CAP and in the wider context of rural development. The Afforestation Grant and Forest Premium schemes introduced under Council Regulation 2080/92 are part of the accompanying measures to CAP reform, and support the afforestation of agricultural land. Through these schemes Ireland hopes to increase it's forest cover from the relative low level of 9% of the land to 17% by the year 2030, an objective which will require the annual planting of 20,000 hectares. A further objective is to increase broadleaf planting to 30% of total afforestation by the year 2006. Ireland is still the least forested country in the EU, where the average is over 30%.

BECOMING INVOLVED

To encourage private afforestation an attractive planting grant scheme exists whereby up to 100% of approved costs are grant aided. These grants help overcome the initial start up costs associated with planting trees. To help counteract the lack of short term return from forestry investments, the Forest Premium Scheme is available as an annual tax free payment for farmers.

Due to the increasing level of activity in the forestry sector, the Forest Service Inspectors can no longer assess individual projects for private afforestation. Farmers interested in afforestation should contact the Forest Service at Johnstown Castle Estate, Wexford who will forward a national list of Approved Forest Companies and Approved Foresters. The farmer can now choose a Forest Company or Approved Forester from the list to arrange a site inspection and to apply for grant approval. When the application is approved a letter issues detailing the conditions and specification for the proposed development. Preplanning approval is subject to the farmer using the contractor/forester who prepared the application. If the farmer wishes to use a different contractor/forester a new application must be submitted.

Once a decision is taken to proceed one must choose how the afforestation and maintenance will be undertaken.

COMPANY MANAGED

The first option available is to enter into a contract with a private forestry company. Normally the contract entails the company undertaking to prepare the site, plant the trees and maintain the plantation for four years. In many cases the cost of a plantation and the first four years maintenance will be covered by the afforestation and maintenance grants which the farmer will mandate to the planting company. This means that he will not have to lay out any money whatsoever.

The entire management of the plantation is in the hands of the company for the critical first four years. The better companies will also handle insurance, mapping and the drawing up of the forestry management plans as required by the Forest Service.

It is essential to only deal with a well established company who have been around for some time and who have a significant number of established plantations which can be seen. An advantage of dealing with a reputable company is that it will have the resources to finance the work, so saving the farmer bridging finance. They will also undertake to maintain the plantation during the crucial first four years.

FARMER MANAGED

The second option is to undertake to carry out the planting and maintenance oneself. This will depend on circumstance and preference. It is quite feasible for a farmer to undertake the task. However, he must employ an approved forester to apply for grant approval and will also require the services of a professional forester to certify maps etc. for grant payment. In any case it is essential that expert advice on site preparation, tree purchase, tree planting and maintenance is obtained and farmers undertaking to establish a plantation should in all cases employ the services of a professional forester to advise on and oversee operations.

To successfully establish a plantation the farmer must inform himself of what is required for good forestry practice and he must be involved in the day to day management of his plantation. With the help of a professional forester any farmer can manage his own plantation and draw the grants himself.

LAND SUITABILITY

Many people associate bad land with forestry which is generally true but nonetheless the land must be capable of producing a commercial crop of wood. Low-lying wet, mineral soil types, with a grass rush vegetation cover are ideal for forestry and only marginal for agriculture with a very short grazing season.

In the past forestry was confined to the most marginal land. However with so many agricultural crops in surplus, planting medium to good land is becoming increasingly attractive. This will help to reduce surplus produce and provide a raw material that is in short supply. The tax free return from forestry is an added incentive. For example premiums for planting broad leaves on enclosed land, e.g. ash, can now amount to €467/ha. per annum for 20 years, which could be equivalent to €952/ha. gross income subject to tax, PRSI and levies.

YIELD CLASS

The forest potential of land is measured in terms of its yield class (Y.C.). This is the average number of cubic metres of timber the land can produce per hectare per annum. Therefore Y.C. 24 means the land can produce 24 m^3 of timber per hectare per annum on average over a rotation grown to the age at which the mean annual increment begins to decrease. In other words the Y.C. is the maximum mean annual increment which the site and the species can produce. On the type of grass rush lowland referred to earlier, one would expect to grow Sitka spruce to Y.C. 24. Such land can be ideally suited to forestry and with Ireland's excellent climate for tree growth, private afforestation can be a worthwhile long-term investment.

TAXATION

All profits from forestry including grants, premiums and timber sales are exempt from income tax and capital gains tax. Similarly, woodlands that are inherited or gifted are eligible for agricultural relief for capital acquisitions tax purposes.

FARM-FORESTRY PARTNERSHIPS

An alternative option for farmers who do not want the responsibility of establishing and maintaining a forest plantation is a farm forestry partnership such as that offered by Coillte Teoranta. The farmer enters into a partnership agreement with Coillte whereby he/she retains ownership of the land and receives a tax free annual income for the life of the crop, as well as an upfront payment of €635/ha. The land owner benefits from Coillte's management and marketing skills throughout the life of the crop and enjoys the larger share of the clearfell profits. The current partnership schemes offer the partner a choice of advance payments and a share of the crop revenue as follows:

- Advance payments of €635/ha. at the start of the scheme.
- Full Forest Premium. This will be for 15 or 20 years depending on the landowners circumstances (farmer/non farmer).
- 80% of the thinning profit. This amount will be apportioned annually from the time premium payments cease until clearfell. This is known as the thinning annuity.
- The landowner receives 55% of the clearfell profits.

Coillte will be willing to discuss other options in relation to increasing the annual annuity by bringing forward the thinning and or clear fell revenues.

COILLTE FBD PIP

Coillte in conjunction with FBD life has established a group Pension and Investment Plan (PIP) exclusively for those who have joined the Coillte Farm Partnership scheme or who have contracted their private forestry planting scheme to Coillte. The landowner contributes part or all of the annual premium/annuity to FBD Life who invest it in either the Coillte FBD Pension PIP or the Coillte FBD Investment PIP. The Coillte FBD Pension PIP is a tax efficient savings plan which provides the landowner with a tax free lump sum and a pension when he/she retires. The Coillte FBD Investment Plan allows the landowner to make regular contributions into an investment plan which offers excellent returns.

INSURING PLANTATIONS

All plantation owners should ensure that they have adequate and proper insurance cover. Cover is available through most of the general insurance companies but more tailor made policies are available from FBD.

FORESTRY COSTS AND RETURNS

The cost of establishing a forestry plantation varies widely. It depends on the nature of ground preparation required, the tree species selection and the need for maintenance in the early years of establishment. There are economies of scale and small areas are more expensive to develop irrespective of the nature of the site. As a general rule the costs of establishing sites in excess of 10 ha's will be fully covered by the afforestation grants.

Table 9.1: Projected returns from forestry

10 hectares low lying grass rush land, 20% diverse species, Y.C. 24. 10% broad leaves included.	
Returns Year 0 to Year 37	**€ per ha.**
Year 0 to year 20 : Annual Premium @ €408.86/ ha.	8,177
Year 15 1st. thin : 32m³ timber @ €3.90 / m³	125
Year 20 2nd. thin :61.5 m³ timber @ €14.68 / m³	903
Year 25 3rd. thin : 61.5 m³ timber @ €23.68 / m³	1,456
Year 30 4th. thin : 61.5 m³ timber @ €32.46 / m³	1,996
Year 35 5th. thin : 61.5 m³ timber @ €42.12 / m³	2,590
Year 37 Clearfell : 364.8 m³ timber @ €49.94 / m³	18,218
Total	**33,465**

The timber prices used in this example is for timber standing in the wood at historically averaged prices. Premiums and volumes per hectare are adjusted to allow for 20% larch and 10% ash, and have been reduced by 15% to allow for roads and open spaces. The prices at roadside or factory gate are much higher. It is worth noting that of the total money generated, premiums account for approximately 25% and timber sales 75%. Income from premiums and timber sales is not subject to income tax.

SPECIES SELECTION

The potential yield class of a tree species on a particular site is the main factor in determining species selection. Sitka spruce has traditionally been the predominant species in this country, because of its particular suitability to Irish soil and climatic conditions and its rapid growth characteristics. Other species are also of interest. Norway spruce is suited to more fertile sheltered sites, particularly frost prone sites, and produces a better quality timber than Sitka spruce. Douglas fir produces excellent timber but the availability of suitable sites is more limited. Larch has a high amenity value and should be used for landscaping and conservation purposes.

If the selection of species is well planned, game promotion, amenity landscape, environmental aspects, as well as the production of commercial timber, can all be included in the plan.

DIVERSIFICATION OF SPECIES

While diversification in species may prolong the rotation, higher grant and premium rates are payable for diverse species in order to:

- Increase the species range, diversity and value of timber end uses
- Reduce the threat which disease or harmful insects would pose in monoculture situations
- Increase the percentage of broadleaf plantations for both commercial end use and for aesthetic, landscape and environmental reasons

Broad-leaved species have a significant role to play in forestry development as they have a tremendous amenity value. While hardwood timber is highly valued broad-leaved species generally have long rotations and do not have the same rate of return as fast growing coniferous plantations. When premiums payments finish at the end of 20 years, there is not the same return from thinnings to ensure continuity of income. However higher planting grants and a more attractive premium scheme are available to encourage broad-leaved plantations.

Oak and beech have rotations of over a 100 years and because of the time scale involved give a very poor return on investment. Ash, sycamore and cherry can have rotations of less than 70 years. At present very high prices can be achieved on the export market for good quality hardwoods, and the return on investment for the shorter rotation hardwoods can compare favourably with the faster growing conifers. As supply of native hardwood increases due to the increased level of planting in recent years, the processing industry will also grow ensuring premium prices for the product in Ireland.

The power of
forestry

Forestry is both a valuable national asset and an excellent source of income.

Substantial grants are available for broadleaf and conifer plantings, even those of modest area, and also ancillary development such as roads and recreational amenities.

Premiums are paid tax-free.

*For further information, contact
The Forest Service,
Department of the Marine
and Natural Resources,
Johnstown Castle Estate,
Co. Wexford
Tel 053 60200
Locall 1890 200 223
Fax 053 43834*

**Department of Communications,
Marine and Natural Resources**

NATIONAL DEVELOPMENT PLAN

Supported by the EU under the
National Development Plan 2000-2006

AFFORESTATION GRANT SCHEME

Forestry has been identified as an industry capable of making a significant contribution to regional economic development. A range of grant schemes have been formulated to create and develop new and existing forests. If the site is greater than 2.5 ha. the application is advertised in the local press. If the site is greater than 25 ha. the application is referred to the relevant local authority. For developments of over 50 ha. an environmental impact assessment and planning permission are required. There are various guidelines and controls to deal with the environmental impact of forestry developments. In certain environmentally sensitive cases there may be a public consultation process whereby non personal information relating to the application may be made public.

The afforestation grant scheme has as its aim the promotion of afforestation as an alternative use of agricultural land. It is hoped that this will lead to an eventual improvement in forest resources and countryside´management in a manner compatible with the environment.

The scheme applies throughout the State, to the afforestation of agricultural land suitable for forestry. *Written approval for afforestation projects must be obtained from the Department of the Marine and Natural Resources prior to the commencement of work.* No grant aid will be approved where work has already commenced. The application for pre-planting approval on Form 1, must be submitted to the Forest Service, Johnstown Castle Estate, Co. Wexford, by an approved Forestry Company or approved Forester.

Grant aid under the scheme is available for activities such as:
- Preparation of ground
- Scrub clearance
- Plants and planting
- Fertilisation
- Fencing
- Fire protection
- Weed control
- Supervision/consultancy/management
- VAT, where applicable

GRANT PAYMENT APPLICATION
In order to apply for grant aid after planting the applicant must forward the following documentation:

- Fully completed and signed application form
- Certified species map
- Invoices for costs of work as per activities outlined above
- Tax clearance certificate(s) for contractor(s) used
- Provenance declaration form(s)
- Where the grant is mandated to a contractor or bank, a valid mandate

CONDITIONS OF PAYMENT

The afforestation grant is payable in two installments. The first installment is due for payment on completion of the site and submission of a completed application signed by both the applicant and the approved forester to whom the pre-planting approval issued.

The 2nd installment is due for payment four years after the completion date of the plantation. An application for payment form issues from the Forest Service and must be completed and signed by both the applicant and the approved forester.

If the entire plantation is up to the required standard then payment of the grant issues.

PLANTATION RULES

Rule 1 - 10% broad leaves: Plantations on improved/enclosed land must contain a minimum of 10% broad leaves, site permitting. The broad leaves making up this 10% must comply with the minimum width criteria when the plantation area is 3.0 ha. or more. In areas less than 3.0 ha. the broad leaves can be planted on boundaries, riparian zones, in groups or intimate mixtures, or can be used as part of the 20% diverse content.

Rule 2 - 20% Diverse Conifers: Where conifers constitute all or part of a plantation the conifers must contain a minimum of 20% diverse conifers (i.e. conifer species other than Sitka spruce or lodgepole pine. In intimately mixed plots the diverse conifer species may be substituted by suitable broad leaves.

GRANT PREMIUM CATEGORIES

Each plot within a plantation must fit into one of the following grant/premium categories (GPC's) and comply with rules 1 and 2 above.
- **GPC 1- Unenclosed Land:** must be planted with no more than 80% Sitka spruce or lodgepole pine. The remainder should be made up of a suitable

diverse conifer such as Japanese larch. Broadleaves may also be introduced as part of the 20%. (unenclosed land)

- **GPC 2 - Non-Diverse:** is made up of Sitka spruce or lodgepole pine. For landscape purposes it may be appropriate to introduce a small number of other species into this plot. *This plot on its own is not grant aided, it does not conform to the rules above, but can be a component of a plantation that conforms.* (enclosed/improved land)
- **GPC 3 - 20% Diverse:** is made up of an intimate mix of Sitka spruce or lodgepole pine and a suitable diverse conifer (normally Japanese or hybrid larch). The diverse content must be greater than 20%. This 20% intimate mix can be made up of trees scattered throughout the plantation, trees planted in small groups through the plantation or a combination of each. Alder and birch may also be used in intimate mixture with SS/LP. (enclosed/improved land)
- **GPC 4 - Diverse:** is made up of 100% acceptable conifer species other than Sitka spruce or lodgepole pine. (enclosed/improved land)
- **GPC 5 - Broadleaf Non Oak/Beech:** is made up of acceptable broad leaves other than oak and beech. (enclosed/improved land)
- **GPC 6 - Oak:** is made up of pure oak or oak/conifer mix. The acceptable conifers are Scots pine and European larch. (enclosed/improved land)
- **GPC 7 - Beech:** is made up of pure beech and/or a beech conifer mix. The acceptable conifers are Scots pine and European larch. (enclosed/improved land)

MAXIMUM GRANT LEVELS

Table 9.2: Maximum grant rates per hectare

Grant/premium Category (GPC)	1st. Installment Grant € / ha.	2nd. Installment Grant € / ha.	Total Grant € / ha.
GPC 1 - Unenclosed	2,031.58	698.36	2,729.94
GPC 2- Non Diverse	2,031.58	698.36	2,729.94
GPC 3 - 20% Diverse	2,158.55	698.36	2,856.91
GPC 4 - Diverse	2,412.50	761.84	3,174.35
GPC 5 - Broadleaf	3,809.21	1,142.76	4,951.98
GPC 6 - Oak	4,825.00	1,523.69	6,348.69
GPC 7 - Oak and Beech	5,078.95	1,650.66	6,729.61

OWNERSHIP

In order to qualify for the afforestation grant and premiums applicants must own, lease, or be in joint management of the lands proposed for planting. All applicants must provide documentary evidence of ownership, leasing and joint management. The one exception to this is where the applicant is purchasing land subject to obtaining preplanting approval. In these cases documentation must be submitted before payment of the afforestation grant. In the case of commonages, consent forms can be submitted allowing one of the owners to apply on behalf of all the owners for the afforestation grant. Documentary evidence identifying the owners is required. All the owners are entitled to premiums and are all assessed. All consent forms must be witnessed and stamped by a solicitor.

TAX CLEARANCE PROCEDURES

Applicants are asked to supply their PPS number and their tax district code. Contractors employed must produce tax clearance certificates before the grant will be paid.

LAND ELIGIBLE FOR PLANTING

The term afforestation means the planting of land not previously under forest. The afforestation scheme applies to agricultural land only. Lands in other uses such as hotel grounds, golf courses and other non-agricultural activities are not entitled to grant aid.

Both conifer and broadleaf sites proposed for planting must be capable of producing a commercial sawlog crop of wood. This means the land must be capable of producing Sitka spruce of at least yield class 14, and yield class 4 for oak/beech.

ACCESS

The applicant must own or have written permission to use or have right of way on the access route to the plantation. It is essential that there is access from a public road to the proposed plantation which will at least accommodate a tractor and trailer in an unrestricted manner.

MINIMUM AREA
- A conifer plantation must be not less than 1 ha.
- Conifer plantations adjoining existing forests, minimum size 0.25 ha.
- A conifer plot must not be less than 0.25 ha.

- A broadleaf plantation must not be less than 0.1 ha.

MINIMUM WIDTH

The minimum width applies to the actual planted area and does not take into account areas left unplanted (e.g. buffers along roads, rivers, streams, etc.). The minimum width of any plantation should not normally be less than 40 metres. Where sites do not meet this requirement but are in the following categories they may be submitted for approval.

- areas where more than 50% of the proposed plantation will exceed 40 metres in width
- areas where more than 50% of the proposed plantation will exceed a width of 30 metres while adjoining an existing woodland
- areas where more than 50% of the proposed plantation will exceed a width of 30 metres for small (under 0.16 ha.) broadleaf areas.

FOREST PREMIUM SCHEME

Investment in forestry is by its nature long term, coniferous plantations typically being suitable for harvesting after 35 to 40 years. The Forest Premium Scheme has been introduced to provide farmers and non-farmers with a short term income from forestry and thus increase the attractiveness of private afforestation.

ELIGIBLE FARMERS

Premiums are payable only for plantations which qualify for an afforestation grant. Applicants must be over 18 years of age. The scheme has two rates, the farmer and the non-farmers rate of premium. The premium is paid following the approval of the afforestation grant. Each of the 4 conditions listed below must be met to qualify for the farmer rate of forest premium, otherwise the non-farmer rate applies. The farmer must:

- practice farming within the state
- reside within 70 miles of the plantation
- own, lease, or be in joint management of at least 3 ha. of agricultural land

- derive at least 25% of their total income from farming in one of the three years prior to planting

Income calculation

- Only the income of the applicant is included in the 25% calculation, spouses income is not included.
- Farming income includes agricultural aids, premiums, subsidies and farm forest premiums
- Land letting on less than the 11 month basis (conacre letting) is eligible as farming income provided the applicant has other farming income.
- All Social Welfare payments, pensions/disability benefits, are excluded from total gross income.
- An applicant who has already been assessed as a farmer under the CAP premium scheme, i.e. has submitted documentary evidence of farmer status does not have to be reassessed for further applications under the CAP scheme for new plantations.

DOCUMENTARY EVIDENCE REQUIRED

- A tax assessment form for one of the three years prior to the completion of the plantation showing farming income as 25% of total income.

or

- If farming income on the tax assessment is not 25% of total income, a statement showing gross farming income in the form of a farm profile or farm accounts and certified by the Revenue Commissioners is acceptable. In these circumstances if gross farming income is 25% of the total income the farmer qualifies.

or

- An income assessment and declaration, TF1 completed by either the local Teagasc Land Use Advisor, or by an Agricultural Consultant, registered with the Department of Agriculture, Food and Rural Development confirming that 25% of total income is derived from farming

The non farmer rate applies to applicants who do not meet one of these conditions.

PREMIUM LEVELS

Table 9.3: Forest Premium Rates per hectare

Grant / Premium Category (GPC)	Farmer Premium (annual payment for 20 years) € / ha. Plantation area			Non-Farmer Premium (a.p.15 years) € / ha.
	<6ha	>=6ha	>=12ha	
GPC 1 - Unenclosed	209.51	209.51	209.51	171.41
GPC 2 - Non Diverse	336.48	349.18	361.88	
GPC 3 - 20% Diverse	391.08	403.78	416.47	
GPC 4 - Diverse	416.47	429.17	441.87	
GPC 5 - Broadleaf (except oak and beech)	441.87	454.57	467.26	184.11
GPC 7 - Oak	473.61	486.31	499.01	
GPC 7 - Beech	473.61	486.31	499.01	

PAYMENT DETAILS

The first premium is due for payment, at the same time as the 1st. installment of the planting grant. The farmer rate is payable for a period of 20 years, and the non-farmer rate for a period of 15 years.

CHANGE OF OWNERSHIP

The Forest Service must be informed if there is a change of ownership of a grant aided plantation. Once a change of ownership has been reported to the Forest Service, all premium payments stop until the ownership has been resolved.

In the case of a change of ownership due to death, one premium payment may be made to the representatives of the estate. The issue of ownership will then have to be resolved before any more premiums are paid.

If the person who inherits the land is an immediate family member, namely husband/wife, sons, daughters, brothers and sisters, the premium continues to be paid at the same rate as paid to the original owner once ownership documentation is provided. The new owner is not assessed for eligibility under the scheme.

If the person who inherits the land is not an immediate family member and the land was in receipt of the farmer rate of premiums the new owner will have to provide documentary evidence of farmer qualification.

In the case of a change of ownership due to sale, the new owner will have to provide documentary evidence of farmer qualification and documentary evidence of ownership. Only when the relevant documentation is received is the name changed on the file and the outstanding premium payments processed.

If the premium paid in respect of the plantation to the original applicant is the non farmer rate, this rate will always apply to the plantation, even if the new owner qualifies as a farmer.

ADDITIONAL SUPPORT MEASURES

- Reforestation Grant Scheme
- Woodland Improvement Scheme
- High Pruning of Conifers
- Reconstitution of Woodlands Scheme
- Formative Shaping of Broadleaves
- Forest Road Grant

REFORESTATION GRANT SCHEME

This scheme applies to land replanted following a clearfell. An EIA is required for areas of broadleaf greater than 10 ha. that are to be replaced with conifers.

The same silvicultural and environmental standards as for afforestation are applicable.

APPROVAL
Complete and submit an application form. Enclose a species map. Following a satisfactory site inspection from a Forestry Inspector written approval will issue. Work should not commence until written approval has been received.

GRANT RATE

- €1015.79 / ha. for broad leaves

- €634.87 / ha. for conifers

The grant is paid in two installments 75% after planting and 25% four years later. No premiums are paid on reforestation sites.

NATIVE WOODLAND SCHEME

Native woodlands occupy about 1% of Irelands land area and are not alone an essential part of our heritage, but also a valuable resource in terms of biodiversity and the general appearance of our landscape. In acknowledgment of the need to protect and enhance our native woodlands the Native Woodland Scheme was launched on 7 November 2001. The scheme is available to both private and public owners of woodlands and unplanted areas with the aim of enhancing existing native woodlands and establishing new ones, using 'close to nature' silviculture.

GRANT AID
Cost based grants are available for woodland improvement subject to a maximum of €4,444 / ha.. Cost based grants are also available for native woodland establishment subject to a maximum of €6,731 / ha.

NATIVE WOODLAND SCHEME PREMIUMS
Applicants for native woodland establishment may also be eligible for afforestation premiums under the general Afforestation Grant and Premium Schemes.
Applicants for Native Woodland Conservation on sites deemed to have an ecological benefit may be eligible for a an annual native woodland premium up to a maximum of €120/ha. paid on a contract basis. This premium is only available to private land owners

WOODLAND IMPROVEMENT

This scheme applies to areas of existing woodland that have had little management in the past and have little economic value. The woodland under consideration should have the potential to be improved through treatment of the existing woodland, enrichment planting or a combination of both.

The same silvicultural and environmental standards as for afforestation are applicable. The elements below refer to activities that may be carried out that are unique to the Woodland Improvement Scheme.

- improvement felling of malformed trees and over mature trees. (a felling license will be required)
- felling of additional trees if necessary to create planting gaps
- pruning to improve stem quality
- enrichment planting to improve species composition and crop quality
- thinning to promote growth
- removal of invasive species that threaten regeneration (such as rhododendron or laurel)
- removal of over dominant ivy
- management and respacing of natural regeneration

Approval procedure as for reforestation. Work should not commence until written approval is received.

GRANT RATES

- Costs to a max. of €4444.08 / ha. for broad leaves.
- Costs to a max. of €2539.48 / ha. for conifers.

The grant is paid in two installments, 75% after planting and 25% four years later. There are no premiums associated with this scheme.

HIGH PRUNING OF CONIFERS

This is an element of the Woodland Improvement Scheme which applies to young (13 to 22 years) conifer woodland. The scheme is directed towards the high pruning of commercial coniferous crops to select suitable stands. The following criteria should be used.

- selected trees within a stand must be capable of increasing their mean diameter by a factor of 2.5
- stands will usually be between 13 and 22 years old
- stands of yield class 18 or more should be selected
- stands should be stable with a low risk of windthrow

- minimum area 0.4 ha.

The objective is to produce a stand of conifers that will have 6 metres of branch/knot free stem. This will increase the value and quality of the crop significantly.

- prune a minimum of 500 stems/ha. (lodgepole pine would require 600 stems/ha)
- the first lift involves the removal of all branches on the selected stems to a height of 3.5 m.
- two to four years after the first lift the second lift from 3.5 to 6.0m may be done.
- Prune an inspection path every 100m.

On completion of the pruning a certificate will be issued from the Forest Service indicating, for future sales purposes, the area pruned, the number of stems per hectare pruned, pruning height etc.

Approval procedure as for reforestation. Work should not commence until written approval is received.

GRANT RATES
- €698.35 / ha. for the first lift (high prune to 3.5m)
- €825.33 / ha. for the second lift (high prune from 3.5 to 6.0m)

RECONSTITUTION OF WOODLANDS SCHEME

This grant applies when a natural disaster causes damage to a plantation. In such cases the Forest Service grant aids the reconstitution of such a plantation if the plantation has been well managed up to the time it was damaged. Examples of natural damage that often effect plantations include fire, frost, disease and windblow.

In the case of windblow a grant is normally allowable if the windblow occurred before the plantation reaches 2/3 of its specified rotation length. Exceptions may be made in the event of catastrophic windblow where the value is significantly reduced.

The objective of the grant is to repair the damage to plantations by replacing the elements that have been damaged. It does not compensate for increment or timber loss and it would be prudent for owners to insure their forestry investment.

Application procedure on Form 1 **within 8 weeks of the occurrence of damage**. Work should not commence until written approval is received.

GRANT RATES
- Costs to a max. of €3174.35 / ha. for conifers.
- Costs to a max. of €6729.61 / ha. for broad leaves.

The grant is paid in two installments, 75% on completion and submission of documentation, and 25% after 4 years.

FORMATIVE SHAPING OF BROAD LEAVES

This element of the Reconstitution of Woodlands scheme applies to broadleaved plantations that are aged between 3 and 6 years and require formative shaping. Formative shaping is required when young trees have multiple leaders or disproportionately large side shoots. This occurs mainly as a result of frost or wind damage. Plantations planted after the 1/11/97 are not entitled to this grant as increased afforestation grants that apply from that date allow the applicant to include this operation in the overall costs.

The objective of the scheme is to produce broadleaved plantations with single straight stems leading to eventual high quality butt lengths of valuable broadleaf timber.

TIMING OF SHAPING

Table 9.4: Optimum periods for shaping

Species	Best Period for Shaping	2nd Best Period for Shaping
Oak	December	Mid Winter
Ash	June to October	Mid Winter
Beech	June to August	Mid Winter
Sycamore	June to August	Mid Winter
Cherry	June to August	Mid Winter

Application procedure as for reforestation. Work should not commence until written approval is received.

GRANT RATES
- 1st shaping   max. €253.95 / ha. (once off payment)
- 2nd shaping   max. €253.95 / ha. (once off payment)

FOREST ROAD SCHEME

The Forest Service grant aid the construction of harvesting and development or management roads. The following criteria are used to assess which plantations receive grant aid.

- The roading scheme does not provide for other purposes i.e. turbary, residential entrances, farm roads etc.
- Co-operative ventures with neighbouring forests are advised.
- Access roads and internal roads are treated in the same for grant purposes.
- All proposed new entrances/lay byes from public roads should be discussed with the County Councils Local Engineer, and written approval supplied.
- For all applicants adjoining a public road, a bell mouth entrance must be provided.
- From a grant point of view the provision of a bell mouth, turntable or hammerhead is equivalent to the addition of 10m of road.
- For areas greater than 20 hectares specifications drawn up by an engineer /surveyor will be required.
- Added funding will be considered in exceptionally difficult conditions (e.g. rock breaking, bridges, etc.).
- Road construction must be compatible with Forest Service published environmental guidelines.

DEVELOPMENT AND MANAGEMENT TRACKS

At planting stage it is important to leave areas unplanted and uncultivated in order to provide access through the plantation by tractors or 4 wheel drive vehicles. These areas can be used to build harvesting roads when the crop approaches first thinning.

Where large sites are involved or where access is difficult a development grant is available.

HARVESTING ROADS

In order to facilitate the successful thinning and clearfelling of a crop access by timber trucks is essential. Roads are built just before harvesting to a density of around 20m/ha. Approval will be processed after receipt of a completed application form available from the Forest Service. No works must take place before written approval is received.

GRANT RATES

Grants of up to 80% of the cost incurred in the construction of a forest road are available subject to the maximum as detailed in the table below.

Table 9.5: Forest road construction grant rates

Road	€ / Linear Metre	Density Metre / Ha.
Harvesting	28.57	20
Harvesting upgrade (where development road grant was previously recorded)	28.57	13
Development and management	28.57	7

NEW DEVELOPMENTS

POPLAR - A FAST GROWING BROADLEAF

More tree species must be identified to ensure the continued future development of a silviculturally sound, environmentally sensitive, and economically vibrant timber industry in Ireland. Poplar (Populus) is one species that may contribute to this development. Hybrid poplars have been bred to be fast growing and disease resistant. Poplars are planted as unrooted cuttings or setts, and will develop roots four to six weeks after planting. One or two thinnings may be carried out ten to fifteen years after planting and all trees are felled at 25 to 30 years of age.

RESEARCH AND FUNDING

Teagasc and the Waterford Institute of Technology are currently involved in EU funded projects identifying the type of land suitable for poplar growing. Market opportunities are being examined in a project funded by COFORD, the National Council for Forest Research and Development. Interim results show that poplar has a wide range of uses including, architrave and skirting boards, fencing rails, tongue and grooved floor boards and furniture.

The Forest Service has agreed to fund a further 200 hectares. Funding will cover the full establishment and maintenance cost and an annual premium payment to the landowner of €442 per ha. for 12 years,

For further information on poplar and on farm demonstrations, contact: Mr. Tom Kent, Course Leader-Forestry, Waterford Institute of Technology, Cork Road, Waterford.

FORESTRY AND RELATED SCHEMES

AFFORESTATION AND REPS
Since 1997 a REPS participant is free to plant land without incurring any penalties. However he/she will not receive REPS payments on the planted lands but will be entitled to the afforestation grants and premiums.

AFFORESTATION AND THE EARLY FARM RETIREMENT SCHEME (ERS)

- A transferor who already has land planted before retiring from farming and is entitled to a forest premium may retain that land and continue to receive the premium. If this forestry land is transferred with the holding the transferee who obtains it can apply for the premium.
- A retiring farmer who wishes to retain some of the land for forestry will need to have the planting completed before he/she transfers the remaining lands. In this way he/she can avail of the forestry premium on the land and the retirement pension on the remainder of the land.
- A farming transferee may use the land for forestry provided he/she practices farming as a main occupation on his/her enlarged holding.
- Maximum aid under the ERS can be obtained when 24 hectares or more is transferred. Many farmers contemplating participating in the ERS have over 24 hectares and could significantly enhance their tax free income by planting land prior to retiring from farming and by holding on to it post farm retirement to benefit from annual premium payments.
- A farmer intending to apply for the ERS who can satisfy the Department that he failed to find an eligible tenant may afforest these lands and draw the ERS pension on them. However he will not be entitled to receive the Forest Premium until the ERS pension expires and then only at the non farmer rate.

ADVISORY, TRAINING AND SUPPORT SERVICES

Advice and assistance on forestry is provided by the Forest Service, Teagasc, Private Consultants and Forest Contracting Companies. For details of Teagasc forestry courses and Forest Service schemes, contact your local Teagasc or Forest Service Office, or the Forest Service, Department of the Marine and Natural Resources, Johnstown Castle Estate, Co. Wexford. Tel 1890 200223.

Society of Irish Foresters Consultant Foresters Regional Group Approved foresters

Frances Burke, 30 Corcoran Terrace, Ballina, Co Mayo. Tel: 096 72791
Michael Costello, Mockmoyne, Boyle, Co Roscommon. Tel: 079 62348
Michael Cregan, 6 Brookville Park, Blackrock, Co Dublin. Tel: 01 2892130
Padraig Dolan, Derrybeg, Killeigh, Tullamore, Co Offaly. Tel: 0506 52609
Patrick Donovan, Prospect, Maree, Oranmore, Co Galway. Tel: 091 792392
William English, Knockballynoe, Kilfeacle, Co Tipperary. Tel: 062 52356
Ted Farrell, "Sequoia", Mart Lane, Foxrock, Co Dublin. Tel: 01 7067716
Paul Finnegan, Newline, Ballycrissane, Ballinasloe, Co Galway. Tel: 0905 75287
Donal Fitzpatrick, Trees to Timber, Lifford House, Ennis, Co Clare. Tel: 065 6821518
Eamon Flanagan, Slí na hAbhann, Tarmonbarry, Co Longford. Tel: 043 26440
Sean Galvin, Cluain Doire, Listowel, Co Kerry. Tel: 068 21182
Aeneas Higgins, Ashmead, Oldcourt Road, Bray, Co Wicklow. Tel: 01 2862747
Michael Hoban, Thomas Street, Castlebar, Co Mayo. Tel: 094 22817 Email:
Dermot Houlihan, 27 Bushy Park Lawn, Circular Road, Galway. Tel: 091 527580
Jim Kinsella, Bishopswood, Dundrum, Co Tipperary. Tel: 062 71472
Sean Lenihan, Kestrel For. Cons, Coolgreany, Gorey, Co Wexford. Tel: 0402 37519
Daragh Little, FEL, 29 Lr. Leeson Street, Dublin 2. Tel: 01 6622479
Michael Macnamara, "Domara", Fossabeg, Scarriff, Co Clare. Tel: 061 921563
Tony Mannion, Ballyweelin, Rosses Point, Co Sligo. Tel: 071 77549
Tom McDonald, Upper Main Street, Portarlington, Co Laois. Tel: 0502 23643
Aidan McKenna, Cavanmoutry, Killybrone, Co Monaghan. Tel: 047 86995
Sean McNamara, Woodside Lodge, Cratloe, Co Clare. Tel: 061 357008
Melissa Newman, Aghaclogher, Strokestown, Co Roscommon. Tel: 078 34883
Peter O'Brien, Glenmore, The Spa, Tralee, Co Kerry. Tel: 066 7136506
John O'Connell, Glenasack Tree Services, Block Road, Portlaoise, Co Laois. Tel: 0502 21669
Kieran O'Connell, Castlematrix, Rathkeale, Co Limerick. Tel: 069 63278
Timmie O'Sullivan, Ahane Cross, Brosna, Co Kerry. Tel: 068 44125
Michael O'Sullivan, Bank House, Main St., Carrick-on-Suir, Co Tipperary. Tel: 051 640398
Patrick Purser, Purser Tarleton Russell, 36 Fitzwilliam Square, Dublin 2. Tel: 01 6625621
Morgan Roche, Sillahertaine, Kilgarvan, Co Kerry. Tel; 064 85631
Fionan Russell, Purser Tarleton Russell, 36 Fitzwilliam Square, Dublin 2. Tel: 01 6625621
Mark Tarleton, Purser Tarleton Russell, 36 Fitzwilliam Square, Dublin 2. Tel: 01 6625621
Donal Whelan, 54 Foxrock Avenue, Foxrock, Dublin 18. Tel: 01 2350988
Colman Young, "Ashlu", Newpark, Portlaoise, Co Laois. Tel: 0502 21678

IRISH TIMBER GROWERS ASSOCIATION

The Association Representing the Interests of Private Woodland Owners

ITGA aims to promote the development and expansion of private sector forestry, in the Republic of Ireland, to ensure that forestry maximises it's economic, environmental and social potential.

Providing forestry information and back-up services to members, including:

- Field Trips to Members Forests
- Annual Seminar
- A Forestry Directory/Yearbook
- A Quarterly Newsletter
- A Representative Voice

For more information contact:
The Secretary,
Irish Timber Growers Association,
84 Merrion Square,
Dublin 2
Tel: (01) 676 4783   Fax: (01) 662 4502
E-Mail: itga@icos.ie

Part 10 - Farm Business Matters

EMPLOYING FARM LABOUR

Deciding to employ a farm worker is not as simple a matter as it might have been in previous generations. There are two principal areas that a farmer should be aware of before a decision is made, these are:

- The true cost of employing a farm worker
- The obligations placed upon the employer and the workers' rights

AGRICULTURAL WAGES AND CONDITIONS OF EMPLOYMENT

Agricultural workers' remuneration and conditions of employment are set down by way of an Employment Regulation Order by the Agricultural Workers Joint Labour Committee. The order covers workers in agriculture, horticulture and forestry but does not cover persons working in the mushroom growing industry, grooms or domestic workers in farm households.

STATUTORY MINIMUM REMUNERATION
The following rates are effective from 23 April 2002:

Table 10.1: Minimum wages based on a 39 hour week

Age of Worker	Per Week	Per Hour
Experienced adult worker	€254.00	€6.51
Under age 18	€177.80	€4.56
Job entrants		
First year after first employment over 18	€203.20	€5.21
Second year after first employment over 18	€228.60	€5.86
Workers in structured training		
First 1/3 period (not exceeding 12 months)	€190.50	€4.88
Second 1/3 period (not exceeding 12 months)	€202.20	€5.21
Third 1/3 period (not exceeding 12 months)	€228.60	€5.86

CONDITIONS OF EMPLOYMENT

WORKING HOURS

The normal number of hours to be worked is 39. The 39-hour week may be implemented in any of the following ways, depending on the needs of the business:

- A 39 hour week on a year-round basis
- 38 hours for 6 consecutive months
  40 hours for 6 consecutive months
- 36 hours for 3 consecutive months
  40 hours for nine consecutive months

Normal pay should not vary in relation to hours worked in the shorter/longer periods, but will be paid as though a 39-hour week was worked.

Where hours worked (including overtime) exceeds 48 per week, the total number of hours in any seven day period must not exceed 48, averaged over a period of six months. The months of the averaging period must be consecutive, but the employer may choose which six months they will be.

SHORT DAY

Only a half day shall be worked on Saturdays unless the contract of employment provides otherwise, or 24 hours notice of a requirement to work after 1.00 p.m. on Saturday is given to the worker by the employer.

OVERTIME RATES

The following are the arrangements that apply after normal working hours have been worked:

- For all time worked in excess of the normal hours of work on any day other than a Sunday, and including after 1.00 p.m. on the short day, the minimum time rate is time and one third.
- For all time worked on Public Holidays, the minimum time-rate is time and one third.
- For all time worked on Sundays, the minimum time rate-rate is time and two thirds.

BENEFITS AND ADVANTAGES

If a worker receives board and lodgings, board only or lodgings only from his employer, the following amounts may be deducted from his pay:

- €54.13 for full board and lodgings per week (7 day week) or €7.73 per day
- €32.14 for full board only per week (7 day week) or €4.60 per day
- €21.85 for lodgings only per week (7 day week) or €3.14 per day

HOLIDAYS

The leave year is the year commencing 1 April and ending 31 March. and holiday entitlements are calculated by one of the following methods:

- 4 working weeks in the leave year in which the worker works at least 1,365 hours (unless it is a leave year in which the worker changed employment);
- 1/3 of a working week per calendar month that the worker works at least 117 hours;
- 6% of the hours worked in a year, subject to a maximum of 4 working weeks.

Where a worker falls ill during annual leave and furnishes to his employer a medical certificate in respect of the illness, the days to which the certificate refers shall not be regarded as annual leave. The annual leave of a worker who has 8 or more months of service shall include an unbroken period of two weeks.

WET TIME

Wet time means all absences from work due to inclement weather where the employee is not paid full wages. For the purpose of calculating holiday entitlements, wet time shall be deemed to be hours worked up to a maximum of 480 hours in the leave year or 40 hours in a month.

SHORT TIME AND PART TIME WORKERS

Holiday entitlements are calculated in the same manner as set out above for full time employees. Entitlement to public holidays leave shall only apply where the worker has worked for at least 40 hours in the 5 weeks before the public holiday

CESSER PAY

Where a worker ceases to be employed and the whole or any portion of annual leave remains to be granted to him, the worker shall be paid an amount equal to the pay that he would have received if he had been granted that leave.

SICK PAY SCHEME

All agricultural workers having a minimum of one years service with their current employer shall be covered by a Sick Pay Scheme which entitles them to payment during absences due to illness. This scheme shall be provided by the employer, and shall be non-contributory. The details are as follows:

- No payment shall be made in respect of the first 3 days of any absence on sick leave.
- Entitlement to payment shall require a medical certificate, produced after the third day of any absence on sick leave, and specifying the nature of the illness. Certificates must be produced weekly thereafter for the duration of the illness.
- Entitlement to benefit under the scheme will apply only during a 12 month period in any Scheme year, and will not carry over from one year to another.
- Full time staff after one years service, and working in excess of 18 hours per week, will be entitled to 3 weeks pay less Social Welfare entitlement. Part-time staff will be entitled to 2 weeks pay less Social Welfare entitlement.
- The worker will be responsible for claiming Social Welfare entitlements while on sick leave, and for paying over such payments to the employer.

EMPLOYER'S OBLIGATIONS AND WORKER'S RIGHTS

An employer has certain obligations which he owes to his employee. The employee also has certain rights which he is legally entitled to and there is a substantial body of legislation in place to protect the worker's rights.

REGISTERING EMPLOYEES

All employees earning more than seven €7.60 a week must be registered under the PAYE system. Failure to do will cause problems for both the employer and employee.

PENALTIES

The penalty for paying less than the statutory minimum agricultural wage is a fine not exceeding €952 for each offence. A similar penalty applies for non compliance with the statutory conditions of employment.

DISMISSAL NOTICE

An employee who is in continuous employment for sixteen weeks or more is entitled to certain minimum notice in the event of dismissal as follows:

Table 10.2: Minimum dismissal notices

Length of Service	Minimum Notice
Thirteen weeks to two years	One week
Two years to five years	Two weeks
Five years to ten years	Four weeks
Ten years to fifteen years	Six weeks
More than fifteen years	Eight weeks

UNFAIR DISMISSAL

An employee who works for eight hours per week or more and is employed for a year or more is entitled to claim unfair dismissal if he should be so dismissed or should the conditions of work be made so difficult that he or she feels obliged to leave. In order to justify a dismissal, an employer must show that it resulted from one or more of the following causes:

- the capability, competence or qualifications of the employee
- the redundancy of the employee
- the fact that continuation of the employment would contravene another statutory requirement
- that there were other substantial grounds for dismissal

Should unfair dismissal be proven the employer will have to:
- reinstate the person in their old job, or
- reinstate them in an alternative job that the adjudicating bodies consider reasonable, or
- provide financial compensation to a maximum of two years' pay

An employee found to have been unfairly dismissed but who has suffered no financial loss, i.e. found suitable alternative employment, may be awarded up to four weeks' pay.

REDUNDANCY

An employee who is employed for two years or more is entitled to statutory redundancy as follows:

- A half week's pay for each year of continuous service between the ages of sixteen and forty-one. (a week's pay is subject to a ceiling of €381).
- One week's pay for each year of continuous service over the age of forty-one plus an additional week's pay.

Employers are entitled to a rebate of 60% of statutory redundancy paid provided they observe certain conditions as follows:

- The requisite two weeks notice must be given to the employee on the prescribed form R.P.1. A copy of this notice must be sent to the Department of Enterprise, Trade and Employment at the same time.
- When dismissal actually takes place, the employee must be given a Redundancy Certificate (form RP2).
- The actual claim by the employer for the 60% rebate should be made to the Department of Enterprise, Trade and Employment on form RP3 accompanied by copies of the Redundancy Certificate.

All of the forms referred to above are available from the Department of Enterprise, Trade and Employment.

SAFETY STANDARDS IN THE WORKPLACE

The employer must ensure that certain safety standards are maintained to protect the good health and safety of the worker. See Farm Safety Section page 266.

NATIONAL MINIMUM WAGE

The National Minimum became law on 1 April 2000. The Act applies to full time, part time and casual employees. The Act does not apply to close relatives of the employer such as s spouse, father, mother, son, daughter, brother or sister, It also does not apply to certain apprentices to various trades, however in the case of farm apprenticeships the Farm Apprenticeship Board lays down the rates of remuneration payable.

MINIMUM HOURLY RATE OF PAY
From 1 October 2002 the national minimum rates are as follows:
- an experienced adult worker is entitled to €6.35 per working hour. An experienced adult worker is over 18 years and has been working for more than two years from the date of their first employment.
- A person under 18 is entitled to €4.45 per working hour.
- A person in the first year of employment over 18 years of age is entitled to €5.08 per working hour.

WORKING HOURS
Working hours of an employee include any overtime hours worked, any time spent on standby in the workplace and any training during normal working hours. Working hours for the purposes of the Act do not include the time that the employee is absent from work on annual leave, or sick leave.

FARM RELIEF SERVICES

Farm Relief Services now have over 20,000 customer farmers and over 3,000 operators supplying a wide range of services.

ANNUAL FEES
Farmers pay an annual registration fee of €40 – €60 and then pay for each individual service as they use it.

CHARGE OUT RATES

Rates will vary between the different FRS areas and the following charges are those as charged in 2002 by the Kilkenny Carlow and District Farm Relief Services Ltd.

Table: 10.3

Relief Milking	Single morning or evening €31- minimum two hours. Daily Milking €61 - minimum four hours. Sunday single €38....Sunday daily €76
Dairy Relief Work	€8 to €9.50.per hour.
General Farm Relief Work	€8.76 to €10.29 per hour. including work for agricultural contractors.
Hoof Care	€32,1st. hour, €25.39 per hour thereafter.
Calf Dehorning	€12.70 minimum charge, €1.90 to €2.54 per head thereafter.
Sheep Scanning	€42.86 per call charge plus €0.57 per ewe thereafter. (quotations for large numbers).
Cow Scanning	€45.72 for first six cows and €2.85 per cow thereafter.
Freeze branding	Two digits-€50.79 for first ten animals, €4.12/hd thereafter. Three digits-€57.14 for first ten animals, €5.08/hd. thereafter.
Home Relief	€8 per hour.
Other services	Quotation on request

SERVICE PLUS

FRS are currently promoting a new concept – 'Service Plus'. The concept is quite simple and should prove very attractive to farmers. A farmer with some spare time and spare capacity on his own machinery provides a service to other farms in his area, such as fertiliser spreading, topping, rolling, weed spraying, etc. Some farmers have purchased specialised machinery such as ATVs, Bob-Cats and Diet Feeders to provide a greater range of services. These are ideally suited to doing work which was previously done manually and is most time consuming.

Service Plus can reduce the need for a General Farm Worker on many farms by supplying the man and machine as a package. It also proves very attractive to the supplier who is now getting a better return on his own machinery and also on his time.

FARM PLASTIC COLLECTION
FRS have been appointed as the national agents for collecting waste farm plastic. They are now collecting approximately 7,000 tonnes each year, which is then sent to Dumfries in Scotland for recycling. There is no charge for the collection service as farmers have already paid a levy incorporated into the price of the plastic.

HEALTH & SAFETY
National Co-Op FRS have employed a national health & safety officer and are promoting a number of safety initiatives including:

- A safety statement service where trained personnel will go out to the farm, carry out a detailed survey and prepare the safety statement for the farm
- Tractor driving skills course aimed at 14 – 16 year olds
- Health and safety training for all FRS operators
- Health and safety training for other bodies and organisations

FORESTRY
FRS Forestry Services are being further extended in conjunction with the Forest Service. The latest initiative is the employment of seven forestry team leaders to promote and deliver forestry services to the farm forestry sector.

EMPLOYMENT AGENCY
FRS have set up an employment agency – FRS people placements – to supply people for employment in the industrial and commercial sectors. A separate division – FRS agricultural appointments – specialise in the agribusiness sector and also placing full-time staff on farms.

LOCAL OFFICES

- Mogeely/Seandun FRS, Unit 1 Enterprise Park, Dwyers Rd., Middleton,Co. Cork. Ph: 021-4613501
- Bride & Blackwater FRS, 5 McCurtain Street, Fermoy, Co. Cork. Ph: 025-32646

- Donegal FRS, Oakfield Demesne, Raphoe, Co. Donegal, Ph: 074-45386
- Galway FRS, The Mart, Athenry, Co. Galway. Ph: 091-844551
- Meath & District FRS, Dunshaughlin, Co. Meath. Ph: 01-8259116
- Monaghan FRS, Main Street, Ballybay, Co. Monaghan. Ph: 042-9741288
- South Tipperary FRS, Carrigeen Ind. Est. Cahir, Co. Tipperary. Ph: 052-41598
- Kilkenny, Carlow & District FRS, Barrack Street, Kilkenny. Ph: 056-61671
- Kerry FRS, Moanmore Ind. Est. Tralee Road, Castleisland, Co. Kerry. Ph: 066-7141099
- Mallow FRS, Island, Burnfort, Mallow, Co. Cork. Ph: 022-29195
- Cavan FRS, Granard Road, Ballyjamesduff, Co. Cavan. Ph: 049-8545100
- Wicklow FRS, Tinahely, Co. Wicklow. Ph: 0402-38427
- Roscommon FRS, The Crescent, Boyle, Co. Roscommon. Ph: 079-62781
- Mid & West Cork FRS, Shinagh House, Bandon, Co. Cork. Ph: 02341271
- Limerick/North Cork FRS, Lottera, Bruree, Co. Limerick. Ph: 063-90666
- Duhallow FRS, Percival Street, Kanturk, Co. Cork. Ph: 029-50750
- Wexford FRS, Dublin Road, Enniscorthy, Co. Wexford, Ph: 054-36222
- Mid-Tipperary FRS, Ballycurrane, Thurles, Co. Tipperary. Ph: 0504-23310
- Waterford FRS, Faha, Kilmacthomas, Co.Waterford Ph. 051 - 294277
- Laois FRS, Bank Place, Portlaoise, Co. Laois, Ph: 0502-61916
- Louth FRS, Ardee Business Park, Hale Street, Ardee, Co. Louth.
- Mayo FRS, Ballindine Road, Claremorris, Co. Mayo. Ph: 094-62226
- South Midlands FRS, Parkmore, Roscrea, Co.Tipperary. Ph. 0505 - 21166
- Westmeath FRS, Dublin Road, Mullingar, Co. Westmeath, Ph: 044-43077

EMPLOYING NON E.U. WORKERS

FRS and other independent agencies now supply non-nationals to work on Irish farms. Fees for procuring workers will vary from agency to agency but can be up to €1,300 for each worker procured. The agency will pay for all costs incurred before the worker arrives and will deal with matters such as work permits and short term visas. Persons applying for workers should give the agency a clear and honest specification of the job in question and the kind of experience sought.. Generally it will take 6 to 8 weeks after applying for the worker to arrive and he/she will usually get a one year work permit which can be extended to two years after which they will have to return home.

Labour law as it applies to nationals also applies to non national workers. Accordingly, minimum wage rates and working conditions must be strictly observed and any form of discrimination will not be tolerated by the reputable agencies.

INSURANCE ON THE FARM

Protecting your investment and your livelihood is not just desirable – it is a necessity. Every farmer's circumstances will vary so it is important to be aware of the options available and the cost of these options. General farm insurance should be reviewed regularly. A calculation using the figures set out in table 10.4 will provide a quick indication of the likely cost in any individual situation.

Table: 10.4. Typical cost of cover for various farming assets.

Item	Insured Value	Typical cost
Farmhouse and contents	€230,000	€360
Out Buildings (all risks)	€101,600	€305
General farm property	€50,800	€150
Livestock	€101,600	€280
Tractor (comprehensive)	€19,000	€300
Employer's liability	€5,000	€300
Public liability		€180
Personal Accident		€330
Total cost of farm insurance		**€2,205**

FARM INSURANCE WHERE THE FARM IS RENTED OUT

Where a farmer has his farm rented out insurance is still very necessary particularly in the areas of public liability, dwelling and farm buildings. A typical policy cost for a 100 acre farmer with a house worth €140,000 and an average range of outbuildings would be in the region of €850.

FARM SAFETY

STARTLING STATISTICS

Typically more than one in three fatal accidents at work in Ireland occur in the farming sector. Of particular significance is the staggering increase in the number of children killed in farm accidents. In recent years 56 children died in farm accidents between 1990 and 2000. Seven children lost their lives in the 10 months to end October 2001. The loss of innocent life cannot and must not be allowed to continue.

It is principally vigilance by adults which can prevent more tragedies this year and the entire farming community must get involved in preventing these accidents. Most child fatalities happen when there is an adult present and adults must take responsibility for exercising a safety regime for their children on the farm. Not bothering with the safeguards could cost a child's life.

Farmers must also think of their own safety too. And while the number of fatal accidents which occur each year is alarming and very tragic, it should not blind us to the cost of non-fatal accidents. Each year, approximately 2,000 people require medical treatment in hospitals following accidents on Irish farms with the cost to Irish farmers running into millions in terms of lost time, farm relief costs etc. Even the loss of a week's labour as a result of a minor accident can have significant implications for the financial security of the farm, not to mention the personal costs to the farmer and his family.

THE LAW AND YOU

The object of health and safety law is to reduce human suffering and losses, due to accidents and ill health at work. The benefits which will accrue from complying with the law far outweigh the effort involved. It is difficult to quantify the degree of suffering and hardship that the victims of these accidents and their families endure, much of which could be avoided by safe farm layouts and proper work practices.

The Safety, Health and Welfare at Work 1989 and Regulations made under that Act apply to all farmers.

The law requires a farmer to provide, insofar as is reasonably practicable,

- a safe farm to work in.
- safe tractors, machinery and equipment.
- safe working practices.
- prepare a Safety Statement.
- report all farm accidents that cause absences of 3 or more days to the HSA.

263

SAFETY STATEMENT

The Safety Statement is central to farm safety, it is the written statement as to how you intend to manage safety on your farm. **Guidelines for the Preparation of a Safety Statement for a Farm** is a new publication available from Health and Safety Authority offices nationwide which will assist you in drafting up your safety statement. Free copies are available from the contact numbers listed below.

HEALTH AND SAFETY AUTHORITY

The Health and Safety Authority has overall responsibility for the administration and enforcement of health and safety at work in Ireland. The HSA monitors compliance with legislation at the workplace and can take enforcement action (including prosecutions). They also provide information, advice, education and training.

Further information on any aspect of workplace health and safety can be had from the help line at Tel: (01) 6147010 or e-mail: infotel@hsa.ie . Information can also be accessed through a web-site at www.hsa.ie

⚠ Beware of overhead lines

- Look up and look out for overhead power lines before you start using machinery on your farm.
- Make sure that everyone observes safe working practices where overhead lines cross your farm.
- Remember, contact or even near contact, with power lines can be fatal.
- Always keep your electrical installation in good repair. Never take chances.

Take particular care with:

✓ Tractors with front end loaders

✓ Slurry Spreaders

✓ Trailors with high loads

✓ Electric fences

✓ Harvesters

Supporting Safety on the Farm.

ELECTRICITY IS A GREAT FORCE OF NATURE. RESPECT ITS POWER. Network

FARMERS AND THE LAW

Many aspects of the farmers business brings him into contact with the public. This places certain responsibilities on him to ensure the safety of those with whom he comes in contact. The following topics are dealt with in this section:

- Public liability
- Farmer liability for animals
- Farmers and the land
- Farmers and public roads
- Farm vehicles
- Pollution bye-laws
- Nuisance
- Injunctions
- Judicial Reviews

PUBLIC LIABILITY

Farmers/occupiers liability to invitees, licensees and trespassers has been the subject of much discussion in recent years. In the distant past, the law distinguished the duty of care which an occupier of land (owner of land or lessee of land) owed to various categories of person entering on his or her lands. There was a different duty of care for invitees, for licensees and for trespassers. However, since the late 1960s and 1970s the difference between the duty of care owed to these different categories of persons was practically done away with by the Supreme Court, to such an extent that an occupier owed practically the same duty of care to all persons who entered upon his lands. That duty was to take such care and measures for the safety of all persons entering upon his land and not to allow obvious or hidden dangers to remain on the land which would cause injury to a person that has entered upon his land.

The Occupiers' Liability Act 1995 became law on the 17 July 1995 and implemented some of the recommendations contained in the Law Reform Commissions' Report on Occupiers' Liability. An occupier of premises now owes a duty of care to the following classes of persons who enters on his premises or land:

VISITORS

The duty owed to visitors is to take reasonable care that they and their property do not suffer injury or damage by reason of any danger existing on the land/premises of the occupier.

RECREATIONAL USERS

The duty owed to recreational users not to injure them intentionally or act with reckless disregard for them. The Occupier's Liability Act 1995 provides that where a structure on a land or premises has been used mostly by recreational users the occupier must take reasonable care to maintain the structure in a safe condition.

TRESPASSERS

The duty owed to trespassers is similar to that owed to recreational users i.e. not to injure them intentionally or act with reckless disregard for them. However an occupier may not be liable for injury or damage unintentionally caused to a person who enters upon land or premises for the purpose of committing an offence, unless the Court determines otherwise.

CONTRACTORS

An occupier who has taken all reasonable care when engaging an independent contractor, will not be liable for injury or damage caused to a person entering on the land or premises, or for the contractor's negligence, unless the occupier knows or ought to have known that the work had not been properly done.

CHILDREN

An important category of person entering upon the farmer's land are children. The law usually holds that a child under the age of seven is not responsible for his or her actions as their comprehension of danger is far less than that of an adult. The important test, however, is the test of foreseeability. Is it reasonably foreseeable that injury would be caused to a person entering upon the lands? If injury occurs due to a once off or freak accident then the test of foreseeability will not apply.

NOTICES OR AGREEMENTS

Occupiers are now entitled to modify their duty by agreement or notice and in many cases, depending on the particular circumstances, a warning may be sufficient to absolve an occupier from liability. The Occupier's Liability Act 1995 illustrates the importance of notice in modifying the duty of occupiers to entrants on their lands. Notices will have to be simple, clear, reasonable, placed in prominent positions and carefully drafted to enable occupiers to restrict and modify or exclude their duties under the 1995 Act. The duty of care that the occupier owes to the entrant is tempered by the test of foreseeability in that the law states that where it is foreseeable that a person would enter the land and would be injured, the farmer or occupier of the land would be liable in negligence for such injury caused to a person entering his land. An occupier of land will therefore be responsible for altering his land in such a manner as to prevent injury to persons entering on same. An example of this would be traps laid inside a boundary wall for the purpose of catching a wild animal. The position is similar where the farmer might have hidden caves or unsafe ground on his land near a boundary leading on to a public right of way or lane way or roadway. Obviously the further the land is from the public roadway or places where the public congregate, the less foreseeable the danger would be. For example local beauty spots and places of cultural interest are dotted all around the country and it has to be expected that the public will congregate for picnics or will want to investigate such sites. Accordingly the law requires an occupier to ensure that his land has no hidden dangers that might cause injury to the public.

Apart from eliminating obvious hazards, the greatest precaution a farmer can take is to make sure that he has full public liability insurance cover. The normal farm policy will not cover a farmer for every type of work on the farm, particularly for work which is construed as construction work or farm building. Before commencing such work, a farmer should ensure that the contractor has proper public and employers liability cover.

FARMER LIABILITY FOR ANIMALS

The law imposes certain obligations on farmers in relation to the control of animals.

DOMESTIC ANIMALS

The law lays down that dogs, whether working dogs or pets be always under the control of a person in public. There are some categories of dog that require to be muzzled in public. Recent legislation has done away with the maxim which stated that the 'dog was entitled to his first bite' and the law now imposes liability on the owner of the dog for all injury caused to a third party.

FARM ANIMALS

With regard to farm animals, since the implementation of the Animals Act 1995 there is now an obligation on farmers to safeguard their stock by adequate fencing. However following a successful Supreme Court appeal of the 1995 act, should animals escape onto the roadway and cause damage to cars or persons, the farmer will not be liable for such damage if due care was observed.

MOVING ANIMALS

The law also imposes a duty of care on farmers when moving animals. The more animals that are taken on to the road, the more persons are required to gain control of these animals if a farmer is to comply with his duties under the law. It is essential that an adequate warning system be in place to warn oncoming traffic. Warnings and flags should be provided both in front and behind the cattle that are being moved. Farmers have an extra responsibility for dangerous animals, in particular in relation to bulls. It is not advisable for a farmer to place a bull on land near a public roadway or over which land there is a right of way or where the public is known to congregate.

FARMERS AND THE LAND

A large percentage of disputes that arise between farmers and their neighbours relate to the question of boundaries and rights of way.

RIGHTS OF WAY

This is the right to pass over the land of another. The Right of Way exists not for the owner of the lands which uses it but rather for the lands themselves. Consequently if the property is sold, it carries with it the benefit of the Right of Way. The right maybe confined to the right to walk over land or it may extend to driving animals or the right to bring machinery. The extent of the Right of Way depends on the use to which the Right of Way has been put to.

Rights of Way maybe granted in writing. In such case it is generally clear the lands over which the Right of Way will exist and also the purpose for which the Right of .Way is granted. In many other cases however grows up simply through usage. These are called rights of way acquired by prescription. This in essence is this is a Right of Way acquired by long user. These Rights of Ways must have been used continually for at least twenty years. If the Right of Way has been used for forty or more years then it is deemed absolute and can not be defeated.

A Right of Way can be lost in different ways e.g. If it is released; where the land which enjoys the Right of Way and the land which is subject to the Right of Way become owned by the one person. A Right of Way can also be lost if it is abandoned. There is no strict time periods for this. It is generally believed that a non user for a time in excess of twenty years will result in the Right of Way being deemed to be abandoned.

BOUNDARIES

What is often thought to be the boundary between two neighbouring farms is sometimes not reflected in the legal document. All boundaries should be apparent on the Land Registry folio map or on a map attached to unregistered title of the property but on rare occasions folio maps may contain inaccuracies. Such matters coming to light should always be brought to the attention of the family solicitor.

FARMERS AND PUBLIC ROADS

The 1993 Road Act imposes a number of duties on all owners of lands as follows:

- To take reasonable steps to ensure that any structure or the use of any structure on the land is not a hazard or a potential hazard to persons using the public road
- To take all reasonable steps to ensure that all trees, hedges and other vegetation are not a hazard to persons using the public road
- To take all reasonable steps to ensure that water is prevented from draining on to the public road
- To take all reasonable steps to ensure that water, soil and other material is prevented from flowing onto the public road from the land. If an owner/occupier does not comply with this duty the local authority may serve him with a notice requiring him to carry out specified works

Depending on the nature of the breach, the local authority may carry out the work themselves and recover the cost of same from the owner/occupier of the land or the owner may be prosecuted and fined the sum of €1,270 or a term of 6 months imprisonment may be imposed.

TREES

Where a landowner has trees growing on his boundary fence whether adjoining the public roadway or his neighbour he is obliged to take care as a reasonable and prudent landowner to ensure that such trees are healthy and are not a potential source of danger. Where, for example a tree displays symptoms of possible decay such as the appearance of fungi on the bark , holes in the trunk or dying off of the foliage on the uppermost branches or any other such abnormalities, it behoves the landowner to further investigate the health of the tree and have it removed if evidence of decay is present or if he considers that the tree may present a source of danger to the public. It should be noted that a landowner would be expected to be capable of detecting visible evidence of decay and if he is unsure he should employ a professional to investigate the matter.

FARMERS AND WATER QUALITY

The Local Government (Water Pollution) Acts, 1977 and 1990 impose a number of duties and conditions on all who store or have custody or control of polluting matter. The Acts are designed to preserve, protect and improve water quality. Section 3(1) of the 1977 Act provides that 'A person shall not cause or permit any polluting matter to enter waters'. Under the Acts , prosecutions for water pollution offences in relation to the entry of polluting matter to waters and breech of licence terms may be taken by a local authority, a fisheries board, the Minister for the Marine and any other persons affected .

Examples of 'polluting matter' as related to agriculture would be slurry, silage effluent, herbicide/ pesticide sprays and dips, fuel/lubrication oils, molasses etc. The definition of 'Waters' includes any inland fresh water bodies, whether natural or artificial including underground aquifers/springs and any tidal waters plus any linked/related/associated beach, riverbank and salt marsh or other area , which for the time being is dry but does not include a sewer.

PENALTIES

The maximum penalties which can be imposed on a person found guilty of an offence, depending on the nature of the breech, range from €127 to €31,750 and/or 5-6 months imprisonment.

POLLUTION BYE-LAWS

The quality of drinking water is becoming a major concern for many local authorities. Accordingly special bye-laws governing the use and storage of chemical fertilisers and animal wastes are being drafted and have been passed by some county councils in respect of certain river catchment areas. While the exact composition of these bye-laws may vary slightly from county to county the main thrust is to control the amount of nitrogen and phosphate entering the ground water. The following is a summary of the bye-laws recently passed by Cork County Council relating to the rivers Lee and Gradogue catchment areas:

- Merchants and Co-op's to maintain a phosphate register with farmer names, and quantities and dates of fertiliser purchases. This register must be available to the County Council.
- Farms over 50 acres to be soil tested every five years. Where the P is found to be low the frequency can be less. Sampling to be carried out by approved planners with sample areas varying from 4 to 12 hectares.
- Application of phosphate not permissible where soil levels exceed 15 parts per million.
- No chemical nitrogen to be spread between 1 October and 1 January and a maximum of 60 units in January/February if conditions are dry and no animal wastes are spread in the same period.
- Where groundwater nitrate levels exceed 20mg/l, applications of organic nitrogen cannot exceed 210 kg/Ha. (approx. 3,000 gallons cattle slurry per acre). On all other land the limit is 250 kg/Ha (approx. 4000 gallons of cattle slurry/acre). These figures include the manure deposited by grazing animals.
- Slurry and dung spreading to be avoided during the non growing season and. spreading should cease on 31 October. At least three months slurry storage is required.
- Proper pollution control facilities must be in place.
- Details of slurry and fertiliser use to be recorded by the farmer and made available when requested.
- Imported slurry can only be spread if soil P is less than 15 ppm. and the council is notified.
- No organic fertiliser spreading shall be carried out within the following distances of the following specified locations:
  - Streams and drains - 10 metres
  - Lakes and Main River Channels - 15 metres
  - Domestic Wells - 50 metres
  - Public Water Supply Sources - 100 metres

FARM VEHICLES

It is to be noted that the Road Traffic Acts, whilst affecting all persons, are of particular concern to farmers. All mechanical propelled vehicles, be they tractors or otherwise, that are taken on to a public roadway must be insured and taxed. Too often proper inquiries are not made where the loan of a vehicle is given from one farmer to another or from a farmer to a member of a family.

Where an accident occurs and there is no proper insurance cover, a farmer may find the family farm at risk as the motor insurance bureau will seek to be reimbursed from a farmer for a repayment of any award paid by the motor bureau to an injured party.

Inadequate lighting or lighting inappropriately positioned can often cause confusion for the motorist and may bring about a circumstance where the motorist will make a claim against a farmer.

NUISANCE

The law relating to Nuisance governs interference by one property owner with the rights of another. The definition is an unreasonable interference with another person in the exercise of his rights. If the rights interfered with belong to the person as a member of the public then it is described as Public Nuisance. If on the other hand the rights interfered with relate to ownership or occupation of land then it is described as a Private Nuisance.

Public Nuisances would include blocking the public roadway, leaving railway gates closed longer than is reasonably necessary amongst others.

Private Nuisances include such matters as trees, including the branches and roots encroaching on to the property of another. It would also include noises and noxious odours emanating from a premises.

The courts have said that there must be substantial interference with the rights of the complainant, something trifling will be ignored by the courts. The courts will look at both the seriousness of the harm to the person making the complaint and the benefit, if any, of the conduct of the person against whom the complaint is being made against. The Courts will also look at where the matter occurs e.g. the noise of cattle in a rural area might be tolerated whereas if they were in an urban area it might not.

INJUNCTIONS

An injunction is an order of court which compels the person or company to whom it is directed to act or refrain from acting in a particular fashion. For instance in the case of trespass on to land the court order might be to the effect that the trespasser is not to go on to the land again.

An injunction may be applied for in either the Circuit Court or the High Court. An injunction may be granted permanently or for a limited time. This will depend upon the matter concerned.

A Judge also has a discretion whether to grant an injunction or not-for this reason it is described as a Discretionary Remedy. In exercise of this discretion the Judge will consider whether compensation would be more appropriate for the injured party. If this is the case then the courts will generally refuse to grant an injunction.

JUDICIAL REVIEW

This is the area of law which entitles the person aggrieved by the decision of a public body to quash the decision of the public body. There are many reasons for such an order being granted, including that all parties were not heard before a decision was made or the body making the decision did not have power to do so.

There have been numerous cases brought for Judicial Review e.g. to challenge planning permissions which issued by Local Authority where proper procedures were not followed; issues relating to social welfare entitlements. It can also be issued to challenge a Compulsory Purchase Order.

The time limit in which to make application is either three months or six months from the date the application first arose. The courts can extend these time limits where there is good reason.

The generous assistance of Eamon Hayes Solicitors, Clonmel Road, Carrick on Suir, Co.Tipperary in preparing this section is gratefully acknowledged

COMPULSORY PURCHASE ORDERS & COMPENSATION
(By Richard J. Rea B.Agr.Sc., Dip.E.I.A.,Mgmt.,MACA Agricultural Consultant)

The right of the State to acquire land and other property for infrastrucutral development and housing has been long enshrined in Law. The 1801 Crowdon Railway Act was the first Act authorising compulsory acquisition by a railway

company. The acquisition of land (assessment of Compensation Act) was introduced in 1919 and this set the rules for determining compensation. The 1919 Act is the act that determines the terms of compensation to the present day. Further acts were introduced - the 1966 Housing Act and the 1974 Local Government (Roads and Motorway Act).

In December 2001 a agreement was finalised between IFA and the Department of the Environment which sets down a new and more realistic approach to compensation and the treatment of landowners affected by compulsory purchase.

THE LEAD UP TO COMPULSORY PURCHASE

Prior to C.P.O. being implemented the local authority has to implement a number of procedures as follows.

CONSTRAINTS STUDY
First public consultation and identification of physical or archaeological features that may restrict road design together with identifying the area within which the study will be conducted.

ROUTE OPTIONS
The next phase is a detailed technical and environmental evaluation of a number of route options for the proposed road and further public consultations.

ROUTE SELECTION
A draft *Route Selection Report* is presented to the elected members of the Local Authority and the public as part of a *Second Public Consultation.* Following this, the Route Selection Report, with a road design and route, called the *Emerging PreferredRoute,* is submitted to the Local Authority and published. The Route Selection Report is finalised and presented to the National Roads Authority for approval with the final recommended road design and route. The Local Authority may also amend the County Development Plan to reflect the selected road design and route.

PRELIMINARY DESIGN
Next, a design for the road scheme is prepared which allows for an accurate outline of the land required to be established. Environmental issues are also examined in detail. See Environmental Impact Assessment page 294.

STATUTORY LAND ACQUISITION
The County Manager makes the Compulsory Purchase Order/Motorway Scheme and the following steps in the statutory process then begin -

- Publication of the CPO/Motorway Scheme
- Publication of the Environmental Impact Statement
- Objections or submissions to the CPO/Scheme, or EIS, to an Bord Planala
- An Bord Planala may hold an Oral Hearing
- When confirmed, a CPO/Motorway Scheme Confirmation Notice is published
- A period is granted to challenge the CPO/Motorway Scheme to the High Court
- The CPO/Motorway scheme then becomes operational and a Notice of Operation is issued.

NOTICE TO TREAT

A Notice to Treat must be legally served on each landowner affected with 18 months of confirmation of the CPO/Motorway Scheme. However under the new IFA/Government agreement. Local authorities must now issue the Notice to Treat within 6 months of the CPO becoming operational, however the 2002 cutbacks may delay this. This notice requests landowners to submit their claim for compensation for lands being taken under the CPO/ Motorway Scheme. Under the new agreement, landowners should submit their claims within two months of the Notice to Treat being issued. Land values etc. are assessed with reference to the date of this Notice.

NOTICE OF ENTRY

Once the CPO/Motorway Scheme is confirmed and Notice to Treat served, the Local Authority can take possession of the lands provided each landowner is served with a Notice of Entry. While a Local Authority can take possession without paying compensation, a low rate of interest accrues on the amount of the final settlement from the date of possession up until the claim is finally paid.

ASSESSMENT OF COMPENSATION

It was recognised by the Social Partners that the operation of compensation under the 1919 Act and subsequent Acts was slow and unfair and needed to be updated. Thus, it was agreed in the Programme for Prosperity and Fairness (PPF) that it was necessary to establish additional arrangements and procedures supplementary to those provided in existing legislation. The advantage of this procedure is that it would have immediate effect and it would not be necessary to change existing legislation.

NEW AGREEMENT

A new agreement will apply to land subject to C.P.O. under the National Development Plan 2000 - 2006 where compensation has not been determined. This agreement will not prejudice the rights of landowners, N.R.A. or Local Authorities under the Roads Act 1993. It will not prejudice landowners rights under the existing legislation where the open market value of the land being acquired may exceed the compensation under this agreement. The new agreement brings many welcome changes in relation to specific areas of compensation and these are dealt with in the following paragraphs. In addition the agreement also includes other useful provisions as follows;

- A Liaison Officer will be appointed in respect of each road project to liaise with affected landowners and I.F.A. including the supervision of the agreed accommodation works.
- The NRA and local authorities will meet the reasonable and necessary costs to landowners in advance of the Notice to Treat being issued, including the cost of assessing and agreeing accommodation works.
- A Code of Practice is being prepared in accordance with the I.F.A./NRA agreement which will provide guidance aimed at ensuring better liaison and communication with the farmers.
- Affected landowners are entitled to claim compensation under three broad headings as follows:
- Open market value of the land being acquired
- Severance and other injurious affection to other lands of the owner including damage to viability of farm business.
- Disturbance and other matters including a goodwill payment.

The effect of the IFA/NRA agreement has been to bring more equity and fair play for land owners where property is subject to CPO.

VALUATION ON THE LAND SUBJECT TO C.P.O.

The 1919 Act resulted in the same value being applied to one acre of land as applied to the average value of land as part of an entire holding. This was clearly unfair and not equitable. Under the new arrangements the land being acquired will be valued by reference to the actual size, location and quality of the land. The effect of this new valuation approach will result in lands being valued at a price that more fairly reflects market value.

VALUATION OF REMAINING LAND

The remaining lands will be devalued as a result of the C.P.O.. Claims can still be made for severance, injurious affection and disturbance caused on the entire farm holding as a result of the compulsory land-take as was always the position. It should be noted however that injurious affection has been extended to include damage to viability of farm business.

DISTURBANCE DURING WORKS

Disturbance during site investigations that did not result in a C.P.O. had in the past no legislative compensation guarantee under the 1919 Act. Under these new arrangements payments will be made to farmers where site works or other works involve disturbance to farming activities, livestock and/or crops and full reinstatement shall be made to all lands damaged by site investigations whether it is the subject of a CPO or not.

REPLACEMENT OF BUILDINGS - NEW FOR OLD

Under existing legislation Local Authorities were only entitled to compensate based on the remaining useful life of the building. Under the new agreement the Local Authority recognises a claim for costs of replacing farm buildings, fixtures and other structures acquired with *comparable* new facilities for similar farming purposes.

ROADSIDE FENCING

Under existing rules, a farmer was responsible for roadside fencing and maintenance arising from road works except in the case of motorway fencing where the local authority were responsible for fencing. Under these arrangements, the Local Authority will be responsible for maintenance on all new roads constructed under the National Development Plan 2000-2006.

GOODWILL PAYMENT

A landowner will receive a goodwill payment per acre of land being acquired in addition to all other payments. This payment will amount to €5,000 per acre and is unrelated to the value of land being acquired. To be eligible for this a landowner must not obstruct or prevent the Local Authority, the N.R.A. or their agents in entering lands for the purpose of normal road design or site infrastructural work. It is important to recognise that the NRA and local authorities already have extensive powers to lawfully enter private lands for road design purposes. A landowner is still entitled to utilise the public consultation process and the CPO process to object to or seek amendments to a proposed road design

It should be noted that there is a clear distinction between obstruction and objection. Where a landowner pursues his objection through the legal process and does not obstruct the programme he will still be entitled to the goodwill payment.

ACCOMMODATION WORKS
These works, which include fencing, drainage, planting, underpasses etc. are usually agreed with the Local Authority and carried out as part of the road scheme.

PROFESSIONAL FEES
Landowners costs incurred **before** the CPO/Motorway Scheme has been confirmed are usually not recoverable. Once Notice to Treat has been served, landowners can claim for;
- Solicitors costs for conveyance, reference to arbitration
- Agronomy/Valuer fees to cover negotiation and accommodation works.
- Other professional fees by agreement with the Local Authority

CLAIMS SETTLEMENT PROCEDURE

STEP 1 - NOTICE TO TREAT AND SUBMISSION OF CLAIM
Notice to Treat will be served on landowners by the Local Authority within 6 months of the CPO being confirmed. The landowner has then 2 months to submit a compensation claim.

STEP 2 - FIRST FORMAL OFFER
Landowners will receive a formal offer of compensation from the Local Authority within two months of receipt of a claim for compensation. The acquiring authority should seek to ensure completion of the agreement within four months of receipt of a proper notice of claim. Accordingly the maximum time that should elapse from the issue of a CPO to an agreed compensation amount is six months.

STEP 3 - PAYMENT OF COMPENSATION
Compensation should be paid within 30 days of final agreement. It is essential that landowners instruct their solicitors once the preferred route is known to get landowners title in order. No payment can be made unless title is in order. Thus, no obligation will arise to pay interest if the delay is due to landowners title not being in order.

INTEREST ON LATE PAYMENT

To date Interest was in the order of 4.5% p.a. thus encouraging a Local Authority to delay payment. Under these arrangements, the Local Authority will be obliged to pay interest from the date of agreement to the date of payment where payment is not made within 30 days at the fault of the Local Authority. Present Interest under this Act is 10.74%.

ARBITRATION

In the event that agreement cannot be reached between the landowner and the Local Authority, either side can seek a hearing before a Property Arbitrator to determine the amount of the claim. The amount of the Arbitrator's award cannot be challenged to the courts other than on a point of law. The landowner will bear the costs of the arbitration where the award is less than the amount of an *unconditional offer* made by the Local Authority in advance of the arbitration hearing.

Under the new IFA/NRA agreement an arbitrator can now be appointed from a panel of suitably qualified and competent persons established by the Chairman of the Chartered Institute of Arbitrators, Irish Branch and not appointed by the Government as heretofore. Arbitration will be conducted under the 1954 Act (Rules of Arbitration).

Should the Arbitrator's award be higher than that offered by the Local Authority, then the Local Authority will pay the cost of the Arbitration. Similarly, if his award is lower than that offered, the landowner will pay cost of Arbitration. Should a landowner decide that he did not accept a goodwill payment then his case will be arbitrated on by a Government appointed Arbitrator and in these circumstances the Arbitrator would be governed by the 1919 Compensation Act.

TAXATION TREATMENT OF CPO COMPENSATION

All elements of the compensation claim, apart from interest on late payment, are assessable to Capital Gains Tax (currently 20%) and not Income Tax. However where a farmer reinvests all of the proceeds in land, buildings or machinery within 8 years, in any trade, no tax will arise. . Qualifying investment in the two years prior to the disposal will also count. Also farmers over 55 years can receive up to €476,250 tax free subject to certain conditions. See taxation section for more detailed information on allowances and relief's.

The generous assistance of Jim Devlin and Harvey Jones, IFA Farm Business Committee, in preparing this article is gratefully acknowledged

COMPUTERS ON THE FARM

Like other farm machinery, whether it's cars or tractors, computers are really designed to make life easier for the farmer by increasing efficiency, and by saving time and money. However when shopping for a computer don' t just buy a piece of machinery. Most farm families prefer to invest in a complete package including farm software designed specially for the Irish market.

BENEFITS OF A FARM COMPUTER

- Easier record keeping and elimination of paperwork
- Accurate premium applications to maximise income and avoid unnecessary penalties
- Accurate quota management to milk your quota for all its worth
- Better day-to-day control of farm management tasks
- Assistance with educating children
- Cheaper communications
- Alternative form of entertainment.

Like using a milking machine, you don't need to be a whizz kid to work a computer. However, though they are simple to use, nevertheless like learning to drive a car, it's best to learn from an experienced person as it saves time, minimises frustration and gets you up to speed much faster.

COMPUTERS SUITABLE FOR A FARM

Modern day computers will virtually run any programmes you might wish to run, however its little use simply getting training on how to use Microsoft Word, or how to play games if your principal purpose in buying a computer is to make it work for your farm. It is therefore best to check with your computer supplier if they can provide farm software programmes which come pre-loaded on the computer and also loaded with your own farm records. Furthermore they should be able to provide a thorough introductory training session on your farm at a time which suits you. The training you should receive will be specific to your farm, your animal records and the mix of farming tasks that you have to undertake. Any sales support required is likely to be farm-related so make sure your supplier knows farming and provides first class support.

EQUIPMENT TO SUIT YOUR NEEDS

Computers are comprised of two main elements, namely hardware and software. Hardware describes the actual machinery while software describes the programmes which generally comes pre-loaded onto the machine. You may see ads for different types of computers but you should be aware that most of the Irish farming software programmes are designed for PCs rather than Apple-style computers, but any supplier who is dedicated to Irish farmers will give you the proper advice in this regard.

An adequate system for farm and family use including a printer and scanner should not cost you in excess of €1,300

Computer software for the farm should only be purchased from specialist farm computer companies. (see list page 284)

DAIRY, BEEF, TILLAGE AND PIG PROGRAMMES

Keeping accurate records, as well as processing premium applications, crop traceability, herd management, and routine bookkeeping are some of the many aspects of farming for which a good programme provides assistance. A suitable dairy package should include a quota planner to help you to manage your quota and, by tracking your milk production trends, it provides a warning system which helps you to make more timely decisions on which cows to dry-off and when. Most of the currently available programmes will have a herd register and calf registration system which are easy to use and are department approved.

THE INTERNET

The Internet is extremely useful and can save you money on communications. Increasingly farmers are using the 'net' to check out prices, order supplies and do their banking on-line. The following are some useful Internet sites;

- Department of Agriculture, www.irgov.ie/daff/default.htm
- Teagasc, www.teagasc.com
- Farmers Journal, www.farmersjournal .ie
- Farming Independant, www.independant.ie
- Irish Farmers Association, www.ifa.ie
- ICMSA, www.icmsa.ie
- Coillte, www.coillte.ie
- ICSA, www.icsaireland.com
- Macra na Feirme, http://indigo.ie~macra
- Agricultural Consultants Assoc., www.agriculturalconsultantsassociation.com

- FBD Insurances, www.fbd.ie
- Farm.ie, www.farm.ie

RECOMMENDED SUPPLIERS

The following companies supply farm software programmes which are Department of Agriculture, Food and Rural Development:

- **Kingswood**, Gerry Lynskey, Kingswood Computing Ltd., IDA Business Centre, Whitestown Road, Dublin 24. Ph: 01-4599491.
- **Agridata**, David Mullins, Agridata Ltd., Bansha, Co. Tipperary. Ph: 062-54900.
- **Agrinet**, Pat Downey, Sales Manager, Irish Farm Computers, Kells, Co. Meath, Ph: 1850-247463
- **Farmsoft**, Brendan Bourke, Farmsoft, 15 South Main St., Naas, Co. Kildare, Ph: 045-899448
- **FDC**, Jack Cusack, FDC, Carrick-on-Suir, Co. Tipperary, Ph: 051-640799

Part 11 - Farming with the Environment

RURAL ENVIRONMENT PROTECTION SCHEME

REPS is a scheme, whereby a farmer enters into a five-year contract with the Department of Agriculture, Food and Rural Development to farm in accordance with an agri-environmental plan drawn up by an approved planner. The objectives of REPS include the establishment of environmentally sustainable and friendly farming practices, quality food production methods and the protection of wildlife habitats and endangered flora and fauna. In order to fulfil the objectives of the general REPS Programme the farmer must undertake to comply with eleven measures. These measures promote the control of phosphate use, nitrogen use and stocking rate, the control of waste and effluent around the farmyard, the protection of water quality, hedges, habitats and features of archaeological or historical importance on the farm. Where a farm exceeds 98.84 acres (40 ha), the measures specified in the plan must be complied with on the entire farm area.

FARMERS ELIGIBLE TO APPLY

The scheme is open to both part-time and full-time farmers who are farming at least 3 hectares (7.4 acres). This land can be either owned or leased for a period that encompasses the whole duration of the scheme. *All* lands farmed (owned, leased, rented or used) must be included in the Agri-Environmental plan and must be the subject of an area aid application. There is no off farm income limit. Payments will be made on lands farmed up to a limit of 98.84 acres (40 hectares). The following areas will not be included for payment under the scheme:

- Dwelling house and associated areas not used for agriculture
- Public roads and lake areas
- Commercial forestry
- Land held in fee simple subject to turbary or grazing rights
- Conacre land or leased land where the lease has less than five years to run
- Set-aside lands
- Commonage shares which are leased/rented
- Owned commonage/grazing rights over which farming rights are not exercised

APPLICATION PROCEDURE

The local offices of the Farm Development Service (FDS) provide a list of approved planning agencies. These include Teagasc and private Agricultural Consultants. The FDS office will provide the farmer with an application form which can be used to apply to any of the planning agencies. A planner will assess eligibility for the scheme

Philip Farrelly & Partners

Agricultural Division	Environmental Division

Agricultural Division

- REPS
- Early Retirement Schemes
- Nutrient Management Plans
- Farm Management Plans
- Expert Witness for Legal Cases
- Assessing Impact of Road Development

Environmental Division

- Environmental Impact Statements
- Integrated pollution control licensing
- Waste management plans
- Environmental monitoring
- Site suitability studies
- Environmental law & regulatory issues

Management Consultancy Division

- Business planning and business reviews
- Data collection, research and analysis
- Organisational Reviews
- Business Management Training.
- Business Mentoring and Counselling
- Feasibility Studies
- Employment Consultancy Services

Property & Valuation Services

- Agricultural Impact Assessments of Infrastructural Development.
- Negotiations for Acquisation of Land and Property.
- Attendance at Arbitrations, Oral Hearings & Public Inquiries.
- Maximising Development Land Potential

You can contact us at any of our **10 Nationwide offices** or alternatively E-mail us on *info@pfarrelly.com*

Carrick on Shannon Office	078 21751	**Donegal Office**	072 22954
Mullingar Office	044 49802	**Monaghan Office**	042 9741195
Ennis Office	065 6823449	**Gort Office**	091 632172
Ballyjamesduff Office	049 8544454	**Cork Office**	025 39437
Carrick on Suir Office	051 642006	**Navan Office**	046 71818

Head Office
2 Kennedy Road
Navan
Co Meath
Tel/Fax: 046 71818/ 046 72311
www.pfarrelly.com

and outline the areas that need to be addressed on the farm. The planner will then draw up a five-year farm plan in consultation with the farmer. This plan, with the completed application form, farm map and other supporting documentation, is submitted to the Department of Agriculture, Food and Rural Development. Payment will then follow formal approval.

PAYMENT RATES AND PROCEDURES

The first payment is made in advance following the approval of a valid application and is normally received 6 to 8 weeks after submission of the plan. Subsequent payments are made annually thereafter subject to the participant making an application and compliance with the conditions of the scheme. The payments per hectare for each year up to a maximum of 98.84 acres (40 Ha) of the farm are as follows:

- 165 Euro/ha. per annum on Non Target Area land (i.e. lands which are not part of a commonage/NHA/SAC/SPA) where the area of the holding is equal to or less than 49.42 acres (20 ha).
- 151 Euro/ha per annum on Non Target Area land where the total area of the holding exceeds 49.42 acres (20 ha), up to a maximum eligible area of 98.84 acres (40 Ha).

There are also additional supplementary measures whereby further payments can be received to augment the basic payment.

REQUIREMENTS OF THE SCHEME

- Limits for chemical phosphate and nitrogen fertiliser and nitrogen from animal and other wastes as specified by the REPS Plan must be observed.
- It is mandatory for the participants to attend a suitable training course before reaching the end of the second year in the scheme.
- Farm boundaries must be kept stock proof for the duration of the REPS Plan.
- Up to date and detailed Record Sheets must be kept regarding stock numbers, farm wastes spread and chemical fertiliser purchased and spread for each year of participation in REPS.
- At the end of each year in REPS these record sheets must be certified by an approved planner.
- The area declared in REPS must match the area on the Area-Aid form.
- The Department of Agriculture and Food must be notified in writing within 6 weeks of :
  - an increase/decrease in land area farmed using a REPS 1A form

- an increase of stock numbers greater than that stated on the REPS Plan

DEPARTMENT INSPECTIONS AND PENALTIES FOR NON-COMPLIANCE

A REPS participant can be subject to an inspection at very short notice. A farmer must have documents proving ownership/ leasing/ grazing rights of all lands included in the REPS Plan. Up to date record sheets and fertiliser and/ or lime invoices must be ready for inspection by Department of Agriculture, Food and Rural Development officials at all times. Any breaches in the terms of the scheme or failure to carry out the various requirements as set out in the plan will result in penalties in the form of a reduction or total forfeiture of your REPS payment for that year. The following are some of the penalties that can apply:

- Limits for fertiliser exceeded, whether chemical or organic and lime requirements not applied - 10% to 50% of payment due.
- Late lodgement of REPS 1C Payment Application form - 1% to 25% of payment if less than 25 working days late. 1C Form lodged more than 25 working days after deadline will result in a penalty of 100% of payment.
- Failure to attend a suitable REPS course within the period specified will result in third and subsequent years payments being withheld until satisfactory evidence is provided that a training course has been completed.
- REPS 1A form not lodged within specified period - 20% of payment due.
- Revised/Amended plan not submitted before anniversary date - 30% of payment due.
- Farm Records not kept as prescribed -100% of payment due.
- Planned waste/ silage/ animal housing facilities not provided - 25% of payment due.
- Mismanagement of waste e.g. slurry tanks not emptied as required, discharge in to water bodies/ drains, - 25% to 100% of payment due.
- Stock not wintered as set out on plan and undertakings in respect of farmyard not carried out as planned - 20% of payment due.
- Fencing/ Hedgerow/ Stonewall requirements not carried out as specified -10% to 100% of payment due.
- Listed habitats and monuments/ features not retained as specified - 100% of payment due.
- Requirements for tillage crop production not adhered to - 10% of payment due.
- Non-compliance with Conservation of National Heritage (SMA) - 100% of payment due

- Non-compliance with all other Supplementary Measures - 100% of supplementary payment
- Area of land farmed under/ over declared and/ or farm boundaries are incorrectly shown - 50% of payment due

Note: 100% means that where one or more of these penalties apply, there will be no payment for a year, but the applicant may continue in REPS. In the case of a repeat offence the appropriate penalty will be doubled. Non-compliance a third time will result in a quadrupling of the penalty. Non-compliance a fourth time will result in termination of the REPS contract and a refund of all money's paid.

ANNUAL RETURNS

Participants are required to make an annual return in the shape of a Form 1C which is in effect the application for payment in years two to five.. **Failure to comply with the deadline set down for submission of the Form 1C will result in forfeiture of part or all of payment.**

SIMPLIFIED PLAN FOR EXTENSIVE FARM ENTERPRISES

A new simplified plan format is available for farmers with extensive farming systems. Farmers meeting the following criteria may avail of the new plan format:

- Eligible farmers with fewer than 60 livestock units and a stocking rate of less than 1.4 livestock units per forage hectare in the year previous to joining REPS.
- The farmer must undertake to remain below the 1.4 stocking limit.
- Planned stocking increases may not exceed the stocking rate in the year previous to joining REPS by more than 10%.
- The maximum tillage area allowed is 5 hectares.
- Chemical Nitrogen application cannot exceed 60 kg's for each livestock unit of cattle or sheep on the farm in the previous year.
- Chemical phosphorous applications must not exceed 15 kg's per hectare for soil P index 1 or 5 kg's for soil P index 2.
- Importing or exporting farm wastes will not be permitted.
- Farms consisting of intensive enterprises (pigs, poultry, mushrooms and horticulture) will not be eligible.

THE INTEGRATION OF FORESTRY & REPS

REPS planners will now be required to identify areas suitable for forestry during the preparatory work for REPS plans. Any afforestation of land which is the subject of a REPS plan must provide additional environmental benefits, have a minimum broadleaf species content of 20% where possible and may not disturb or affect or result in the loss of existing habitats.

SUPPLEMENTARY MEASURES

In addition to the basic REPS premium, farmers who undertake supplementary measures will be entitled to an additional payment if they comply with any of the supplementary measures. These measures are open only to farmers who are also participants in REPS. Farmers may undertake to comply with any or all of these supplementary measures but will only be paid in respect of a single supplementary measure. In the case of Measure A as set out above, participants who are receiving payments in respect of land in a target area may also apply for additional payments in respect of the Supplementary Measure on the rearing of registered female animals of Local Breeds in Danger of Extinction.

MEASURE A - NHA'S, SAC'S, SPA'S, COMMONAGES -

Lands farmed in the general REPS scheme are described as non target areas and are outside HHA's, SAC's SPA's and commonages. However land farmed within these areas must undertake Measure A for which they receive increased payments. The objective of Measure A is 'to provide a comprehensive approach to the conservation and/or regeneration of designated target areas'.

There has been no change in the existing scheme farming conditions or rates of payment as agreed with the EU by the Department of Agriculture, Food and Rural Development. These payments apply in all Natural Heritage Areas (NHAs), Special Areas of Conservation (SACs) and Special Protection Areas (SPAs) as well as all Commonages. The payment rates are as follows:

- Target Areas comprising the first 98.84 acres (40 Ha) €98.24 per acre
- Target Areas greater than 98.84 acres (40 Ha) and up to and including 197.68 acres (80 Ha) €9.74 per acre
- Target Areas greater than 197.68 acres (80 Ha) and up to and including 296.52 acres (120 Ha) €7.62 per acre

It should be noted that the payment will only be paid on the actual lands in the NHA, SAC, SPA or Commonage area.

LOCAL BREEDS

The objective of this supplementary measure is to aid in the preservation of certain breeds currently on the FAO List of Endangered Species by assisting REPS farmers who rear female animals of the following local breeds:

- Cattle: Kerry & Irish Maol,
- Horses: Irish draught

In addition to the basic REPS payment, a once-off payment of €400 per Livestock Unit for each newly registered female bovine/equine animal and a once-off payment of €60 per Livestock Unit for each newly registered female ovine of endangered species shall be paid . This additional payment will be made subsequent to the recording year.

LONG TERM SET-ASIDE (20 YEARS)

This applies to the areas along the banks of certain designated rivers at points where the river is greater than 2 metres (6½') wide. The purpose of this measure is to encourage vegetation that will intercept nutrients arising from agricultural land and also to stabilise river banks. The set-aside areas can be made up of strips of land extending for an average width of at least 10 metres (11 yds) and not more than 30 metres (33 yds) from the river bank. The area shall be permanently fenced (non-electric) to exclude livestock but with suitable entry points by hung gates to facilitate machine entry for maintenance work and stiles for access to fishing. The set-aside area shall be subject to a maximum of 2.5 Ha (6.17 acres). on any one holding. A payment of €724.5 /Ha. annually will be made to participants in REPS on the set-aside land for 20 years.

ORGANIC FARMING IN REPS

In order to be eligible for this supplementary measure, participants in REPS must be registered as an organic operator or in the case of animal production/livestock products be registered with an approved organic farming body. The payments, which are based on minimum stocking levels of 0.5 livestock units per hectare and are paid subsequent to the recording year, are set out hereunder.

Table 11.1: Additional payments for organic farming under REPS

Area	Status	Euros per Ha.
Applicants with more than 3 hectares of utilisable agricultural area:	In conversion:	181 (max. 40 ha.)
	Full organic	91 (max. 40 ha.)
Applicants with less than 3 hectares with at least 1.0 ha under vegetables.	In conversion:	242 (max. 3 ha.)
	Full organic:	121 (max. 3 ha.)

NON-COMMONAGE TARGET LAND FARMED OUTSIDE
THE GENERAL REPS PROGRAMME

Farmers with non-commonage land in a target area (NHA, SPA, SAC) who are not applying to participate in the general REPS programme may opt for payment on target area land at the rate of €242/ Ha. up to a maximum eligible area for payment of 10 hectares, subject to complying with the following conditions:

- Farm all lands in the target area in accordance with the relevant measures of the general REPS programme applicable to such lands
- Apply good agricultural practice on all the holding
- Submit documentation and maintain records as specified.

COMMONAGE FRAMEWORK PLANS

All commonage areas have been the subject of an in depth study to identify the level of sheep overgrazing and determine the appropriate stocking levels to ensure the areas are protected. These studies are known as Commonage Framework Plans and on the basis of preliminary calculations the relevant authorities will notify farmers of the options open to them where a requirement to de-stock has been determined. Where farmers are required to de-stock compensation will be payable at a proposed rate of €50 per ewe. Increased stocking will generally not be permitted where over grazing has occurred.

ENVIRONMENTAL IMPACT ASSESSMENT

Environmental Impact Assessment (EIA) is the process which anticipates and evaluates the likely and significant environmental impacts of a development. The concept of Environmental Impact Assessment originated in the United States and its acceptance by the developed world dates from the 1972 UN Environmental Conference in Stockholm. Enshrined in European legislation since 1985 when the European Union established Council Directive 85/337/EEC on the assessment of the effects of certain public and private projects on the environment (as amended by Directive 97/11/EC). The EIA Directive (85/337/EEC, amended by 97/11/EC) led to the requirement of an Environmental Impact Statement (EIS). This is the written document which results from the EIA process. The EIA Directive states 'the environmental impact assessment will identify describe and assess the direct and indirect effects of a project on the following factors:

- *Human Beings.*
- *Flora and Fauna*
- *Soil.*
- *Water.*
- *Air.*
- *Climate.*
- *Landscape.*
- *Material Assets.*
- *Cultural and Archaeological Heritage.*
- *The Interaction of the foregoing.*

FARM RELATED PROJECTS SUBJECT TO AN EIA

In Ireland Environmental Impact Assessment is integrated into the planning process. The following types of developments of relevance to farmers, **may** require an EIA as part of the planning permission application depending on the size, nature and location of the project. Developments of a size greater than the limits indicated will definitely require an EIA.

- Installations for intensive rearing of pigs or poultry (40,000-85,000 places for broilers, 40,000-60,000 places for hens, 2,000-3,000 places for fattening pigs and 400-900 sows.)
- The use of uncultivated land or semi-natural areas for intensive agricultural purposes greater than 100 hectares.
- Quarries (5-25 hectares)
- Peat extraction (50-150 hectares).
- Construction of overhead electrical power lines.
- Waste disposal installations (for hazardous waste).
- Waste disposal installations (for non hazardous waste).
- Afforestation, where the total area including adjacent land planted in any of the three previous years exceeds 70 hectares.
- Reclamation of land from the sea.
- Permanent campsites.
- Wind farms with more than five turbines or having a total output greater than 5MW.
- Installations for the slaughter of animals.
- Sea water fish breeding.

SCREENING

The first thing to do when proposing a development is to decide whether it needs an EIA. This is called *Screening*. If the developer is unsure about the need for an EIA it is worth contacting the competent authority as this will save money in the long run if they decide that an EIA is necessary. The competent authority have the right to demand an EIA for any project which they consider will have likely and significant effects, for example, if the development is proposed for an environmentally-sensitive location.

SCOPING

Having ascertained the need for an EIA, all issues of importance must be identified and those of irrelevance eliminated. This is called *Scoping*. Scoping highlights all of the factors which will require in-depth analysis. The competent authority may be approached at this stage for a scoping opinion and they will identify what they consider the key issues to be assessed in the EIS.

ADVICE AND ASSISTANCE

There are a number of Agricultural Consultancy firms specialising in projects concerning the environment. Details can be had from Ann Marie Clark, Hon.Secretary, ACA, 8 Grattan St., Tipperary.

The generous assistance of Maggie Semple, Martin & Rea Ltd., Agricultural Consultants in preparing this article is gratefully acknowledged.

GOOD FARMING PRACTICE

Under the Agenda 2000 Agreement the integration of environmental concerns is deemed to be central to CAP reform . Good farming practice is common sense farming which cares for the environment and meets minimum hygiene and animal welfare standards. Good farming practise also involves complying with the law on the environment, hygiene, animal welfare, animal identification and registration and animal health.

Observance of the code of Good Farming Practice is now a requirement of all Department of Agriculture, Food and Rural Development grant aid schemes. The following are the key aspects of Good Farming Practise;

NUTRIENT MANAGEMENT

Farmers must observe the following;

- Comply with and be aware of their responsibilities under the law.
- Maintain proper collection and storage of **all** farm slurries, effluents, chemicals and any other waste materials.
- Not spread slurry, dungstead manure or chemical nitrogen in the months of November and December
- Comply with action plans in Nitrate Vulnerable Zones and river catchment areas..
- Be aware of Teagasc recommendations on the spreading of N,P,K and lime.

GRASSLAND MANAGEMENT

Farmers must observe the following;

- The management of animals outdoors should not result in severe poaching, overgrazing or soil erosion..
- Supplementary feeding points should be at least 30 metres from a watercourse well or lake and feeders should be frequently moved so as to prevent excessive damage..
- The burning of growing vegetation on non-cultivated land between 15 April and 31 August is also prohibited.

PROTECT THE ENVIRONMENT

The following practices are not allowed:

- Spreading chemical fertiliser within 1.5 metres of a watercourse.
- Spreading organic manure within 50 metres of a domestic well, 300 metres of a public water supply, 10 metres from a stream or drain and 20 metres from a lake or main river channel.
- Spreading chemical or organic fertiliser on wet, waterlogged, frozen, snow covered or on land sloping steeply towards a watercourse or on any land where heavy rain is forecast within 48 hours.
- Each farmer must comply with the requirements applicable to NHA's, SAC's, SPA's, commonage land and The Wildlife Act, 1976.
- All external boundaries or roadside fences should be stockproof.
- All pesticides and chemicals must be stored safely. They should also be used according to the label instructions with regard to good plant protection practice and pesticide residues. Fertilisers and oil should be stored a safe distance from produce destined for human consumption and animal feeding stuffs.

297

- Farmers must comply with the National Monuments Act 1994. Monuments should not be interfered with by activities such as ground disturbance, excavation, construction or building, or afforestation.
- The visual appearance of the farm and farmyard should reflect the standard of farming which a reasonable farmer would follow. In any farmers must comply with the Litter Pollution Act 1997.

RECORDS

The following records should be kept up to date:

- Herd Register, flock register and animal remedies record
- Records such as invoices and delivery dockets of the date, type and quantity of chemical fertilisers, organic waste or pesticides brought onto or leaving the farm

ANIMAL WELFARE

Farmers should ensure that;

- Animals are adequately nourished and are not exposed to unnecessary suffering.
- Farm animals must be disposed of in accordance with requirements as specified by the local district veterinary office.
- Farmers should comply with the various National and European animal welfare regulations.

HYGIENE

Dairy farmers must comply with the European Communities (Hygiene Production and Placing on the Market of Raw Milk, Heat-treated Milk and Milk-Based Products) Regulations 1996.

NON USE OF PROHIBITED SUBSTANCES AND RESPONSIBLE USE OF ANIMAL REMEDIES.

Farmers must not use prohibited substances and must take care in using lawful remedies to ensure observance of dosing rates and withdrawal periods so as not to lead to unauthorised residues.

COMPLIANCE AND PENALTIES

A schedule of penalties is set down for breaches of good farming practice These penalties range from 10% to 100% (depending on the nature and severity of the breach) reduction or clawback of benefit received or to be received under any of the schemes from which the farmer is entitled to aid. In the case of farm investment and installation aid schemes the total amount of the grant will be deemed to be a five year payment and accordingly the penalty will applied at the appropriate percentage to one fifth of the total payment.

ORGANIC FARMING

The aim of organic farming is to produce food of optimum quality in a manner beneficial to the environment and wildlife. In recent times the number of organic farmers has rapidly increased and there are now over 1,000 certified organic farmers in the Republic of Ireland, farming approximately 24,000 hectares. Of these 850 are livestock producers and the remainder are producing vegetables and tillage crops. The main counties involved in organic farming are Clare, Limerick, Cork, Tipperary and Leitrim.

Organic farmers must comply with organic standards of production as laid down in the relevant EU regulations.

The principles and methods employed result in practices which:

- coexist with, rather than dominate natural systems
- sustain or build soil fertility
- minimise damage to the environment
- minimise the use of non-renewable resources
- ensure the ethical treatment of animals

Systems of organic production must be profitable to be sustainable. Furthermore the returns must be comparable with those from non-organic farming systems in order for this relatively new production method to gain a significant foothold in Irish agriculture.

BECOMING INVOLVED

The Department of Agriculture and Food acts as the authority governing the certification of growers as organic producers. Prospective organic farmers must follow an organic system of production for up to three years before produce can be sold as organic. On-farm inspections constitute part of the certification process. The Department of Agriculture and Food has approved the following inspection bodies:

- **Irish Organic Farmers and Growers Association Ltd (IOFGA)** Harbour Buildings, Harbour Road, Kilbeggan, Co Westmeath. Tel: (0506) 32563
- **Organic Trust Ltd** Vernon House, 2 Vernon Avenue, Clontarf, Dublin 3. Tel: (01) 8530271.
- **Demeter Standards (Irl.) Ltd,** Watergarden, Thomastown, Co Kilkenny. Tel: (056) 54214.

Farmers interested in converting to organic must prepare a plan which includes proposals for:

- a balanced rotation
- appropriate manure management
- appropriate cultivation's
- any changes to livestock numbers or variety during conversion

METHODS OF PRODUCTION

The main features of organic production are:

- The prohibition of the use of synthetic chemicals, fertilisers, pesticides and herbicides
- Balanced rotation systems
- The use of organic materials as manure
- Specific cultivation techniques: mulching, stale seedbeds
- Beneficial ecological practices

Well-planned rotations are regarded as an essential part of successful organic production and help to maintain soil fertility, minimise weeds, pests and disease, provide sufficient organic feed for stock and reduce risks by maximising the range of cash-crops grown.

WELFARE AND HOUSING
- The permanent housing of all stock is prohibited.
- The prolonged confining and tethering of animals is prohibited.
- Bedding materials, preferably organic, must be provided.
- Provided floors are well bedded, up to 25% of the floor area may be slatted.

Castration and dehorning are permitted where it is judged to be necessary for considerations of safety and welfare.

LIVESTOCK NUTRITION
Organically grown feedstuffs should be fed to livestock.
- Conventional sources of concentrate feeds must not make up more than 10% of the total fed to non-dairy ruminants and 20% for dairy stock.
- Only where a known dietary deficiency exists in home-grown feeds is mineral supplementation permitted.
- In-feed additives and medications are prohibited.

VETERINARY
- Only where a known farm problem exists may specific drugs be administered. However strict identification procedures and withdrawal periods must be observed.
- Treatment of healthy animals and the routine use of prophylactic drugs is prohibited.
- Antibiotics are not generally permitted.
- Growth promoters and fertility drugs are prohibited.

PURCHASE OF LIVESTOCK
Ideally all purchased livestock should be sourced from organic producers. However, in practice, due to limited availability, producers are permitted to buy-in livestock from conventional sources and these animals must undergo a conversion period.

CONVERSION TO ORGANIC FARMING
Conversion to organic farming is achieved over a period of time, normally two to three years. The most fundamental change in husbandry practices is the provision of a sustainable grass/clover sward. Organic farming on an all-grass sward is not sustainable. The system must ensure that soil fertility is maintained. Recent studies

and experience suggest that supplementation of phosphate is necessary in livestock and dairy systems. This can be achieved by the application of basic slag every three to four years. Organic farming requires a more extensive system of farming. Stocking rates of 1.5 acres per livestock unit or less are not sustainable.

ECONOMICS OF ORGANIC FARMING

At present the value of the organic farming industry in Ireland is estimated at 2 million pounds per annum and it is expected that there will be a significant volume growth of organic produce in the next few years. However, while some of the production from organic farms is sold at normal produce prices an increasing amount is commanding a premium over non-organic produce. The occurrence of the BSE and FMD crises allied to a number of other food residue issues have led to a renewed interest in organic produce. Gross margins per livestock unit from organic milk, beef and lamb production can be comparable to those achieved from conventional production. However, due to the extensive nature of organic farming, gross margins per acre tend to be significantly lower than those achievable from non-organic systems.

GRANTS FOR ORGANIC FARMING

Rural Environmental Protection Scheme: Financial assistance is currently available through The *Rural Environmental Protection Scheme (REPS)* which includes an optional supplementary measure whereby organic farmers or farmers involved in conversion to organic status can avail of additional annual payments under this scheme. The basic annual payment for participants in REPS is €64.33 per acre up to a maximum of 98.8 acres.

Farmers with more than 3 ha. (7.4 acres) of UAA can avail of the following:

Conversion status:	€181 per hectare. (max. 40 ha.)
Full organic status:	€91 per hectare (max. 40 ha.)

Farmers with less than 3 hectares (7.4 acres) of UAA and at least 1 ha. under vegetables can avail of the following:

Conversion status:	€242 per ha. (max. 3 ha.)
Full organic status:	€121 per ha. (max. 3 ha)

Scheme of Grant Aid for the Development of Organic Farming under the National Development Plan 2000 - 2006. Under the National Development Plan approval has been granted to provide grant assistance towards development of the organic sector in Ireland. €7,620,000 will be provided under the Regional Programmes for the Border, Midlands and Western Southern and Eastern Region. The funding will be used to provide grant assistance for both on farm and off farm investment. For on farm projects costing over €2,540 the Department will provide 40% grant assistance, up to a maximum of €50,800, towards investment in equipment and facilities for the production, improved presentation, grading, packing and storage of organic crop products. For off farm projects costing over €2,540 the Department will provide 40% grant assistance, up to a maximum of €254,000, towards developing facilities for the preparation, grading, packing and storage of organic products.

Application forms are available from The Organic Farming Unit, Department of Agriculture, Food and Rural Development, Johnstown Castle Estate, Wexford. Tel 1890 200 509.

ADVANTAGES OF ORGANIC FARMING
- It is a healthy, environmentally friendly method of food production.
- There is an increasing consumer demand for organically produced food and produce commands a premium price.
- It is a low input system of farming, based on low stocking which is conducive towards availing of extensification subsidies.
- There is scope for further expansion in the industry.
- Animal health problems are reduced due to greater animal welfare considerations.
- There is an attractive subsidy under the REPS scheme for organic farming.

DISADVANTAGES OF ORGANIC FARMING
- Many consumers are as yet unwilling to pay a premium price for organically grown beef and lamb.
- Unless supply is continuous, marketing of organic produce is difficult.
- A higher degree of husbandry and farm management skills are necessary to successfully farm organically.
- Organic farming is sustainable only at lower stocking rates than conventional farming; thus returns per acre will be lower also.

Dúchas The Heritage Service

Special Areas of Conservation and Special Protection Areas collectively form part of 'Natura 2000', a network of protected areas throughout the European Union.

Special Areas of Conservation include many of the prime wildlife conservation areas in the country, and are considered to be important on a European as well as Irish level. The legal basis on which SACs are selected and designated is the "Habitats Directive" (92/43/EEC). This directive was transposed into national legislation by the European Union (Natural Habitats) Regulations, 1997. It lists certain habitats and species that must be given protection in SACs. This list includes priority habitats, which require particular attention. Priority Irish habitats include raised bogs, active blanket bogs, turloughs and machair (flat plains near coastal areas). Other habitats include sea bays, estuaries, rivers, heaths, lakes and woodlands amongst others. The directive also requires protection of habitats of certain animals and plants, including salmon, lamprey, freshwater mussel and crayfish.

Special Protection Areas are areas of importance to birds (and often are important for other types of wildlife). The Birds Directive (79/409/EEC) requires designation of SPAs for:

- Listed rare and vulnerable species such as Whooper Swan, Greenland White-fronted Goose, Peregrine Falcon, Corncrake and Terns.

- Regularly occurring migratory species, such as ducks, geese and waders.

- Wetlands, especially those of international importance, which attract large numbers of migratory birds each year. (Internationally important means that 1% of the population of a species uses the site, or more than 20,000 birds regularly use the site.)

In most cases where lands are included in a SAC, or SPA, farmers will not have to change their farming methods; it is likely that farmers will be requested to carry on in the traditional way. In some situations changes may be necessary. Dúchas consults with farmers and advises them on the appropriate changes that may need to be made. Where a farmer is required to take particular action to protect the wildlife interest of the site, compensation may be payable, either through the Rural Environment Protection Scheme, or a Dúchas farm plan.

A list of activities that might damage the wildlife interests of the site, and measures required to protect the site, are also provided. These are called the "Notifiable Actions". Landowners have to consult Dúchas before any of these actions are carried out on their lands. They include such things as ploughing or reseeding lands that were not altered in such a way before; removal of rock, soil or scrub; new drainage works; and a range of other activities.

Dúchas has a network of local conservation rangers located right across the country. They can discuss queries in relation to conservation issues affecting lands in their areas. Their names, contact details, and areas that they serve can be accessed at the freephone number 1800-40-5000. Further contact details on page 254.

The following pages contain a list of the protected areas throughout the Republic of Ireland.

European Nature Conservation Designations

TYPE	CODE	SITE NAME
Co.Cavan		
SPA	2207	Lough Kinale and Derragh Lough
SPA	2216	Lough Oughter
SPA	2208	Lough Sheelin
cSAC	584	Cuilagh -Aneirin Uplands
cSAC	6	Killyconny Bog (Cloghbally)
Co.Clare		
cSAC	14	Ballyallia Lake
SPA	2215	Ballyallia Lake Wildfowl Sanctuary
cSAC	2246	Ballycullinan, Old Domestic Building
cSAC	994	Ballyteige
cSAC	996	Ballyvaughan Turlough
cSAC	20	Black Head/Poulsallagh Complex
cSAC	2250	Carrowmore Dunes
cSAC	1021	Carrowmore Point to Spanish Point and Islands
SPA	2311	Cliffs of Moher
cSAC	30	Danes Hole, Poulnalecka
cSAC	32	Dromore Woods & Loughs
cSAC	1926	East Burren Complex
cSAC	268	Galway Bay Complex
cSAC	1912	Glendree Bog
cSAC	1013	Glenomra Wood
SPA	2343	Illaunonearaun
cSAC	36	Inagh River Estuary
SPA	2240	Inner Galway Bay
cSAC	2264	Kilkee Reefs
SPA	45	Loop Head
SPA	2220	Lough Derg (Shannon)
cSAC	51	Lough Gash Turlough
cSAC	308	Loughatorick South Bog
cSAC	2165	Lower River Shannon
SPA	53	Mattle Island
cSAC	54	Moneen Mountain
cSAC	57	Moyree River System
SPA	59	Mutton Island
cSAC	2157	Newgrove House
cSAC	2091	Newhall & Edenvale Complex
cSAC	2010	Old Domestic Building (Keevagh)
cSAC	2245	Old Farm Buildings, Ballymacrogan
cSAC	2126	Pollagoona Bog
cSAC	37	Pouladatig Cave
cSAC	64	Poulnagordon Cave (Quin)
SPA	2327	River Shannon & River Fergus Estuaries
cSAC	1321	Termon Lough
cSAC	2131	Awbeg Rive
Co.Cork		
SPA	2307	Ballycotton Bay
cSAC	77	Ballymacoda (Clonpriest & Pillmore)
SPA	2285	Ballymacoda Bay
cSAC	2171	Bandon River
cSAC	1040	Barleycove To Ballyrisode Point

TYPE	CODE	SITE NAME
Co.Cork contd.,		
SPA	2224	Blackwater Callows
SPA	2286	Blackwater Estuary
cSAC	2170	Blackwater River (Cork/Waterford)
CSAC	93	Caha Mountains
cSAC	2037	Carrigeenamronety Hill
cSAC	1547	Castletownshend
cSAC	1043	Cleanderry Wood
cSAC	91	Clonakilty Bay
SPA	2333	Clonakilty Bay
SPA	2267	Cork Harbour
cSAC	1230	Courtmacsherry Estuary
cSAC	1873	Derryclogher (Knockboy) Bog
cSAC	2189	Farranamanagh Lough
cSAC	1879	Glanmore Bog
cSAC	90	Glengarriff Harbour & Woodland
cSAC	1058	Great Island Channel
cSAC	2158	Kenmare River
SPA	2230	Kilcolman Bog
cSAC	1061	Kilkeran Lake & Castlefreke Dunes
cSAC	365	Killarney N.P./Magillicuddy's Reeks/Caragh River
cSAC	97	Lough Hyne Nature Reserve & Environs
cSAC	1890	Mullaghanish Bog
cSAC	1070	Myross Wood
SPA	2319	Old Head of Kinsale
cSAC	101	Roaringwater Bay & Islands
cSAC	102	Sheep's Head
SPA	2348	Sovereign Islands
cSAC	106	St Gobnet's Wood
SPA	2325	The Bull and the Cow Rocks
cSAC	108	The Gearagh
SPA	2226	The Gearagh
cSAC	109	Three Castle Head To Mizen Head
cSAC	584	Cuilcagh-Anierin Uplands
cSAC	6	Killyconny Bog (Cloghbally)
Co. Carlow		
cSAC	770	Blackstairs Mountains
cSAC	2146	Derreen River
cSAC	2162	River Barrow & River Nore
cSAC	781	Slaney River Valley
Co. Dongeal		
cSAC	111	Aran Island (Donegal) Cliffs
cSAC	115	Ballintra
cSAC	116	Ballyarr Wood
cSAC	1975	Ballyhoorisky Point To Fanad Head
cSAC	1090	Ballyness Bay
cSAC	2047	Cloghermagore Bog & Glenveagh National Park
cSAC	1107	Coolvoy Bog
cSAC	129	Croaghonagh Bog
cSAC	133	Donegal Bay (Murvagh)

European Nature Conservation Designations

TYPE	CODE	SITE NAME	TYPE	CODE	SITE NAME
Co.Donegal contd.,			**Co.Donegal contd.,**		
SPA	135	Dunfanaghy/Rinclevan	cSAC	2259	Tory Island Coast
cSAC	1125	Dunragh Loughs/Pettigo Plateau	SPA	2284	Tory Island
cSAC	138	Durnesh Lough	cSAC	194	Tranarosan & Melmore Lough
cSAC	140	Fawnboy Bog/Lough Nacung	SPA	195	Trawbreaga Bay
cSAC	142	Gannivegil Bog	cSAC	197	West of Ardara/Mass Road
SPA	2195	Glenveagh Naitonal Park	**Co.Dublin**		
SPA	146	Greers Isle	cSAC	199	Baldoyle Bay
cSAC	1141	Gweedore Bay & Islands	SPA	2282	Baldoyle
SPA	2255	Horn Head	SPA	2308	Broadmeadow/Swords Estuary
cSAC	147	Horn Head & Ringclevan	cSAC	1209	Glenasmole Valley
SPA	149	Inch Lake and Sloblands	cSAC	202	Howth Head
SPA	2228	Inishbofin, Inishdooey & Inishbeg	SPA	2192	Howth Head Coast
			cSAC	2193	Ireland's Eye
SPA	2344	Inishduff	SPA	203	Ireland's Eye
SPA	1146	Inishkeel	cSAC	725	Knocksink Wood
cSAC	154	Inishtrahull	cSAC	204	Lambay Island
SPA	2212	Inishtrahull	SPA	2328	Lambay Island
cSAC	1151	Kindrum Lough	cSAC	205	Malahide Estuary
cSAC	2176	Leannan River	SPA	2312	North Bull Island
cSAC	158	Lough Akibbon & Cartan Lough	cSAC	206	North Dublin Bay
SPA	161	Lough Barra Bog	SPA	2317	Rockabill
SPA	2222	Lough Derg (Donegal)	SPA	2278	Rogerstown
cSAC	163	Lough Eske & Ardnamona Wood	cSAC	208	Rogerstown Estuary
SPA	2206	Lough Fern	SPA	2276	Sandymount Strand/Tolka Esutary
SPA	2138	Lough Foyle	SPA	2347	Skerries Islands
cSAC	2164	Lough Golagh & Breesy Hill	cSAC	210	South Dublin Bay
cSAC	428	Lough Melvin	cSAC	2122	Wicklow Mountains
cSAC	2135	Lough Nageage	**Co.Galway**		
cSAC	164	Lough Nagreany Dunes	cSAC	2244	Ardrahan Grassland
cSAC	165	Lougn Nillan Bog (Carrickatlieve)	cSAC	474	Ballymaglancy Cave, Cong
SPA	2341	Lough Nillan Bog (Carrickatlieve)	cSAC	2118	Barnahallia Lough
cSAC	2287	Lough Swilly	cSAC	231	Barroughter Bog
SPA	2305	Lough Swilly	cSAC	1242	Carrownagappul Bog
cSAC	168	Magheradrumman Bog	cSAC	242	Castle taylor Complex
cSAC	1880	Meenaguse Scragh	cSAC	248	Cloonmoylan Bog
cSAC	172	Meenaguse/Ardbane Bog	cSAC	2034	Connemara Bog Complex
cSAC	173	Meentygrannagh Bog	cSAC	218	Coolcam Turlough
cSAC	1179	Muckish Mountain	cSAC	252	Coole-Garryland Complex
cSAC	2159	Mulroy Bay	SPA	2231	Coole-Garryland
cSAC	2012	North Inishowen Coast	cSAC	2110	Corliskea/Tri en/Cloonfelliv Bog
cSAC	2046	Owendoo & Cloghervaddy Bogs	cSAC	1251	Cregduff Lough
cSAC	2210	Pettigo Plateau Nature Reserve	cSAC	255	Croaghill Turlough
cSAC	181	Rathlin O'Birne Island	cSAC	261	Derrycrag Wood Nature Reserve
SPA	2330	Rathlin O'Birne Island	cSAC	1257	Dog's Bay
SPA	2346	Roaninish	cSAC	2181	Drummin Wood
cSAC	2283	Rutland Island & Sound	cSAC	1926	East Burren Complex
cSAC	185	Sessiagh Lough	cSAC	268	Galway Bay Complex
cSAC	1190	Sheephaven	cSAC	2213	Glenloughaun Esker
SPA	1827	Sheskinmore Lough	cSAC	2180	Gortacarnaun Wood
cSAC	189	Slieve League	cSAC	1271	Gortnandarragh Limestone Pavement
cSAC	190	Slieve Tooey/Tormore Island/Loughros Beg Bay	SPA	2332	High Island (Galway)
cSAC	191	ST. John's Point	cSAC	278	Inishbofin & Inishshark
cSAC	1992	Tamur Bog	cSAC	1275	Inisheer Island
cSAC	1195	Termon Strand	cSAC	212	Inishmaan Island
SPA	192	Tormore Island	cSAC	213	Inishmore Island

European Nature Conservation Designations

TYPE	CODE	SITE NAME	TYPE	CODE	SITE NAME
Co.Galway contd.,			**Co.Kerry contd.,**		
SPA	2240	Inner Galway Bay	SPA	2229	Akeragh, Banna & Barrow
cSAC	2111	Kilkieran Bay & Islands			Harbour
cSAC	285	Kilsallagh Bog	cSAC	335	Ballinskellig Bay & Inny Estuary
cSAC	286	Kiltartan Cave (Coole)	cSAC	2112	Ballyseedy Wood
cSAC	1285	Kiltiernan Turlough	cSAC	2173	Blackwater River (Kerry)
cSAC	2265	Kingtown Bay	cSAC	2172	Blasket Islands
CSAC	295	Levally Lough	SPA	2314	Blasket Islands
SCAC	296	Lisnageeragh Bog & Ballinastack	cSAC	93	Caha Mountains
		Turlough	cSAC	343	Castlemaine Harbour
cSAC	1774	Lough Carra/Mask Complex	SPA	2322	Castlemaine Harbour
cSAC	297	Lough Corrib	cSAC	1342	Cloonee & Inchiquin Lough,
SPA	2217	Lough Corrib			Uragh Wood
cSAC	2117	Lough Coy	cSAC	2187	Drongawn Lough
SPA	2205	Lough Cutra	SPA	354	Eirk Bog
SPA	2220	Lough Derg (Shannon)	cSAC	1879	Glanmore Bog
cSAC	2241	Lough Derg, North-East Shore	cSAC	2158	Kenmare River
cSAC	606	Lough Fingall Complex	cSAC	2263	Kerry Head Shoal
cSAC	301	Lough LurgeenBog/Glenamaddhy	cSAC	364	Kilgarvan Ice House
		Turlough	cSAC	365	Killarney N.P./Magillicuddy's
SPA	524	Lough Mask			Reeks/Caragh River
cSAC	2119	Lough Nageeron	SPA	2073	Killarney National Park
cSAC	304	Lough Rea	SPA	342	Lough Gill
SPA	306	Lough Scannive	cSAC	370	Lough Yganavan & Lough
cSAC	308	Loughatorick South Bog			Nambrackdarrig
cSAC	2008	Maumturk Mountains	cSAC	2165	Lower River Shannon
SPA	4096	Middle Shannon Callows	cSAC	2261	Magharee Islands
cSAC	2129	Murvey Machair	SPA	2191	Magharee Islands
cSAC	1309	Omey Island Machair	cSAC	1881	Maulagowna Bog
cSAC	318	Peterswell Turlough	cSAC	375	Mount Brandon
cSAC	319	Pollnaknockaun Wood Nature	cSAC	1371	Mucksna Wood
		Reserve	cSAC	1890	Mullaghanish Bog
cSAC	322	Rahasane Turlough	cSAC	2098	Old Domesti c Building, Aski ve
SPA	2209	Rahasane Turlough			Wood
cSAC	216	River Shannon Callows	cSAC	2041	Old Domestic Building,
SPA	2338	River Suck Callows			Curraglass Wood
cSAC	1312	Ross Lake & Woods	cSAC	353	Old Domestic Building, Dromore
cSAC	1313	Rosturra Wood			Wood
cSAC	1311	Rusheenduff Lough	SPA	380	Puffin Island
cSAC	326	Shankill West Bog	SPA	2327	River Shannon & River Fergus
cSAC	328	Slyne Head Islands			Estuaries
SPA	2331	Slyne Head Islands	cSAC	382	Sheheree (Ardagh) Bog
cSAC	2074	Slyne Head Peninsula	SPA	2313	Skelligs
cSAC	1913	Sonnagh Bog	cSAC	2185	Slieve Mish Mountains
cSAC	1321	Termon Lough	SPA	387	Tralee Bay
cSAC	2031	The Twelve Bens/Garraun	cSAC	2070	Tralee Bay & Magharees
		Complex			Peninsula, West to Clo
cSAC	2130	Tully Lough	cSAC	2262	Valencia Harbour / Portmagee
cSAC	330	Tully Mountain			Channel
Co.Kildare			**Co.Kilkenny**		
cSAC	391	Ballynafagh Bog	cSAC	831	Cullahill Mountain
cSAC	1387	Ballynafagh Lake	cSAC	2137	Lower River Suir
cSAC	396	Pollardstown Fen	cSAC	2162	River Barrow & River Nore
cSAC	1398	Rye Water Valley/Carton	cSAC	849	SPA Hill & Clomantagh Hill
Co.Kerry			cSAC	407	The Loughans
cSAC	332	Akeragh, Banna & Barrow			
		Harbour			

European Nature Conservation Designations

TYPE	CODE	SITE NAME	TYPE	CODE	SITE NAME
Co.Laois			**Co.Mayo contd.,**		
cSAC	2256	Ballyprior Grassland	cSAC	484	Cross Lough (Killadoon)
cSAC	859	Clonaslee Eskers & Derry Bog	SPA	1489	Cross Lough (Mullet)
cSAC	869	Lisbigney Bog	cSAC	457	Derrynabrock Bog
cSAC	2141	Mountmellick	cSAC	492	Doocastel Turl ough
cSAC	2162	River Barrow & River Nore	cSAC	1497	Doogort Machair /Lough Doo
cSAC	412	Slieve Bloom Mountains	cSAC	495	Duvillaun Islands
Co.Leitrim			SPA	2342	Duvillaun Islands
cSAC	1403	Ar r oo Mountain	cSAC	1501	Er ris Head
cSAC	623	Ben Bulben, Gleniff & Glenade	cSAC	497	Flughany Bog
		Complex	cSAC	500	Glenamoy Bog Complex
cSAC	584	Cuilcagh-Anierin Uplands	cSAC	503	Greaghans Tur lough
cSAC	1919	Glenade Lough	SPA	505	Illanmaster
cSAC	1976	Lough Gill	SPA	2334	Inishglora & Inishkeeragh
cSAC	428	Lough Melvin	cSAC	507	Inishkea Islands
Co.Longford			cSAC	2238	Inishkea North
SPA	2235	Ballykenny-Fisherstown Bog	cSAC	1513	Keel Machair / Menaun Cliffs
SPA	2207	Lough Kinale & Derragh Lough	cSAC	504	Kilglassan/Caheravoostia Turlough
SPA	2223	Lough Ree			Complex
Co.Louth			cSAC	458	Killala Bay/Moy Estuary
cSAC	1957	Boyne Coast & Estuary	SPA	2324	Killala Bay/Moy Estuary
cSAC	1862	Boyne River Islands	cSAC	516	Lacken Saltmarsh & Kilcummin
cSAC	453	Carlingford Mountain			Head
cSAC	1459	Clogher Head	cSAC	1529	Lough Cahasy, Lough Baun &
cSAC	455	Dundalk Bay			Roonah Lough
Co.Limerick			SPA	518	Lough Carra
cSAC	432	Barrigone	cSAC	1774	Lough Carra / Mask Complex
cSAC	2037	Carrigeenamronety Hill	SPA	2219	Lough Conn
cSAC	930	Clare Glen	cSAC	297	Lough Corrib
cSAC	174	Curraghchase Woods	SPA	2217	Lough Corrib
cSAC	646	Galtee Mountains	SPA	2204	Lough Cullin (Mayo)
cSAC	1432	Glenstal Wood	cSAC	2177	Lough Dahybaun
SPA	2327	River Shannon & River Fergus	cSAC	522	Lough Gall Bog
		Estuaries	cSAC	633	Lough Hoe Bog
cSAC	439	Tory Hill	SPA	524	Lough Mask
Co.Mayo			cSAC	527	Moore Hall (Lough Carra)
cSAC	2268	Achill Head	cSAC	470	Mullet / Blacksod Bay Complex
cSAC	416	Ardkill Turlough	cSAC	1932	Mweelrea/Sheerfry / Erriff Complex
cSAC	463	Balla Turlough	cSAC	2144	Newport River
cSAC	2081	Ballinafad	cSAC	532	Oldhead Wood
cSAC	1922	Bellacorick Bog Complex	cSAC	534	Owenduff-Nephin Complex
cSAC	466	Bellacorick Iron Flush	SPA	2339	Owenduff-Nephin Complex
cSAC	2005	Bellacragher Saltmarsh	cSAC	2006	Ox Mountains Bogs
SPA	2253	Blacksod Bay/Broadhaven	cSAC	525	Shrule Turlough
cSAC	471	Brackloon Woods	cSAC	541	Skealoghan Turlough,
cSAC	472	Broadhaven Bay	cSAC	542	Slieve Fyagh Bog
cSAC	475	Carrowkeel Turlough	SPA	4072	Stags of Broad Haven
Spa	2203	Carrowmore Lake	cSAC	547	Tawnaghbeg Bog
cSAC	476	Carrowmore Lake Complex	SPA	4093	Termoncarragh Lake & Annagh
cSAC	2243	Clare Island Cliffs (formerly			Machair
		Clare Island 477)	cSAC	2179	Towerhill House
cSAC	1482	Clew Bay Complex	cSAC	1571	Urlaur Lakes
cSAC	1899	Cloonakillina Lough	**Co.Meath**		
cSAC	479	Cloughmoyne	cSAC	1957	Boyne Coast & Estuary
cSAC	485	Corraun Plateau (extension to	SPA	4080	Boyne Estuary
		Corraun)	SPA	2326	Carlingford Lough
cSAC	1955	Croaghaun/Slievemore	SPA	2320	Dundalk Bay

European Nature Conservation Designations

TYPE	CODE	SITE NAME	TYPE	CODE	SITE NAME
Co.Meath contd.,			**Co.Roscommon contd.,**		
SPA	2336	Stabannan-Braganstown	cSAC	216	River Shannon Callows
cSAC	1862	Boyne River Islands	SPA	2338	River Suck Callows
cSAC	6	Killyconny Bog (Cloghbally)	cSAC	1571	Urlaur Lakes
cSAC	2120	Lough Bane & Lough Glass	**Co.Sligo**		
SPA	4065	Lough Sheelin	cSAC	622	Ballysadare Bay
cSAC	1398	Rye Water Valley/Carton	SPA	2350	Ballysadare Bay
cSAC	1810	White Lough, Ben Loughs & Lough	cSAC	623	Ben Bulben, Gleniff & Glenade
Co.Monaghan					Complex
CSAC	1786	KilrooskyLough Cluster	cSAC	1656	Bricklieve Mountains &
Co.Offaly					Keishcorran
cSAC	566	All Saints Bog & Esker	cSAC	625	Bunduff Lough &
SPA	2233	All Saints Bog			Machair/Trawalua & Mullagh
cSAC	571	Charleville Wood	SPA	1994	Cummeen Strand
cSAC	572	Clara Bog	cSAC	627	Cummeen Strand/Drumcliff Bay
cSAC	575	Ferbane Bog			(Sligo Bay)
cSAC	576	Fin Lough (Offaly)	SPA	2251	Drumcliff Bay
cSAC	2236	Island Fen	cSAC	497	Flughany Bog
cSAC	2147	Lisduff Fen	SPA	2326	Inishmurray
SPA	2337	Middle Shannon Callows	cSAC	458	Killala Bay/Moy Estuary
cSAC	580	Mongan Bog	SPA	2324	Killala Bay/Moy Estuary
SPA	2239	Mongan Bog	cSAC	1669	Knockalongy & Knockachree Cliffs
cSAC	581	Moyclare Bog	cSAC	1673	Lough Arrow
cSAC	1776	Pilgrim'sRoad Esker	SPA	2218	Lough Arrow
cSAC	582	Raheenmore Bog	SPA	2202	Lough Gara
cSAC	919	Ridge Road, SW of Rapemills	cSAC	1976	Lough Gill
SPA	2335	River Little Brosna Callows	cSAC	633	Lough Hoe Bog
cSAC	216	River Shannon Callows	cSAC	634	Lough Nabrickkeagh Bog
cSAC	585	Sharavogue Bog	cSAC	2006	Ox Mountains Bog
cSAC	412	Slieve Bloom Mountains	cSAC	1680	Streedagh Point Dunes
cSAC	925	The Long Derries, Edenderry	cSAC	636	Templehouse & Cloonacleigha
Co.Roscommon					Loughs
cSAC	588	Ballinturly Turlough	cSAC	637	Turloughmore (Sligo),
cSAC	592	Bellanagare Bog	cSAC	638	Union Wood
SPA	2234	Bellanagare Bog	cSAC	1898	Unshin River
cSAC	597	Carrowbehy/Caher Bog	**Co.Tipperary**		
cSAC	1625	Castlesampson Esker	cSAC	2133	Aherlow River
cSAC	600	Cloonchambers Bog	cSAC	2125	Anglesey Road
cSAC	614	Cloonshanville Bog	cSAC	641	Ballyduff/Clonfinane Bog
cSAC	218	Coolcam Turlough	cSAC	2124	Bolingbrook Hill
cSAC	2110	Corliskea/Trien/Cloonfelliv Bog	cSAC	930	Clare Glen
cSAC	604	Derrinea Bog	cSAC	646	Galtee Mountains
cSAC	457	Derrynabrock Bog	cSAC	1197	Keeper Hill
cSAC	607	Errit Lough	cSAC	647	Kilcarren-Firville Bog
cSAC	448	Fortwilliam Turlough	cSAC	934	Kilduff, Devilsbit Mountain
cSAC	1637	Four Roads Turlough	SPA	2220	Lough Derg (Shannon)
cSAC	2214	Killeglan Grassland	cSAC	2241	Lough Derg, North-East Shore,
cSAC	609	Lisduff Turlough	cSAC	2165	Lower River Shannon
cSAC	1673	Lough Arrow	cSAC	2137	Lower River Suir
SPA	2218	Lough Arrow	SPA	2337	Middle Shannon Callows
cSAC	610	Lough Croan Turlough	cSAC	2248	Mutleen River
cSAC	1818	Lough Forbes Complex	cSAC	216	River Shannon Callows
cSAC	611	Lough Funshinagh	cSAC	939	Silvermine Mountains
SPA	2202	Lough Gara	**Co.Waterford**		
cSAC	440	Lough Ree	cSAC	2123	Ardmore Head
SPA	2223	Lough Ree	SPA	2224	Blackwater Callows
cSAC	612	Mullygollan Turlough	SPA	2286	Blackwater Estuary

European Nature Conservation Designations

TYPE	CODE	SITE NAME
Co.Waterford contd.,		
cSAC	2170	Blackwater River (Cork/Waterford)
cSAC	1952	Comeragh Mountains
SPA	2323	Dungarvan Harbour
SPA	2190	Helvick Head Coast
cSAC	667	Lismore Woods
cSAC	2137	Lower River Suir
cSAC	668	Nier Valley Woodlands
cSAC	2162	River Barrow & River Nore
SPA	2321	Tramore Backstrand
cSAC	671	Tramore Dunes & Backstrand
cSAC	787	Waterford Harbour
Co.Westmeath		
SPA	2340	Garriskil Bog
cSAC	679	Garriskil Bog
SPA	2199	Glen Lough
SPA	2197	Lough Derravaragh
SPA	2198	Lough Ennell
SPA	2200	Lough Iron
SPA	2207	Lough Kinale & Derragh Lough
SPA	2201	Lough Owel
SPA	2223	Lough Ree
SPA	2208	Lough Sheelin
SPA	2337	Middle Shannon Callows
cSAC	2120	Lough Bane & Lough Glass
cSAC	685	Lough Ennell
cSAC	2121	Lough Lene
cSAC	688	Lough Owel
cSAC	440	Lough Ree
cSAC	216	River Shannon Callows
cSAC	692	Scragh Bog
cSAC	1831	Split Hills & Long Hill Esker
cSAC	1810	White Lough, Ben Loughs & Lough
Co.Wexford		
cSAC	695	Ballyhack
cSAC	696	Ballyteigue Burrow
SAP	2318	Ballyteigue Burrow
cSAC	697	Bannow Bay
SPA	2260	Bannow Bay
cSAC	770	Blackstairs Mountains
cSAC	2269	Carnsore Point
cSAC	764	Hook Head
SPA	2316	Inish & Sgarbheen
SPA	2345	Keeragh Islands
cSAC	1741	Kilmuckridge-Tinnaberna Sandhills
cSAC	1742	Kilpatrick Sandshills
cSAC	704	Lady's Island Lake
SPA	2315	Lady's Island Lake
cSAC	2161	Long Bank
cSAC	710	Raven Point Nature Reserve
cSAC	2162	River Barrow & River Nore
cSAC	707	Saltee Islands
SPA	2310	Saltee Islands
cSAC	708	Screen Hills
cSAC	781	Slaney River Valley
cSAC	709	Tacumshin Lake
SPA	2227	Tacumshin Lake

TYPE	CODE	SITE NAME
Co.Wexford contd.,		
SPA	2266	The Raven
SPA	2304	Wexford Harbour
SPA	2309	Wexford Nature Reserve
Co.Wicklow		
cSAC	714	Bray Head
SPA	715	Broad Lough
cSAC	729	Bukcroney-Brittas Dunes & Fen
cSAC	717	Deputy's Pass Nature Reserve (in Glenealy Woods)
cSAC	2146	Derreen River
cSAC	719	Glen of the Downs
SPA	723	Kilcoole Marshes
cSAC	725	Knocksink Wood
cSAC	1766	Magherabeg Dunes
SPA	2221	Poulaphouca Reservior
cSAC	2249	The Murrough Wetlands (formerly The Murrough 730)
cSAC	1852	Tomnafinnoge Wood
cSAC	733	Vale of Clara
SPA	2349	Wicklow Head
cSÅC	2122	Wicklow Mountains
SPA	2196	Wicklow Mountains
cSAC	2274	Wicklow Reef

Further Information available from:

Dúchas The Heritage Service
7 Ely Place, Dublin 2.

Site Designations Helpline: 1800-405000
Tel: LoCall1890-321 421
Fax: +353-1-6620283
E-mail: npw@duchas.ie
Web: www.duchas.ie
www.heritagedata.ie

Dúchas The Heritage Service

Part 12 - Quotas

MILK QUOTA

National milk production is restricted to the extent of the national milk quota. Each of the country's milk purchasers (co-op's and dairy plc's) is responsible for applying a super levy on those producers who exceed their individual quotas after the reallocation of unused quota. The super levy amounts to 115% of the target price for milk and is currently €1.6678 per gallon.

Current milk policy regulations are based on Statutory Instrument No. 94 of 2000 which is available from the Government Publications Office. The following section attempts to identify the principal matters contained in the statutory instrument that may affect quota holders .

ATTACHMENT OF QUOTA TO LAND (REGULATIONS 4 & 5)
- With a number of exceptions (see below) the quota continues to attach to land, but does not always transfer with it.
- Quota attaches to land used for milk production, i.e. land used for grazing cows and replacement heifers and land used to grow fodder for same, in the last quota year in which 90% of the quota was produced.
- Where owned quota has been produced on leased land, the quota will not attach to that land, and may be attached by the Minister to other land upon application in writing by the producer.

FAMILY TRANSACTIONS (REGULATION 6)
Land and quota may be sold, leased or transferred by way of inheritance or gift between blood relatives (children, parents, siblings, grand parents, uncles and nephews) however quota may be transferred only once in every two years unless approval for such a transfer is granted by the Minister.

PERMANENT TRANSFERS OF LAND AND QUOTA AS A GOING CONCERN (REGULATION 7)
Land and quota can be sold by the producer or his or her heir but subject to the following:

- Transfers are subject to a certificate being issued by the Minister which may be subject to a fee.

- The producer has been producing milk on the holding for the previous three quota years and has ceased production no more than six months prior to the sale.

PARTNERSHIPS (REGULATION 9)

Farm partnerships involving separate individual producers are now possible subject to certain conditions. See page....

PURCHASE OF MILK QUOTA BY LESSEE (REGULATION 9)

Subject to agreement with the lessor, the lessee (provided he is a producer) can buy out the quota on expiry or earlier termination of the lease. This applies only to leases which have existed prior to 13 October 1999 and expire on or after 31 March 2000.

RENEWALS OF LAND AND QUOTA LEASES (REGULATION 10)

Existing land and quota leases may be renewed within six months of the date of expiry. **Where the lessor is involved in the Early Retirement Scheme and the lessee is unable, due to reasonable cause, to renew the lease, a new lease may be drawn up with a new eligible transferee.** However such cases will be subject to the Minister's approval.

IMPOSITION OF LEVY (REGULATION 15)

A super levy will be charged where milk is delivered against milk quota which is not fully legally transferred, whether or not the country is over quota.

QUOTA ATTACHED TO LAND SITUATED IN LESS FAVOURED AREAS (REGULATION 16)

Milk quota is ring fenced within 30 miles in Less Favoured Areas in the case of land and quota transfers.

TRANSFERS OF LAND WITHOUT MILK QUOTA (REGULATION 18)

It is possible to transfer land without milk quota provided an application is made with the appropriate documentation to the Minister.

DORMANT MILK QUOTAS - PART SURRENDER TO THE NATIONAL RESERVE (REGULATION 24)

Where less than 70% of the milk quota is not filled in a production year either by way of production or leasing or a combination of both, the Minister may decide to add all or part or that quota to the National Reserve except in cases where just cause can be proven. When the producer resumes or increases production he or she will be reallocated the said quota.

MILK RESTRUCTURING SCHEME

Each year, arrangements are put in place for the purchase of milk quota surrendered under the Milk Quota Restructuring Scheme.

SELLING THE MILK QUOTA INTO RESTRUCTURING

Persons selling their entire quota into restructuring must cease milk deliveries by 31 March. They will not be entitled to milk quota under a subsequent restructuring scheme. It is possible to sell part of the quota into restructuring however such a part sale will eliminate entitlement to any future allocations of restructured milk, temporary leasing or flexi milk.

TRANSFER OF RESTRUCTURED QUOTA

Milk Quota purchased under a restructuring scheme since April 2000 cannot be transferred in the case of a transfer of land and quota by way of sale.

PRICE

The maximum price of quota under the 2002 scheme was 31cent per litre (€1.41 per gallon) .

PRIORITY CATEGORIES
The following categories of farmer received priority access to restructured milk in 2002 in the order listed:

(1) Successors to persons who sold their quota under the 2000 or 2001 restructuring scheme
First priority is granted to a son or daughter of a person who sold their quota under the 2000 or 2001 restructuring scheme. To qualify they must have acquired the land to which the quota was attached during the year 1 April 2000 and 31 March 2002 and they must have commenced milk production by 31 December 2002.

(2) Producers who were unable to renew land and quota leases
Second priority is granted to producers whose land and quota leases expired on 31 March 2002 on the following basis:
> (a) two thirds of milk quota (net) leased with land where the lease expired on 31 March 2002 and will not be renewed because the lessor is resuming milk production.
> (b) one third of milk quota (net) leased with land where the lease expired on 31 March 2002 and the lease was not renewed.

(3) New and recent entrants to Dairying
20% of the restructuring pool remaining after the allocation of 1 & 2 above must be set aside for new or recent entrants. The minimum allocation to new entrants must be 50,000 litres (10,998 gallons). The following eligibility conditions apply;

- New entrants must meet the educational and training criteria set down for producers entering milk for the first time.
- In the case of an existing producer, be under 35 years on 1 April 2001.
- The total quota of each applicant following the allocation of additional quota must not exceed 180,000 litres (39,594 gallons).
- New entrants buying milk quota from the restructuring scheme must start production within one year and three months of purchase. Furthermore new entrants must be registered under the hygiene regulation when they start production.

(4) Allocation of the remainder of the pool
The remaining quota will be allocated to producers who applied for quota under the 2002 Milk Restructuring Scheme on the following basis:

- Category 1 - suppliers of 0 - 180,000 litres (0 - 39,594 gallons)

- Category 2 - suppliers of 180,000 litres - 275,000 litres (39,594 - 60,492 gallons).
- Category 3 - suppliers over 275,000 litres (60,492 gallons).

TEMPORARY LEASING

Each quota year the Department of Agriculture offers through the Co-ops the option to temporary lease in or out of milk. There are three phases of temporary leasing ending in the months of May, September and December each year.

A number of conditions (regulation 27 S.I. 94 of 2000) apply to temporary leasing as follows:

- A person no longer engaged in milk production cannot temporary lease his or her quota for more than three consecutive years. After that period has elapsed they may resume production or sell the quota to restructuring. However, an exception may be made for persons who temporary leased and were unable to produce milk in the three years due to exceptional circumstances.
- A quota holder who has leased privately with land for three years or more can only lease their quota into temporary leasing for one year.

PRICE
The maximum price payable in 2002 was 4 cent per litre (18 cent per gallon), whether leasing in or out.

ALLOCATION OF QUOTA
Producers whose entitlements under the 2002 Restructuring Scheme have not been fully satisfied have priority to Temporary Leasing. A producers entitlement is calculated on his or her entitlements under the 2002 Restructuring Scheme **minus** the quantity of quota purchased under that scheme.

The remaining quota was granted to all those producers who applied for the first stage of the 2002/2003 Temporary Leasing Scheme on the following basis:

- Category 1 applies to suppliers of 0 - 180,000 litres (0 - 39,594 gallons) .

- Category 2 applies to suppliers of 180,000 - 275,000 litres (39,594 - 60,492 gallons).
- Category 3 applies to suppliers over 275,000 litres (60,492 gallons).

MILK QUOTA APPEALS TRIBUNAL

The establishment of a Milk Quota Appeals Tribunal was announced by the Minister for Agriculture and Food on 12 March 1990. The functions of the tribunal are:

- To assist individual producers who have suffered hardship, or are small scale producers who find it impossible to expand, or younger producers with a limited quota size. Such assistance can take the form of allocation of Restructured Quota or Temporary Leasing
- To adjudicate on quota disputes and make recommendations to the Minister about allocation of quota to small scale producers

The members of the tribunal are drawn from ICOS, ICMSA, IFA and Macra na Feirme. The Secretary/Advisor is a member of the Department's Milk Policy Division. It should be noted that allocations are quiet small due to the small amounts of quota available in the national reserve.

Milk quota legislation is very complex and advice should always be sought from a professional who is an expert in this area before making any decision in relation to milk quotas.

MILK PRODUCTION PARTNERSHIPS

Partnerships between unrelated persons holding milk quotas will be permitted from the commencement of the 2002/2003 production year subject to certain conditions. The Farm Apprenticeship Board will be the registration body for milk production partnerships and will issue a certificate of compliance which will be valid for one year and will be renewed annually. Only bona fide partnerships will be permitted and partnerships cannot be viewed as a form of 'leasing by the back door'.

CONDITIONS FOR ENTERING A PARTNERSHIP

- The partnership must be for at least five years
- The partnership is limited to the pooling of two separate milk quotas.
- The partnership shall include the pooling of all agricultural assets of each partner, in other words a partner may not maintain a separate farming operation.
- Both partners must be under 55 years when the partnership agreement is signed.
- The partnership must apply for a new herd number.
- The ratio of quota size of each partner cannot be greater than 4:1 where the larger quota is under 325,000 litres (71,500 gallons), or where the larger quota is over 325,000 litres the ratio cannot be greater than 3:1.
- The holdings operated by each partner must be within 20 kms (12 miles) of each other.
- Each partner is subject to an annual off farm income limit of €20,000.
- A partner may not be eligible if they have acquired or disposed of land (exceeding a hectare) within a three year period of application for registration.
- A partnership may only be registered where each partner made deliveries of milk amounting to 70% of their quotas during each of the three milk production years prior to the year of registration
- An application fee of €500 applies. A further €250 per year is payable for a certificate of compliance
- Each partner will continue to have access to milk quota in their own right

ADVICE AND ASSISTANCE

Entering into a Milk Production Partnership is a very serious matter and deserves thorough research and consideration. There are a small number of farm consultancy firms dealing with this scheme. They will advise on the suitability of the proposed partnership and will detail the information to be included in the partnership agreement and may arrange to have it drawn up. They will also complete and submit the application. Names of such firms can be had from Ms. Anne Marie Clarke, Hon. Secretary, ACA, Tel. 062 52166. For application forms and full details of the scheme contact the Farm Apprenticeship Board, Teagasc, Moorpark, Fermoy, Co.Cork, Tel 025-42244..

SUCKLER COW QUOTA

The rules relating to the use of suckler cow quota are as follows:

- Farmers with more than 7 quota rights must use at least 90% each year or loose the unused ones to the National Reserve. Farmers with 7 or less must use 90% in one of two consecutive years. Consideration may be granted to farmers who can prove exceptional circumstances surrounding their failure to reach the 90% limit.
- Leasing out quota rights to other farmers is considered to be the same as if the farmer used them himself.
- Quota may not be leased out for three consecutive years. After leasing the quota the farmer must use it for the next two consecutive years.
- Farmers in the Early Retirement Scheme may lease for more than three years. Evidence of participation in ERS must accompany the leasing form.
- There is no deduction for the National Reserve when quota is leased.

CONDITIONS RELATING TO TRANSFERS OF SUCKLER COW QUOTA

- All transfers of suckler cow quota must be notified jointly by the transferor and the transferee to the Department of Agriculture and Food in advance of the application for premium. The Department of Agriculture, Food and Forestry will set a closing date for receipt of notification.
- Where a partial transfer of quota occurs, the following minimum number of quota rights must be transferred:- 3 for farmers who have a quota of more than 25 , - 1 for farmers with quotas of less than 26.

- A farmer who transfers his quota, without at the same time transferring his holding, must surrender some of the transferred quota to the national reserve without compensation as per table 12.1.

Table 12.1: Deductions to national reserve

Quota Transaction	Deduction
1 to 6 premium rights	5% (rounded to one decimal place)
7 to 13 premium rights	1 premium right
14 to 20 premium rights	2 premium rights
21 to 27 premium rights	3 premium rights
Each further 7 premium rights	1 additional premium right

- A farmer who transfers the entire holding along with his quota will not suffer any deduction to the National Reserve.
- Suckler Cow quota cannot be transferred out of a disadvantaged area.
- The closing date for transfers of quota is the date of the Suckler Cow premium application.
- Quotas may not be bought and leased out in the same year.
- Quota cannot be sold if the seller received additional quota from the National Reserve in the previous three years.

CONDITIONS - TEMPORARY LEASING OF SUCKLER QUOTAS

- All leasing agreements must be notified jointly to the Department of Agriculture and Food.
- A leasing arrangement must be for at least a full calendar year.
- Leases cannot run indefinitely as the owner has to use the quota himself for at least two consecutive years in a five-year period.
- Leasing of premium rights from disadvantaged areas to non-disadvantaged areas is not permitted.
- Quota may not be leased in and out in the same year.
- The minimum number of quota rights that may be leased are as follows:
  - 3 for farmers who have a quota of more than 25
  - 1 for farmers who have a quota of fewer than 26
- Premium rights received from the National Reserve are amalgamated with the existing Quota, none of which may be leased out for the following three years except in 'duly justifiable circumstances'.

Note: The same minimum number of quota rights that apply to leasing also apply to transfers.

APPLICATIONS FROM THE NATIONAL RESERVE

A national reserve has been established by making a deduction from individual quotas. For the year 2003 there are 1500 quota rights available for distribution to farmers who applied by 31 August 2002. This allocation is targeted to a number of defined priority categories who have more suckler cows than quota units:

- **Category A:** Farmers under 35 years on 1 January 2002 who apply for the Suckler Cow Scheme for the first time in 2003 and whose income (including spouse's income) does not exceed €25,600 of which off farm income must not exceed €12,700. Such farmers cannot have total livestock units in excess of 50 and must have at least 150 hours of farm training if born after 1 January 1968.
- **Category B:** Farmers who live on offshore islands (including Valentia and Achill) and who satisfy the income limits as set out in A above.
- **Category C:** Organic producers who were registered with the Department on or before 30 June 2002 and satisfy the age and income conditions under Category A and who are applying for the first time.
- **Category D:** Farmers who regularly submit applications for the Suckler Cow Scheme, including first time applicants in 2002 and who will apply again in 2003 and who can demonstrate that the viability of their holdings will be jeopardised by lack of quota. They must satisfy the age and income limits as outlined in category A above..

Application forms for quota from the national reserve are available annually from the Department of Agriculture Food & Rural Development, Michael Davitt House, Castlebar, Co. Mayo.. Documentary evidence to support one's claim must accompany the application.

EWE QUOTA

Producers must use at least 70% of their quota each year or else surrender the unused quota to the National Reserve. This rule does not apply to participants in the Early Retirement Scheme.

APPLICATIONS FROM THE NATIONAL RESERVE

For the year 2002 there were almost 500,000 of reserve quota and accordingly there were no restrictive criteria for eligibility. However priority will be given to producers with less than 20 livestock units. Applications for quota from the National Reserve were required to made by 30 August in 2002.

TRANSFERRING AND LEASING QUOTA

The following are the minimum number of quota rights which can be leased/transferred:

Table 12.2: Minimum number of quota rights eligible for transfer

QUOTA	MINIMUM
Less than 20	1
Between 20 and 99	5
100 or more	10

The quota at the time of the current lease determines the minimum number. There is no loss of premium rights when quota is leased. Where quota is transferred 15% of the quota being transferred (subject to a minimum of one), will be deducted for the national reserve. For family transactions the amount clawed back is 1%, again subject to a minimum of one quota unit.

Quota cannot be leased or transferred outside the disadvantaged areas. Where a quota includes an allocation from the national reserve, it cannot be leased or transferred within three years from the year of allocation. If a farmer is a participant in the Rural Environment Protection Scheme (REPS) they may be restricted from leasing or transferring quota. It will be necessary for the REPS participant to forward a copy of their REPS plan before any proposed transaction can be approved.

Application forms for the transfer and lease of quota are available from the Department of Agriculture and Food, Quota Section, Michael Davitt House, Castlebar, County Mayo. Tel. 094- 35300.

INCOME TAX

Every farmer has an obligation to register for tax regardless of whether they might think that their enterprise is of a size that dose not warrant doing so. The local tax inspector will make that decision for you and may exempt you from making an annual tax return if he decides that the scale of operations would not justify a return.

REGISTERING FOR A PERSONAL PUBLIC SERVICES NUMBER (PPSN)
A personal public service number (PPSN), formerly known as an RSI number is required not alone for tax purposes but also for a variety of purposes, many of which are to the benefit of the individual as follows:

- Headage payments
- Disease eradication payments
- VAT refunds on capital investment
- Early farm retirement scheme
- Forestry grants and premia

- Social Welfare Payments
- Health Board Payments
- Pension entitlement
- Education grants
- REPS (may be required)

To acquire a PPSN the farmer will be required call in person to the local Social Welfare to complete a PPSN application form. Once you have received your PPSN you should contact your local tax office and they will issue you with a Form STR which is the registration form for tax.

RELIEF'S CREDITS AND ALLOWANCES

There are numerous relief's and allowances that can serve to reduce a farmer's tax liability. These can be categorised as follows:

- Personal Tax Credits
- Capital allowances
- Other allowances

In all cases the allowances referred to are those available in the 2001/2002 tax year unless otherwise stated.

PERSONAL TAX CREDITS

Personal tax credits have now replaced the old system of tax free allowances. The distinction between the two is that tax credits are a direct reduction from your tax liability, whereas tax free allowances reduced your taxable income.

Table 13.1 Tax Credits 2003

	2003
Personal Allowance	Euro €
Single person	1,520
Married couple	3,040
Widowed person (in year of bereavement)	3,040
Widowed person (subsequent years)	1,820
Widowed person with dependent child (additional)	
First year after bereavement	2,600
Second year after bereavement	2,100
Third year after bereavement	1,600
Fourth year after bereavement	1,100
Fifth year after bereavement	600
Child Allowance - Incapacitated	500
Widow, Widower - with dependant children, addtl.	1,520
Single parent - with dependant children, addtl.	1,520
Dependent relative allowance	60
Blind person	800
Both spouses blind	1,600
Age Allowance - Single / widowed	205
- Married man	410
Home carer	770
Employee allowance	800

HOME CARERS CREDIT

This credit is available to married persons who are jointly assessed and where a spouse works at home to care for children, the aged or incapacitated persons. The Carers spouse's income cannot exceed €5,080 to avail of the full credit.

MORTGAGE INTEREST RELIEF

Relief is available in respect of interest on money borrowed for the purchase, erection or improvement of a principal private residence, or the residence of a former or separated spouse, or the residence of a dependent relative who is living in the house rent free. The relief is relieved only at the lower 20% rate of tax. In addition to the restriction in the rate of tax at which mortgage interest is allowable there is a ceiling on the amount that can actually be claimed. The position is summarised in the following table.

Table 13.2: Calculation of mortgage interest relief in 2003 for a first loan

		SINGLE	WIDOWED	MARRIED
First Loan Prior to 6/4/99	Ceiling	2,540	5,080	4,000
	Tax credit	508	1,016	800
[1]First time buyer	Ceiling	4,000	8,000	8,000
	Tax credit	635	1,270	1,270
[1]	Applies to first seven tax years only.			

From 1 January 2002 the tax credit are netted off the interest payable by the lending institution. However where the mortgage or part thereof was taken out for purposes other than the purchase or construction of a principal private residence the tax credit applied by the lending institution should be restricted accordingly. If the money borrowed was for business or farm purposes there will be no restriction in the amount of interest allowable against your profits.

FEES PAID TO CERTAIN PRIVATE COLLEGES

Relief is granted towards fees paid for approved courses in certain private colleges. The courses will have to be full time undergraduate courses of at least two years, duration. The relief is allowed only at the standard 20% tax rate and is also available to persons repeating and persons doing post graduate courses. Relief is also confined to the standard rate. in the form of a tax credit.

FEES PAID TO EU AND US COLLEGES

Tax relief at the standard rate is granted in respect of fees paid to publicly funded universities or similar third level colleges in the EU and US. The course must of at least two years.

FEES PAID FOR TRAINING COURSES

Relief for fees is available to individuals who partake in approved courses in the areas of information technology and foreign languages subject to the following conditions:
- the course is of less than two years duration.
- the course is approved by FAS as to quality and standards.
- the course will result in the awarding of a certificate of competence.

CREDIT FOR PAYMENT OF SERVICE CHARGES

From 2002 onwards service charges are allowed at the 20% tax rate on payments made in the previous tax year, in the form of a tax credit on the full amount paid, other than for refuse collection based on the 'tag' system.

PERSONAL PENSION PAYMENTS RELIEF

For persons under 30 years payments to approved personal pension schemes amounting to no more than 15% of the tax payer's relevant income are fully allowable against tax for persons with non-pensionable incomes. The limit is 20% for persons aged 30 to 40 and 25% for persons aged 40 to 50 and 30% for persons aged 50 and over. An important condition is that the income referred to has to be 'earned income' as distinct from 'unearned income'. In other words the earnings must be from a trade, profession or employment that does not carry with it any pension rights such as farming.

ALLOWANCE FOR RENT PAID ON PRIVATE ACCOMMODATION

Persons paying rent for private accommodation where the accommodation is the taxpayer's only principal residence, are entitled to the following tax credits:

	Persons over 55 years	Others
Single person	€508	€254
Widowed person	€1,016	€508
Married person	€1,016	€508

RENT A ROOM RELIEF
This relief was introduced in the December 2000 budget. It entitles home owners to up to €7,620 tax free rent when they rent a room as residential accommodation.

MEDICAL EXPENSES
Tax relief is available on non–recoverable medical expenses incurred by the tax payer, his spouse and children. Certain items are not allowed such as ophthalmic or dental treatment. The first €125 claimed in the case of individuals or €250 in the case of families is not allowed.

HEALTH EXPENSES: DEPENDANT RELATIVE
Medical expenses incurred by an individual in respect of a dependant relative can be claimed against tax provided none of those expenses can be recouped. In the case of a dependant relative being maintained at a nursing home or hospital the allowable amount is reduced by 60% of the dependant's old age pension. Full allowances are granted in the case of expense incurred on once–off treatment such as a serious operation.

MEDICAL INSURANCE
Payments made to recognised medical insurers are allowable against tax. at the 20% rate of tax in the form of a tax credit. From 6 April 2001 the tax credit is deducted from the premium at source and will be shown on the invoice from the health insurer.

PERMANENT HEALTH INSURANCE PREMIUMS
Payments made to a health insurance scheme which provides regular income in the event of sickness or disability are fully allowable against tax. The premiums being paid must not exceed 10% of current income.

RELIEF FOR INVESTMENT IN FILMS
Expenditure of up to €31,750 per annum in an approved project is 80% tax allowable.

DEEDS OF COVENANT
As a general rule tax relief on covenants to children is no longer be available. The types of covenant payments that are still allowed are as follows:

- payments to permanently incapacitated adults.
- payments to permanently incapacitated nieces, nephews or other unrelated children.
- payments to elderly individuals who are not incapacitated. The amount allowable is restricted to 5% of the income of the person making the payments.
- payments for research and teaching of natural sciences and to certain bodies for the promotion of human rights. The amount allowable is restricted to 5% of the income of the person making the payments.
- payments which are part of a maintenance agreement between separated spouses.

EMPLOYEE TAX CREDIT -FAMILY MEMBERS
Family members who are full time employed on the farm are entitled to the Employee Tax Credit (formerly known as the PAYE Allowance) provided they earn farm wages in excess of €4,571

TAX ALLOWABLE LIFE ASSURANCE
Tax relief on life assurance premiums was fully abolished as and from the 1992/93 tax year with one notable exception, namely S.235A life assurance policies. These are policies that can be stand-alone policies or be included in a personal pension contract.

Payments to these policies are allowable against income tax up to 5% of relevant income. However where tax relief is also being claimed for personal pension payments the overall limit which applies to pension premiums also covers the combined payments. Certain restrictions apply to these policies:

- The policy is straightforward life cover and cannot include any savings
- Cover must be taken on a single life basis only
- The term has to end between age 60 and 70
- This type of policy is non–assignable i.e. it cannot be assigned to a bank as security against borrowings

Where a 42% tax paying farmer is contributing say €1,000 per annum towards straight life cover he would save €420 if his policies were S.235A policies.

INVESTING IN COMMERCIAL PROPERTY

The 1998 Urban Renewal Scheme and the 2000 Town Plan Scheme provided a scheme of incentives for investment in commercial property in many urban and rural town around the country. If you are an owner occupier or a lessor, 50% of construction or refurbishment cost can be claimed at once or as the tax payer wishes and 4% per year thereafter up to a total of 100%.

INVESTING IN CERTAIN RESIDENTIAL PROPERTY

The 1998 Urban Renewal Scheme and the 2000 Town Plan Scheme provides a scheme of incentives for investment in residential property in many urban and rural towns around the country. If you erect or refurbish residential accommodation for letting you can offset 100% of the deemed cost against all Irish rental income from all sources. This could be of interest to farmers who are in receipt of letting income from land. In family situations where tax is a major issue leasing or renting some of the farm to a family member could be an interesting option where the relief available on rented residential property could be used to offset the rental income from the rented land, while at the same time providing valuable tax relief for the family member who has the land rented.

If you happen to be an owner occupier of such residential property as referred to above you can claim 5% of the deemed construction cost against all of your income for ten years. In the case of a house that you refurbish you can claim 10% of the cost against all of your income for ten years. This relief could be of interest to retiring farmers who wish to move off the farm, particularly where there is a qualifying town or village nearby.

INVESTING IN NON DESIGNATED RESIDENTIAL PROPERTY

Interest arising on and from 1 January 2002 on borrowed moneys employed in the purchase, improvement or repair of rented residential properties by an individual, partnership or company will be allowed as a deduction for tax purposes against rental income.

INVESTING IN STUDENT ACCOMMODATION

Expenditure incurred between 1 April 1999 and 31 March 2003 on the construction or refurbishment of rented residential accommodation for third level students qualifies for relief against total rents received. The accommodation must conform to certain guidelines and must be within 8 km. of the main campus.

INVESTING NURSING HOMES

Capital expenditure incurred on private convalescent facilities qualifies for capital allowances at the rate of 15% per annum for six years and 10% in the seventh year.

INVESTING IN THE BUSINESS EXPANSION SCHEME

This scheme was introduced in 1994 to encourage investment in certain private companies. The scheme works on the basis of investing money i.e. purchasing shares in a qualifying company for a period of five years. Full tax relief on sums up to €31,750 is available annually. At the end of the five-year period the investor is in theory free to realise his investment. However the investment is not guaranteed and the company may not survive the five–year period. Furthermore, it may not be difficult to dispose of the shares after the five year period..

BES investments do carry some risk and one should always seek good professional advice from somebody who is well versed in BES investments. The scheme runs to 31 December 2003.

OTHER FARM TAX RELIEF'S

AVERAGING OF FARM PROFITS

Due to the fluctuation of farm incomes from year to year a concession was introduced in 1981 whereby a farmer could opt to be taxed on an average of three years' profits, the current year and two previous years. This means that an unusually high profit in a given year could be reduced by adding it to the profit of the two previous years and taking an average figure for the three years. The problem with the system is that once you opt onto it, it is not easy to opt out again. A farmer is obliged to remain in the system for a minimum of three years and thereafter opting out may result in the benefit that was gained in the two previous years being clawed back.

Example

Profit year ended 31 December 2001	= €30,000
Profit year ended 31 December 2000	= €20,000
Profit year ended 31 December 1999	= €15,000
The average of the three years	= €21,666

By opting for averaging the profit can be reduced in the tax year 2001 by €8,334. This could reduce the resultant tax bill by up to €3,917.

NOTE: Income averaging requires forward planning. It may be useful to have a nine month appraisal of your profit carried out in respect of the current years accounts in order to determine if is beneficial to remain on, or opt out of averaging in respect of the previous years accounts before they are submitted to the Revenue.

AVERAGING - POINTS TO NOTE
- Averaging may effect a permanent saving in tax only if profits continue to rise in the years subsequent to opting in to the system.
- Where profits are falling, income averaging will result in a profit that is higher than the income for the current year. In a year of small profits this may have serious cashflow implications as the resources may not be present to pay a tax bill which is in effect the result of a postponement of an earlier tax liability.
- **Capital Allowances:** Capital allowances are not subject to averaging.
- **Stock Relief:** As stock relief is treated as if it were a trading expense, profits for averaging purposes are the profits after deduction of stock relief.
- **Opting out of Averaging:** A farmer may opt out of averaging only if he has been on averaging for the three years prior to the year he wants to opt out. No revision will be made to the last year of averaging but the two years prior to the last year are reviewed and if the existing assessment for either year is less than the amount of the assessment for the last average year, an additional assessment is made for the difference.

STOCK RELIEF

There are currently three systems of stock relief in place.

GENERAL RELIEF
A system of stock relief to replace the old system was introduced on 6 April 1993 for all farmers and is currently in place until 5 April 2003. Under this scheme, a deduction of 25% of the increase in value in trading stock is allowed against trading profits in the accounting year. There is no clawback provision and the main effect of the present scheme is that a farmer is taxable on three quarters of his increased stock value.

However, were he to dispose of his stock he would be taxed only on the amount by which the sale proceeds exceed the actual value that had been placed on those stock for tax purposes.

RELIEF FOR YOUNG QUALIFYING FARMERS

A system of stock relief claimable at 100% for young qualifying farmers is available for four years from commencement. The scheme is due to cease for new entrants from 31 December 2002 as no extension was granted in the December 2002 budget. Qualifying farmers must meet the following conditions:

- have qualified for grant aid under the Scheme of Installation Aid for Young Trained Farmers, **or**
- commenced farming in the year in which the claim is made
- be under 35 years **and**
- meet the following agricultural training criteria;
  (a) a third level qualification from Teagasc or the Farm Apprenticeship Board, a university degree in agriculture or an agricultural certificate from the NCEA along with a Teagasc certificate confirming participation in a farm management course of not less than 80 hours duration.
  (b) has completed any full time third level course of not less than two years duration and holds a Teagasc certificate confirming completion of a farm management course of not less than 180 hours duration.
  (c) if born before 1 January 1968 holds a Teagasc certificate stating that he or she has satisfactorily attended an agricultural or horticulture training course of not less than 180 hours duration.

It should be noted that the 100% relief for young trained farmers is also permanent and cannot be clawed back if stock levels subsequently reduce.

CREATIVE USE OF STOCK RELIEF

The existing 25% scheme of stock relief offers the farmer an opportunity to effect significant savings particularly in light of the fact that the relief is never clawed back This relief coupled with the 100% relief for young trained farmers (available to 31 December 2002) makes a strong case for leasing or transferring a part of the farm to the son or daughter working on the farm for the purpose of maximising the benefits of stock relief.

STOCK RELIEF - POINTS TO NOTE

- Stock relief cannot be claimed to create or increase a loss
- Where stock relief is claimed it is not permitted to carry forward prior year losses or excess capital allowances against future profits.
- Stock Relief is not available in the year in which a farmer ceases to farm.

COMPULSORY DISPOSAL OF LIVESTOCK

A relief for farmers is available in respect of profits resulting from total herd depopulation due to statutory disease eradication measures. The relief applies to profits arising from the compulsory disposal of livestock which took place on or after 21 February 2001. There are two separate relief's:

- The farmer may elect to have the *excess* i.e. the difference between the amount of compensation received and the opening stock value in that accounting year, excluded from the computation in the year in which it arises and to have it taxed in four equal instalments in each of the four succeeding accounting periods. Or he may elect, if it suits him, to have the excess taxed in four equal instalments in the year in which it arises and the three immediately succeeding accounting periods. Farmers who suffered compulsory disposals which occurred prior to 21 February 2001 are only entitled to a two year deferral period in respect of taxation of the *excess*.
- Where the receipts from the compulsory disposal of livestock are reinvested in livestock, the farmer may elect to claim stock relief at 100% during the four (or two if before February 2001) year deferral period. However, where he does not invest the full amount received the stock relief will be reduced proportionately.

It should be noted that in the case of compulsory disposal under the Brucellosis Eradication Scheme, total herd depopulation is not necessary to avail of the relief.

CAPITAL ALLOWANCES

Expenditure on farm machinery, motor vehicles and farm buildings are not allowed as deductible expenses in the way that direct costs such as feedstuffs or fertilisers are.

They are allowable over a number of years and the amount that is allowed is called, in the case of farm buildings and land improvement, **Farm Buildings Allowance** and in the case of plant and machinery or motor vehicles, **Wear and Tear Allowance.**

PLANT AND MACHINERY
From 1 January 2001 to 4 December 2002, the rate of write off is 20% per year over five years. From 4 December 2002 the rate is 12.5% over eight years.

FARM BUILDINGS AND LAND DRAINAGE/RECLAMATION
Farm buildings erected after the 26 January 1994 may be claimed against profits at a rate of 15% of the cost price for the first six years and 10% in the seventh year.

For the purposes of claiming capital allowances the cost of a farm building is taken after deduction of all grants and VAT refunds.

FARM BUILDINGS ALLOWANCE - POLLUTION CONTROL
For new farm buildings and structures associated with pollution control 50% of the net cost may be written off in the first year subject to a maximum expenditure of €50,800. The following conditions apply to the relief:

- the work must be carried out between 6th. April 1997 and 5th. April 2003.
- a farm nutrient management plan must be drawn up by an agency or planner approved by the Department of Agriculture & Food. A plan drawn up for the REPS or under the Erne Catchment Nutrient Management Scheme will satisfy the requirement.
- the plan must be submitted to the Department of Agriculture and Food. The farm may be subject to a random compliance check.
- for each year in which farm pollution control allowances for capital expenditure are sought, record sheets must be completed and retained in a manner set down on form Schedule II.
- the concession will not extend to new pig and poultry buildings but will apply to expenditure on waste storage facilities for these enterprises where there is no increase in housing capacity.

MILK QUOTA

Capital allowances at 15% per year for six years and 10% in the seventh year are granted on the purchase of milk quota from a restructuring scheme of from another producer. The relief is allowed against profits from the tax year 2000/2001 tax year onwards.

MOTOR VEHICLES

From 1 January 2001 Motor cars are treated similarly to other plant and machinery. The allowance granted for cars purchased between 1 January 2001 and 3 December 2002 is 20% of the cost each year for five years. From 4 December 2002 the allowance is 12.5%. The Revenue Commissioners set a maximum figure on which capital allowances can be claimed. The limit for cars purchased after 1 January 2002 is €22,000. in the case of new cars and second hand cars.

The wear and tear allowance will not be allowed in full as a deduction will be required for personal use. This deduction usually varies between 1/3 and 1/4. Furthermore exceeding the €22,000 limit may result in some of the allowable car expenses being disallowed. The amount to be deducted will depend on the amount by which the cost of the car exceeds the particular limit and also the amount of the actual motor expenses. Capital allowances on other road vehicles such as jeeps or pick-ups are granted in the same way as motor cars but are not subject to any restriction.

TAX-FREE OR TAX EFFICIENT ACTIVITIES

STALLION FEES

The income from the sale of services of mares by a stallion within the state is tax free. As for other tax free activities the expenses that are incurred on maintaining the stallion are not allowable against other taxable income.

GREYHOUND STUD FEES

From the 6 April 1996 greyhound stud dog within the state are tax free. As for other tax free activities the expenses that are incurred on maintaining the stud dog are not allowable against other taxable income.

RACEHORSES

Horse breeding is a taxable activity in the same way as any other form of livestock farming. However when a horse is transferred to a racing stable the winnings or indeed any sale proceeds are not taxable. The expenses incurred in training are not deductible for tax purposes.

PRIVATE FORESTRY

Profits, including the grants and premiums, from forestry carried out in the state which is managed on a commercial basis are exempt from income tax. However the establishment and maintenance costs are not allowed as a deduction against other income. The sale of growing timber is also exempt from capital gains tax but not the land on which it grows. Forestry is also eligible for agricultural relief in the determination of capital acquisitions tax.

FORESTRY PARTNERSHIPS

Annual payments from forestry partnerships such as those on offer from Coillte are completely free of tax.

LEASING OF FARM LAND

Where a person aged 55 years or over, or a person who is permanently incapacitated by reasons of mental or physical infirmity, leases his/her land for a period of 5 years or more, some or all of that income may be exempt from income tax.

For qualifying leases made on or after 23 January 1996, the first €7,620 is exempt on a lease of 7 years or more. The exemption is €5,080 for a lease of between 5 and 7 years. There are certain important conditions to be aware of:

- The lease must be in writing for a definite term of 5 years or more.
- The land must be leased to individuals who are unconnected with the lessor and who use the land for the purpose of farming.
- The income of a husband and wife is treated separately whether they are jointly assessed or not.

EMPLOYING FULL TIME FAMILY MEMBERS

Where a son or daughter is full time employed on the farm many farmers are paying them a minimum wage usually up to their tax exemption limit whereby no PAYE/PRSI liability is created. This makes little sense where the farmer is paying significant tax at the 42% rate. It would make infinitely more sense to pay a worthwhile wage on the condition that a substantial portion is saved or invested to be used for funding some non allowable expenditure at a future date. The son or daughter could well justify a wage commensurate with a farm managers basic wage of say €20,000. If the farmer had income in excess of €20,000 subject to 42% tax he would effect a saving of nearly €7,580 after paying the son or daughters PAYE/ PRSI. As well as a substantial tax saving this is a very effective means of providing for the future for such things as building a house when the son or daughter gets married. However it is important to point out that the wages must actually be paid and if part of the wage is put by in a deposit account, the son or daughters name must appear on that deposit account

EMPLOYING PART TIME FAMILY MEMBERS

To legitimately claim tax relief on wages to school or college going children, the work has to be done and the payment actually made. It would not be satisfactory to claim that payment was in the form of board and maintenance, nor would it be satisfactory to pay €5,000 for twelve weeks' work during the summer. However many sons or daughters may work full-time during holiday periods and also work significant hours during school term, and it is perfectly legitimate to pay them a reasonable wage in respect of the hours worked. In many cases this money is saved and is available for future tax non-allowable costs such as education that the parent might have to bear in the normal course of events.

Under labour law a young person between 14 and 15 years may be employed for light non–industrial work provided it does not interfere with their schooling. Young people of between 15 and 16 may be employed for up to 8 hours a day or 37½ hours a week.

Costs and savings of registering family members

In the tax year 2003 a single employed part time family member can earn up to €7,600 free of tax, so if a farmer were to pay his son or daughter this amount he would save up to €3,572 in tax PRSI and levies without any tax cost to the son or daughter. Furthermore if the family member is living at home, there is no PRSI cost to either party at this level of wage.

Registering as an employer

In order to claim tax relief on any wages paid, be it to family members or others, it is necessary to register as an employer with the local Inspector of Taxes. This is a simple procedure and involves completing a straightforward application form. As soon as the farmer is registered he will request each employee to complete a simple form known as a Form 12 where the employee was not already in employment in that tax year. This form will form the basis for the employee's 'tax free allowance' and should be submitted to the Inspector of Taxes on completion. The Inspector will then forward a tax deduction card which should be maintained from week to week.

FORMING A LIMITED COMPANY

For the year ended 1 January 2001 the rate of tax payable by limited companies (corporation tax) is 12.5% where the profit does not exceed €254,000, otherwise the rate is 16% (from 1 January 2002) which is also set to reduce to 12.5% by the year 2003. This may present an opportunity to certain farmers to significantly reduce their tax liability. A married farmer with a wife working on the farm earning a profit of €60,000 after paying himself a salary of €37,000 could save €20,700 per annum. The saving can be achieved by structuring his commercial farming activity in a manner whereby the income is earned in a company and subject to corporation tax rather than personal tax.

Transferring all or part of your business to a limited company is a complicated matter and the best available professional advise should be sought.

TAXATION OF QUOTAS

The taxation treatment of buying and selling quotas varies, depending on the type of quota in question.

MILK QUOTA

The purchase of Milk quota is treated as a capital item on which capital allowances at 15% per year for six years and 10% in the seventh year are available for offset against your farm profits. Proceeds from the sale of milk quota up to the amount of any capital allowances claimed are subject to income tax. Where the sale proceeds exceed the amount of capital allowances claimed (or where no capital allowances were claimed) the balance is subject to capital gains tax in the same way as if a part of the farm were sold. Farmers over 55 years may be entitled to retirement relief, see page...

SUCKLER COW & EWE QUOTA

The purchase of Suckler cow or Ewe quota cannot be set off in any way against farm profits for income tax purposes. Where a quota is sold the sale proceeds (less the purchase price, if any) are subject to Capital Gains Tax at the prevailing rate, currently 20%.

SUGAR BEET QUOTA

Purchase or sale or sugar beet quota under the 2001 scheme introduced by Greencore is treated as taxable income or an allowable purchase against your farming profits for income tax purposes. Due to the fact that this matter was not clarified by the Revenue Commissioners until September 2002 it is possible that in many cases the 2001 tax return is incorrect. Affected farmers should contact their accountants if in doubt.

A TAX RELIEF CHECK LIST

Have you claimed or considered claiming the following:

- Family wages
- Income Averaging
- Stock relief
- Dependant Relative Allowance
- Local Authority service charges
- Medical expenses
- Tax allowable life assurance premiums
- Medical expenses for a dependant relative
- Personal Pension payments
- Property, BES or Film Investment Relief
- Age Allowance
- The Limited Company option

TAXATION OF SEPARATED AND DIVORCED PERSONS

The manner in which such persons are taxed will depend on the nature of their separation.

Living Apart: Where the separation is genuine and likely to be permanent and there are no legally enforceable maintenance payments, then the couple are assessed on a Single Assessment basis. i.e. as if they were two totally unrelated individuals. Any maintenance payments made are disregarded. If there are legally enforceable maintenance payments passing between the couple who are both resident in the state and they opt for Single Assessment the payments are allowable against tax for the paying spouse and taxable for the spouse receiving the payments. However maintenance payments in respect of the children are neither taxable or tax allowable. It should be noted that in cases of single assessment where there are dependant children and where custody is shared even to a very limited degree both spouses in such circumstances will be granted the single parent tax allowance

Legal & Judicial Separations: If there is no legally enforceable maintenance agreement in place the individuals are assessed to tax on a Single Assessment basis Any maintenance payments passing between the spouses are not taxable or tax allowable. If there are legally enforceable maintenance payments passing between the couple who are both resident in the state and they opt for Single Assessment the payments are allowable against tax for the paying spouse and taxable for the spouse receiving the payments. However maintenance payments in respect of the children are neither taxable or tax allowable. It should be noted that in cases of single assessment where there are dependant children and where custody is shared even to a very limited degree both spouses in such circumstances will be granted the single parent tax allowance

If the couple are both resident in the country they may opt for Separate Assessment whereby the payments are ignored for tax purposes.

Divorced Couples: The same provisions apply as for separated couples but if either party remarries the option of Separate Assessment no longer applies.

REVENUE AUDITS

Most people have a great fear of revenue audits and probably with justification if they have something to hide. The revenue auditor will always insist on holding the audit at the farmer's residence, which in itself will reveal a certain style and standard of living. He will always have some work done on the returns submitted and will have targeted certain areas for particular attention. He will require to see all the documents from which the accounts were prepared and will not be happy if all purchases and sales are not supported by evidence of receipt or payment.

At the commencement of the audit the farmer will be offered the opportunity to declare any unrecorded sales or income. A declaration at this stage may avoid the imposition of penalties.

There are a number of areas to which the tax auditor may pay particular attention:

- A constant week by week or month by month pattern of personal spending. Any unexplained gaps in this pattern will immediately attract his attention.
- Fluctuations in expenses from year to year that cannot be readily explained.
- Significant purchases of certain farm inputs such as feedstuffs in the last few days of the accounting year may cause a problem if no closing stock is entered for that batch of feedstuffs.
- Loans, creditors, gifts, winnings or awards. These will have to be supported by evidence of origin. To say a loan was received from the uncle in America will require some evidence of the transaction.
- Amounts received for livestock and crop subsidies will have to be consistent with the schedule of livestock and crops for that year. For example, a farmer claiming ewe subsidy where no sheep are present in his accounts will have particular problems.
- Motor vehicles present on the farm but not in the accounts. In some cases the tax auditor will already have details of all motor vehicles registered in the local motor taxation office so explanations will be required if all vehicles are not accounted for.
- Unusually high repairs and maintenance will attract particular scrutiny to ensure that capital expenditure is not being claimed as current expenditure.
- Bank deposits and savings accounts not present in the accounts. These accounts may become evident if the tax auditor requests the farmer to have his bankers complete a Form BD1 which is a declaration of accounts held by the farmer and his wife at that particular bank branch. If the tax auditor is suspicious that there are undeclared deposits he may request a BD1 from all financial institutions that the farmer is conducting business with.

- If any leasing agreements were terminated during the year were the correct procedures adopted ?
- If wages are claimed as an expense in the accounts are they supported by proper PAYE/PRSI returns ?

The farmer should always be represented by his accountant for as much of the period of questioning as possible and certainly at the commencing and concluding stages. If it is established that you have underpaid tax, your name will be printed in the national press if the amount is in excess of €12,700.

If you have nothing to hide you have nothing to fear, as, in the main, the revenue auditor will be found to be pleasant and fair minded.

Never allow the revenue auditor to make groundless accusations or suggestions. If he arrives at conclusions that are incorrect, do not accept the situation and request that the matter be brought to appeal.

VALUE ADDED TAX

Value Added Tax or VAT is, as the name suggests, a tax on the value that is added to a particular product. If a farmer sells a bullock to a factory the payment he receives will include 4.3% VAT. However the farmer will have incurred various costs in maintaining the animal over winter and in providing facilities and equipment and if the amount paid out exceeds the amount received, then there may be a case for considering registering for VAT. However unregistered farmers are entitled to claim back VAT incurred on capital expenditure on buildings and land improvement and also certain items of fixed plant such as bulk tanks, milking facilities, automatic scrapers etc.

REGISTERING FOR VAT

To decide if there is likely to be a benefit from registering for VAT a calculation must be performed to establish if on average more VAT is paid out on expenses than what is taken in on sales. This is best done by your accountant on the most recent year's figures and it will provides an good indication as to the extent of the benefit, if any, of registering.

POINTS IN FAVOUR AND AGAINST REGISTRATION
- There may be a cash benefit in registering.
- Being registered imposes a requirement for the maintenance of excellent records, which can only be for the good of the business as a whole.
- Additional bookkeeping costs may arise.
- The books and records will be subject to scrutiny by the Revenue authorities on a more frequent basis than would apply for unregistered farmers.
- It is possible for unregistered farmers to claim VAT refunds on capital expenditure on farm buildings, land drainage and reclamation and fixed plant and equipment.
- A rebate of VAT is additional income subject to Tax, PRSI and levies.

The option of registering for VAT should be given careful consideration. It is not possible to deregister without repayment of any net benefits gained in the previous three years.

It is only in cases where a farmer engages in significant capital expenditure on machinery and allowable vehicles that registering is justified.

CAPITAL ACQUISITIONS TAX

Capital Acquisitions Tax (CAT) is the broader term covering gift tax and inheritance tax. Inheritance tax arises on the value of property passing to somebody on the death of another person. Gift tax arises on the value of gifts received from another living person.

WHO IS TAXABLE ?
With the exception of gifts or inheritances between husbands and wives and for certain charitable or public purposes, all persons can be liable. Inheritances from a son or daughter taken on or after 12 April 1995 are also exempt provided that the son or daughter had taken a non exempt gift or inheritance from a parent within five years prior to death.

HOW MUCH CAN BE RECEIVED TAX FREE
The amount that can be received tax free will depend on the relationship to the donor. However this tax free amount is a lifetime allowance and not an annual allowance

similar to an income tax allowance. Furthermore gifts or inheritances taken on or after 2 December 2001 are aggregated with all gifts or inheritances received since 5 December 1991.

Table 13.3: Tax free amounts for gift/inheritance tax taken in 2002

Relationship to the donor/testator	Tax free amount
Husband or Wife	All
Child or Favourite Nephew/Niece	€422,148
Brother, Sister or Child of a Brother or Sister	€42,215
Any Other Person	€21,108

RATES OF TAX
The rates of tax is 20% on taxable gifts and inheritances.

AGRICULTURAL RELIEF
Normally, tax is based on the market value of the property comprising the gift or inheritance, and allowance is given for all liabilities, costs and expenses that are properly payable out of the gift or inheritance. However a special concession known as **agricultural relief** applies where the recipient is a farmer within the meaning of the Act, defined as follows,.

Definition of a farmer for Agricultural Relief purposes:
A farmer is defined as someone where. 80% of his or her gross property after receiving the gift or inheritance is **'agricultural property'**. In this case 'gross property' means the value before taking into account any debts.

Agricultural Property
For the purposes of agricultural relief 'agricultural property' includes farm land and woodland situate in the state, crops or trees growing on such land, farm buildings, farm houses and mansion houses (as are of a character appropriate to the property) livestock, bloodstock and farm machinery.

Amount of Relief

Agricultural relief entitles a farmer to a reduction of 90% in respect of the market value of all eligible farm assets being gifted or inherited on or after 23 January 1997. The availability of agricultural relief will ensure a nil tax liability in the vast majority of cases so it is vital that a person about to receive or inherit a farm should have as few non agricultural assets as possible.

Ensuring entitlement to relief

A farmer who is considering willing or gifting his farm and cash reserves to his successor should establish that the successor will be eligible for agricultural relief after receiving the gift or inheritance. The successor may avoid a substantial tax liability if some or all of the cash reserves are converted to agricultural assets prior to receiving the gift or inheritance. Alternatively, the person making the will or gift could direct that after his death (or granting the gift) such cash reserves be invested in whole or in part in qualifying farm assets. Such a direction will have to be carried out within a two year period.

Clawback of Relief

Relief will be withdrawn where land acquired is sold or compulsorily acquired within 6 years from the date of gift or inheritance and is not replaced within four years.

FAVOURITE NEPHEW RELIEF

In certain circumstances a nephew or niece of the disponer who has worked on a full time basis on the farm will be deemed to have a relationship to the disponer as that of a child. To be eligible the following conditions must be satisfied;

- The donee or successor must be a child (including a step child or adopted child) of a brother or a sister.
- The donee or successor must have worked 'substantially on a full time basis' for a period of five years prior to taking the gift or inheritance. Substantially on a full time basis has been defined as to mean more than 15 hours per week where the farming is carried on exclusively by the disponer, his spouse and the donee or successor. Otherwise the lower limit is 20 hours per week.

FAMILY HOME RELIEF

Gift or inheritance tax no longer applies on the transfer of the family home on or after 1 December 1999 subject to the following conditions;

- it is the principal private residence of the disponer and/or recipient.

- the recipient has been living in the home for the three years prior to the transfer.
- the recipient does not have an interest in any other residential property.
- the recipient does not dispose of the home for six years after the transfer.

INHERITANCE TAX INSURANCE

Due to the extent of agricultural relief, Inheritance Tax will very seldom arise in farm family situations . *If Section 60 policies already exist their necessity should be re-appraised by a tax consultant, as apart from the fact that they may be no longer necessary, they can in certain situations render a beneficiary ineligible for agricultural relief.*

GENERAL POINTS TO NOTE

- If a person dies within two years of making a gift, it becomes an inheritance.
- Agricultural relief will be withdrawn if the recipient or successor is not resident in the state for any of the three years following the gift or inheritance.
- There is now no limit to the availability of Agricultural Relief regardless of the number of gifts or inheritances one receives.
- Agricultural Relief is clawed back if the property is sold within 6 years of acquiring it. However if the property is replaced within four years no clawback arises.
- In the unfortunate circumstances of a farm reverting back to the parent as an inheritance where the son or daughter dies, no tax is payable provided the farm was transferred to the son or daughter within the previous five years. If the five year period has been exceeded the same allowance is available as would be available to a son or daughter providing the parents had not received any gift or inheritance since 5 December 1991, in which case the value of all gifts or inheritances are aggregated.
- The value of milk quota may be reflected in the value of the land and as such is entitled to agricultural relief.
- No tax will arise on gifts of up to €1,270 from any one individual in any year regardless of the number of gifts received from different people.
- Agricultural relief is not available where the property passing is shares in a company owning agricultural land.
- If somebody has the use of land rent-free from another person the commercial rental value of the land is deemed to be a gift received by the person who is using the land and therefore may attract gift tax.

CAPITAL GAINS TAX

Where a farmer disposes of certain assets such as land, buildings, shares or certain quotas he or she may be liable to capital gains tax.

ITEMS LIABLE TO CAPITAL GAINS TAX
- Land and buildings (whether sold or transferred during the owner's lifetime).
- Assets of a business carried on in the state.
- Company shares.

RATES OF TAX AND TAX FREE AMOUNT
A rate of 20% applies to all gains. From 6 April 1998 the tax free amount in any year amounts to €1,270 (£1,000) for an individual. Where the asset is in joint names or where both spouses individually make a disposal they will each be entitled to the €1,270 exemption but it is not transferable from one spouse to the other.

TRANSFERRING THE FAMILY FARM
Transferring the family farm can give rise to capital gains tax in certain circumstances. Such circumstances might arise if the period of ownership was not very long or the farmer transferring was under 55 years. However where a farm is being transferred within the family, by a farmer who is over 55 years, to a qualifying son, daughter or favourite niece or nephew, no capital gains tax will arise provided the following conditions are satisfied:

- farm was owned, and was used for farming purposes in the 10 years or more prior to disposal, and
- the transferee does not dispose of it within six years.

Transfers between husbands and wives are not liable to capital gains tax.

TRANSFERRING A SITE TO A FAMILY MEMBER
From 6 December 2000 no liability to Capital Gains Tax will arise on the transfer of a site to a son or daughter subject to the following conditions:

- it is for construction of the son or daughter's principal private residence.

- the market value of the site does not exceed €254,000 (£200,000).
- a parent can only transfer one site to each child for this exemption.

SELLING A SITE OR PART OF A FARM

Where the price realised for land is significantly in excess of the current use value of land in that area, then that land may be classed as **development land**. This is often the case in selling sites and up to 6 April 1995 was the case with lands compulsorily acquired by a local authority. Current use value can be taken to mean prevailing agricultural value in that area. Indexation relief on development land will apply only to the current use value element of the cost.

However, even though the land may be classed as development land, normal capital gains tax rules apply if the total value of disposals does not exceed €19,050 in any tax year. While there are very few situations where a disposal will fall below €19,050, nevertheless a disposal of what would otherwise be classed as development land below €19,050 in value, will qualify for roll over relief and indexation of the full cost value.

SELLING THE FAMILY FARM

In the case of farmers under 55 years, where part or all of the family farm is sold with no intention of replacing it, a liability to capital gains tax may arise. Whether or not this will occur will depend on a number of factors, principally:

- Period of ownership
- Sale proceeds
- Valuation of farm at the time of acquisition
- Amounts spent on capital improvements and additions during the period of ownership

The period of ownership is relevant as account is taken of inflation being a factor in the increased value of the land since the date of acquisition. To adjust the original cost or valuation of the farm to take account of inflation the original value is multiplied by the relevant indexation factor. (See Page 10). The period of ownership of both spouses is regarded as one. This means that if a spouse disposed of land shortly after the death of the other spouse, the period of ownership would extend from the date the deceased spouse acquired it.

Example of a capital gains tax calculation
Farmer Joe, a married man in his forties, sold his 70 acre farm in December 2002. He originally purchased the farm in May 1976 for €45,000.

Table 13.4: Example of a capital gains tax calculation

	€
Sales Proceeds	400,000
Less: Cost as adjusted for inflation i.e €45,000 x 4.996	224,820
Gross Gain	175,180
Less allowable costs	4,200
Gain	170,980
Less: Personal exemption	1,270
Taxable Gain	169,710
Tax Due @ 20%	33,942

If Joe had been 55 no tax would have arisen as the sale proceeds were less than €476,250.

RETIREMENT RELIEF
In the vast majority of cases, farmers who are over 55 years disposing of their farms within the family will not incur a capital gains tax liability. However, given the current price of agricultural land, there are many situations where a liability would arise in the case of disposals outside the family. Nevertheless if the sale proceeds are less than €476,250 a farmers over 55 years may dispose of part or all of his farm free of capital gains tax. This is conditional upon him having owned and farmed the farm (not rented) for the 10 years or more immediately prior to the date of disposal. This particular relief is known as *'retirement relief'* and is available regardless of whether or not the farmer retires. This means that qualifying farmers over 55 years who sell sites or parts of their farm will be free from Capital Gains Tax up to a total disposal sum of €476,250, whether it be by one or more disposals.

351

RETIREMENT RELIEF - FARM RETIREMENT PARTICIPANTS

Persons retired under the Early Farm Retirement Scheme (1994) who lease their lands and subsequently dispose of any part of those lands which forms part of the 'retirement lands' retain their entitlement to this relief. It should be noted that at the time of going to print this concession does not apply to participants in ERS 2000, however it expected that this anomaly will be rectified in the 2003 Finance Act. Check with your solicitor or tax consultant before deciding to sell.

COMPULSORY PURCHASE ORDER COMPENSATION

Compensation under a CPO is subject to Capital Gains Tax. However where a farmer reinvests all of the proceeds in land, buildings or machinery no tax will arise. For disposals on or after 6 December 2001 the farmer has eight years to reinvest the money. Qualifying investment in the two years prior to the disposal will also count. If he does not reinvest the proceeds he will be entitled to indexation relief which takes account of the fact that inflation will have accounted for some of the increased value of the land since it was acquired.

ROLL OVER RELIEF

The gain from a sale of land prior to 4 December 2002, other than development land, may be offset by reinvesting the proceeds in replacement assets. Such assets relevant to farming are;

- Land and buildings occupied for the purpose of farming
- Plant & Machinery used solely for the purposes of farming.

The replacement assets must be acquired one year before or three years after the disposal. If the land which was disposed of was owned for less than ten years the replacement assets must be for the purpose of farming. However where the land was owned for a period of more than ten years and you are ceasing to farm, it is possible to re-invest the sale proceeds in assets for another trade which you intend to set up.

Note: Roll over relief, is discontinued as from 4 December 2002

SOME GENERAL POINTS ON CAPITAL GAINS TAX

- Where the land was acquired prior to 6 April 1974 the deemed cost is the market value that obtained on 6 April 1974.

- A farmer who owns land that was valued at £750 per acre on 6 April 1974 (which will have been a typical value for good land at that time) and now decides to sell would not incur any capital gains tax if the selling price of the land does not exceed €6,600 per acre. This is because of **indexation relief.** The chart at page 10 sets out the indexation factors for all years.
- Development land tax status is not applied to a disposal of lands to a local authority associated with road construction or improvement
- Where a farmer disposes of land that achieves a price well in excess of the current use value it will not be regarded as development land if the farmer can acquire a certificate from the local authority stating that the land being disposed of is subject to a use which is inconsistent with the protection and improvement of the amenities of the general area within which the land is situated, or is otherwise damaging to the local environment. This situation might apply to land adjacent to urban areas.
- Where a farmer leased his lands and ceased farming under the Early Farm Retirement Scheme the requirement under the 'retirement relief' provisions that he should have farmed the land for a ten year period will in such instances be the ten year period prior to the commencement of the lease.
- Capital Gains Tax does not arise in relation to assets owned at the time of death, regardless of who inherits such assets.

STAMP DUTY

Stamp duty is a tax by another name that arises on instruments i.e. written documents, conveying certain assets from one person to another.

RATES OF DUTY ON LAND TRANSFERS

Table 13.5: Rates of stamp duty effective from 4 December 2002

Value of Asset (€)	Rate of Duty	Value of Asset (€)	Rate of Duty
nil - 10.000	not liable	70.001 - 80.000	5%
10.001 - 20.000	1%	60.001 - 100.000	6%
20,001 - 30,000	2%	100,001 - 120,000	7%
30,001 - 40,000	3%	120,001 - 150,000	8%
40,001 - 70,000	4%	Over €150,000	9%

STAMP DUTY ON FARM TRANSFERS

Duty is payable on the value of the land only. The transfer of livestock, machinery and assets that can be transferred by delivery rather than written agreement are not subject to duty. However, where these assets form part of the overall transfer, the total value of assets being transferred will determine the rate of stamp duty applicable to the land.

TRANSFERRING A SITE TO A FAMILY MEMBER

From 6 December 2000 no liability to Stamp Duty will arise on the transfer of a site to a son or daughter subject to the following conditions:

- it is for construction of the son or daughter's principal private residence.
- the market value of the site does not exceed €254,000 (£200,000).
- a parent can only transfer one site to each child for this exemption.

Other than situations as referred to above where the transfer is between related persons the duty is reduced to half the rate that would normally apply.

STAMP DUTY ON LEASES

A rate of 1% of the annual rent payable under the lease applies in most cases. However where the rent payable is considered by the Revenue Commissioners to be less than the market rent they will calculate the gift element of the lease over the entire term and charge the appropriate rate of stamp duty that would apply between non relatives.

Example:

Farmer Joe leases his 100 acres of land to his son for ten years at an annual rent of €6,000. However the Revenue Commissioners consider the rental value to be €130 per acre and calculate that Framer Joe is giving his son a gift to the value of €70,000 over the next ten years. The rate of stamp duty applicable to a gift of this amount is 5% or €3,500 in total. Family leases can cause problems in this regard as if the true market rent is specified on the lease and not subsequently paid over, the lessor could still be liable for income tax on the specified rent.

SPECIAL RELIEF FOR 'YOUNG TRAINED FARMERS'

From the 1 January 2000 a zero rate of stamp duty applies farmers who are under 35 years of age and who have satisfactorily attended a course in farm management. The relief applies to sales and gifts where no power of revocation exists and runs until

31 December 2005. There a number of different categories of young trained farmers with differing training requirements.

Persons born after 1 January 1968: Such persons will be required to be the holder of one of the diplomas or certificates as laid down by the Revenue Commissioners as follows,

- A third level qualification from Teagasc or the Farm Apprentiship Board, a university degree in agriculture or an agricultural certificate from the NCEA along with a Teagasc certificate confirming participation in a farm management course of not less than 80 hours duration.
- Has completed any full time third level course of not less than two years duration and holds a Teagasc certificate confirming completion of a farm management course of not less than 180 hours duration.

Persons born before 1 January 1968: Such persons will require:

- A certificate from Teagasc confirming attendance at a relevant course of not less than 180 hours duration.
- Farming to be the principal occupation for a period of not less than three years.

The reduction applies to purchases of land as well as transfers.

There are a number of important conditions worth noting:

- The young trained farmer must spend not less than 50% of his or her time farming the land for at least five years subsequent to the transfer or conveyance.
- He or she must not dispose of all or part of the lands for a period of five years unless such lands are replaced within one year of disposal.

If a transferee has completed a course of minimum duration of two years at a third level institution and fulfils the further training requirements within three years of the conveyance or transfer they will be entitled to a refund of the appropriate amount of stamp duty without interest.

STAMP DUTY ON RESIDENTIAL PROPERTY
The following table sets out the rates effective since December 2001:

Table 13.6: Residential property rates of stamp duty

Sale/TransferValue of Asset Euro(€)	Residential rate of stamp duty		
	1st. Time buyer	Owner/ occupier	Investor * New or S/H
Up to €127,000	Nil	Nil	Nil
127,001 to 190,500	Nil	3%	3%
190,501 to 254,000	3%	4%	4%
254,001 to 317,500	3.75%	5%	5%
317,501 to 381,000	4.5%	6%	6%
381,001 to 635,000	7.5%	7.5%	7.5%
Over 635,000	9%	9%	9%

* effective from 6 December 2001

INHERITANCES
Where property is acquired by way of inheritance, no stamp duty is payable.

POINTS TO NOTE

- No stamp duty arises on inheritances
- No stamp duty arises in transfers between husbands and wives
- No stamp duty arises on transfers made to former spouses under an order of the Family Law or Family Law Divorce Acts.
- No stamp duty arises on the sale of commercial forestry
- The zero rate for young trained farmers continues until the 31 December 2002
- No stamp duty arises on the sale of a site to a son or daughter

PRSI AND HEALTH LEVY

The PRSI scheme for the self–employed became effective on 6 April 1988 and is known as Class S PRSI. With the exception of persons claiming Unemployment Assistance or Farm Assist on a continuous any self employed person with an income of €3,175 or more per annum is liable. The benefits arising out of paying PRSI are, entitlement to a Contributory Old Age Pension, Contributory Survivors' Pension, Maternity Benefit, Bereavement Grant or Contributory Orphans' Pension.

PAYMENT OF PRSI

From 6 April 2001 PRSI is chargeable at 3% of farm profits after deduction of capital allowances, subject to a minimum payment of €253 per annum. There is no upper limit to the amount of income that is liable to PRSI.

VOLUNTARY CONTRIBUTIONS

Once three years (i.e. 156 contributions) PRSI has been paid, a person may become a voluntary contributor if they cease to be compulsorily insured because of giving up farming or because of earning less than €3,175 per year. Applications to become a voluntary contributor should be made within one year of the end of the tax year in which you ceased to be compulsorily insured. Where no contributions are made because of any of the circumstances outlined, a person may be missing out on vital contributions to ensure full entitlement to contributory old age, survivors or orphans pensions. It is generally not possible to back pay such contributions as the time limit for applying is strictly adhered to. The current rate of voluntary contribution is €253.

PRSI FOR THOSE EXEMPTED FROM MAKING A TAX RETURN

Where a self employed individual on low income is notified by the Inspector of Taxes that he or she is not required to make a tax return, they are obliged to apply to Social Welfare to become contributors to PRSI which will safeguard their eventual entitlements. This type of contributor is described as a **'no net liability contributor'** and the total annual contribution is €157.48 in the 2002 tax year. This amount can be paid quarterly, half yearly or annually.

For people who are in arrears, there is no time limit in operation in which to bring their contributions up to date. It will of course mean paying all arrears applying to any contribution years missed out since 1988/89 which can in certain circumstances attract an interest charge. However the overall cost will be small in relation to the potential benefits.

Further information on voluntary or 'no net liability contributions' can be had from the Department of Social Community and Family Affairs, Government Buildings, Cork Road, Waterford. Tel: 051-874177.

HEALTH LEVY

The Health Levy amount to 2% of profits assessable for tax purposes after deduction of capital allowances. Payment of health levy is obligatory where income exceeds €18,512 per annum in the 2002 tax year. The following self employed people are exempted from these levies: Medical Card Holders, persons to whom the Department of Social Welfare is paying Widow's/Widower's Pension, Deserted Wives' or One Parent Family Benefit.

AI CATTLE BREEDING STATIONS

Progressive Genetics, Kylemore Road, Dublin 12.
Tel: 01 - 4502142
Cork Milk Board Cattle Breeding Society
ODL House, Doughcloyne Ind. Est., Sarsfield
Road, Wilton, Cork. Tel: 021 - 345333
Golden Vale Cattle Breeding Society,
Clarecastle, Ennis, Co. Clare. Tel: 065 - 6828220
North West Cattle Breeding Society
Headquarters, Doonally House, Sligo.
Tel: 071 - 45314
North Eastern Cattle Breeding Society
Headquarters, Ballyhaise, Co. Cavan.
Tel: 049 - 38152/38106
South Eastern Cattle Breeding Society
Headquarters, Dovea, Thurles,
Co. Tipperary. Tel: 0504 - 21755
Castleisland Cattle Breeding Station
Headquarters, Castleisland, Co. Kerry.
Tel: 066 - 7141506
Dairygold A.I. Station
Headquarters, Mitchelstown, Co. Cork.
Tel: 1800 500 321
South Western Services Co-op Society
Headquarters, Bandon, Co. Cork.
Tel: 023 - 41271

AGRICULTURE & HORTICULTURE COLLEGES

Franciscan Agricultural College
Mountbellew, Co. Galway. Tel: 0905 - 79205
Salesian Agricultural College
Pallaskenry, Co. Limerick. Tel: 061 - 393100
**Salesian College of Agriculture and
Horticulture**, Warrenstown, Co. Meath.
Tel: 01 - 8259342
St. Patrick's Agricultural College
Monaghan. Tel: 047 - 81102
Franciscan Agricultural College
Multyfarnham, Co. Westmeath.
Tel: 044 - 71137
Gurteen Agricultural College
Ballingarry, Roscrea, Co. Tipperary.
Tel: 067 - 21282

Rockwell Agricultural College
Cashel, Co. Tipperary. Tel: 062 - 61444**ICA**
Horticultural College An Grianán, Termonfeckin,
Drogheda,
Co. Louth. Tel: 041 - 9822158
College of Amenity Horticulture
National Botanic Gardens, Glasnevin,
Dublin 9. Tel: 01- 8374388
Mellowes Agricultural College
Athenry, Co. Galway. Tel: 091 - 845146
Agricultural College
Ballyhaise, Co. Cavan. Tel: 049 - 4338108
Agricultural College
Darrara, Clonakilty, Co. Cork. Tel: 023 - 33302
**Kildalton Agricultural and Horticultural
College,** Piltown, Co. Kilkenny. Tel: 051 - 643105

AGRICULTURAL CONSULTANTS
See ACA list of members, page 23

AGRICULTURAL SCIENCE ASSOCIATION
Irish Farm Centre, Bluebell, Dublin 12.
Tel: 01-4603682

BORD FÁILTE
Baggot Street Bridge, Dublin 2.
Tel: 01-6024000

BORD GLAS
8 Lower Baggot Street, Dublin 2.
Tel: 01-6763567

COILLTE TEO.
Leeson Lane, Dublin 2. Tel: 01-6615666

DEER AND GOAT ASSOCIATIONS
Irish Deer Farmers' Association
Kevin Mahon, Archers Grove, Kilkenny.
Tel: 086-8286863
Galtee Deer Care Ltd.
Pat or Miriam Mulcahy, Ballinwilliam House,
Mitchelstown, Co. Cork.
Tel: 025 - 24801

DIRECTORY OF USEFUL SERVICES

DEPARTMENT OF AGRICULTURE AND FOOD
Office of the Minister and Secretariat
Kildare Street, Dublin 2. Tel: 01 - 6072000
Accounts Division
Farnham Street, Cavan. Tel: 049-4368200
Headage Division
Davitt House, Castlebar, Co. Mayo.
Tel: 094 - 35300
Special Beef Premium Unit
Portlaoise, Co. Laois. Tel: 0502-74400
Johnstown Castle
Wexford. Lo Call 1890 200509 or 053-42888

LOCAL DEPARTMENT OFFICES
Carlow ERAD & FDS Industrial Estate, Athy Road, Carlow. Tel: 0503 - 70022
Cavan ERAD & FDS Government Offices, Farnham Street, Cavan. Tel: 049 - 4368200
Clare ERAD & FDS Government Offices, Kilrush Road, Ennis. Tel: 065 - 6866042
Cork 3rd.Floor, Hibernian House, South Mall, Cork. ERAD(Cork N/E)Tel: 021 -4 851400
FDS(Cork City) 021-4851400
ERAD(Cork SW) FDS(Mallow/Fermoy NW) Gooldshill, Mallow. Tel:022 - 21153
FDS (Cork W) 1 Emmet Square, Clonakilty. Tel:023 - 33371
Donegal ERAD Meeting House Street, Raphoe, Lifford, Co. Donegal. Tel: 074 - 45990
FDS(Donegal South) Irwinsyard, Milltown, Donegal Town. Tel:073 - 21048
FDS(Donegal North) Govt. Offices, High Road, Letterkenny. Tel:074 - 22199
Dublin ERAD(Dublin/Wicklow E.) St. Johns House, Old Blessington Road, Dublin 24. Tel: 01 - 4149900
FDS Floor 3E, Agriclture House,Kildare Street, Dublin 2. Tel:01 - 6072000
Galway ERAD Hynes Building, St. Augustine Street, Galway. Tel. 091 - 507600
FDS(Galway W) Govt. Offices, Dublin Road. Tel:091 - 771381
FDS(Galway N) The Mall, Tuam. Tel:093 - 24257
FDS(Galway E & S) Main Street, Loughrea. Tel:091 - 841098
Kerry Government Buildings, Spa Road, Tralee, Co. Kerry. ERAD Tel: 066 - 7145042
FDS (Kerry N) Tel: 066 - 7145042

FDS(Kerry S) New Street, Killarney.
Tel:064 - 31013
Kildare ERAD Poplar House, Popular Square, Naas, Co. Kildare. Tel: 045 - 873035
FDS Spring Garden Hse., Sallins Rd., Naas. Tel: 045 - 894044
Kilkenny Government Offices, Hebron Rd., Kilkenny. ERAD Tel: 056 - 72400
FDS   Tel: 056 - 72400
Laois Government Offices, Portlaoise, Co. Laois. ERAD Tel: 0502 - 74400
FDS Tel: 0502 - 74400
Leitrim ERAD Government Buildings, Cranmore Road, Sligo. Tel: 071 - 55030
FDS Govt. Offices, Carrick-on-Shannon.
Tel: 078 - 20030
Limerick ERAD & FDS St.Munchins House, Dock Road, Limerick. Tel: 061 - 208500
Longford Govt. Offices, Ballinalee Road, Longford. ERAD Tel: 043 - 50020
FDS Tel: 043 - 46319
Louth ERAD North Quay, Drogheda, Co. Louth.
Tel: 041 - 9870086
FDS St. Patricks Hall, Dundalk. Tel: 042 - 9334342
Mayo ERAD & FDS (Mayo W) Michael Davitt House, Castlebar, Co. Mayo. Tel: 094 - 35300
FDS(Mayo N) Govt. Offices, Ballina.
Tel: 096 - 21161
FDS(Mayo E) The Square, Claremorris.
Tel: 094 - 71490
Meath ERAD & FDS Government Offices, Kells Road, Navan, Co. Meath.
Tel: 046 - 79030
Monaghan ERAD Main Street, Ballybay, Co. Monaghan. Tel: 042 - 9748800
FDS Plantation, Monaghan. Tel: 047-81452
Offaly ERAD & FDS Government Offices, Clonminch,Tullamore, Co. Offaly.
Tel: 0506 - 46037
Roscommon Circular Road, Roscommon, ERAD Tel: 0903 - 30100
FDS   Tel: 0903 - 27251
Sligo ERAD & FDS Govt. Offices, Cranmore Road, Sligo. Tel: 071 - 55030
Tipperary South ERAD St.Michael's Road, Tipperary. Tel: 062 - 80100
FDS New Quay, Clonmel. Tel: 052 - 21717
Tipperary North ERAD & FDS Government Offices, St.Conlons Road, Nenagh.
Tel: 067 - 50014

DIRECTORY OF USEFUL SERVICES

Tipperary Mid FDS Liberty Square, Thurles. Tel: 0504 - 21664
Waterford ERAD & FDS(Waterford E) The Glen, Waterford. Tel: 051 - 301700
FDS(Waterford W) Davitt's Quay, Dungarvan. Tel: 058 - 41279
Westmeath ERAD Bellview, Dublin Road, Mullingar, Co. Westmeath. Tel: 044 - 39034
FDS Pearse Street, Athlone.
Tel: 0902 - 94794
Wexford ACC Building, Castle Hill, Enniscorthy, Co. Wexford. ERAD Tel: 054 -42008
FDS   Tel: 054 - 42100

ESB ADVISORY SERVICE
Agricultural Unit, ESB Marketing Department, Lr. Fitzwilliam Street, Dublin 2. Tel: 01-6765831

FARM RELIEF SERVICES
Bride & Bladkwater Trish Coughlan, 55 McCurtain Street, Fermoy. Tel: 025-32646
Cavan Michael McHugh, Granard Road, Ballyjamesduff. Tel: 049-8545100
Carlow Philip Kenny, Industrial Estate, Tullow. Tel: 0503-52444
Clare Billy Tynan, Clare Marts, Ennis. Tel: 065-6820275
Donegal Austin Duignan, The Diamond, Raphoe. Tel: 074-45386
Duhallow Dan O' Riordan, Percivan Street, Kanturk. Tel: 029-50750
Galway Thomas Finn, The Mart, Athenry.   Tel: 091-844551
Kerry John Lyons, Moanmore Ind. Estate, Castleisland. Tel: 066-7141099
Laois Pat Coffey, New Road, Portlaoise
Tel: 0502-61916
Limerick North Liam O' Rourke, Lottera, Bruree. Tel: 63-90666
Louth Martin Frayne, Willaim Street, Ardee Tel: 041-6857222
Mallow Michael Looney, Island, Burnfort Tel: 022-29195
Westmeath Michael McHugh, Dublin Road, Mullingar. Tel: 044-43077
Wicklow   Joe O' Brien, Tinahely. Tel: 0402-38427

FARM APPRENTICESHIP BOARD
Teagasc, Moorpark, Fermoy, Co.Cork. Tel: 025-42244

FARM EXAMINER
c/o Cork Examiner, 95 Patrick Street, Cork. Tel: 021 - 4272722

FARMING INDEPENDENT
c/o Irish Independent, 90 Lr. Middle Abbey Street, Dublin 1. Tel: 01 - 8731666

HORSE INDUSTRY ASSOCIATIONS
Association of Racehorse Owners c/o John Brophy, Rossmore House, Kilkenny.
Tel: 056 - 21525
Association of Riding Clubs c/o Helen Mangan, 8 Main Street, Glencormac, Bray, Co. Wicklow. Tel: 01 - 2860196
Association of Riding Establishments Tommy Ryan, Moorepark, Newbridge Co. Kildare. Tel: 045 - 431584
Equestrian Federation Ashtown Hse., Castleknock, Dublin 15. Tel: 01 - 8387611
Riding for the Disabled Assoc. of Ireland c/o Niamh Kingston, 28 Castlepark Rd, Sandycove, Co. Dublin. Tel: 01 - 2857428
Showjumping Association Anglesea Lodge, Anglesea Road, Dublin 4. Tel: 01 - 6601700
Thoroughbred Breeders Association Old Connell House, Newbridge, Co. Kildare. Tel: 045 - 31890
Stallion Owners' Society c/o P.J. O'Reilly, Shraugh Stud, Louisburgh, Co. Mayo. Tel: 098 - 66144

IRISH CREAMERY MILK SUPPLIERS ASSOCIATION
John Feely House, Upper Mallow St, Limerick. Tel: 061-314677

IRISH CO-OPERATIVE ORGANISATION SOCIETY LTD
Plunket House, 84 Merrion Square, Dublin 2. Tel: 01-6764783

DIRECTORY OF USEFUL SERVICES

IRISH FARMERS ASSOCIATION
Irish Farm Centre, Bluebell, Dublin 12.
Tel: 01-450 0266
e-mail: postmaster@ifa.ie

President:
John Dillon, Killuragh,, Pallasgreen, Co. Limerick
Tel: 061-384060
Deputy President:
Ruaidhri Deasy, Fortmoy House, Aglish, Roscrea,
Co.Tipperary. Tel. 067-21102
Vice Presidents:
MUNSTER
Donal Kelly, Lehanmore, Garnish, Beara, West
Cork. Tel. 027-73009
STH. LEINSTER:
Matt Merrick, Shean, Edenderry, Co.Offally. Tel.
0405-31638.
ULSTER/NTH. LEINSTER:
Eugene Sherry, Drumbin, Tydavnet, Co.Monaghan.
Tel. 047-89304
CONNACHT:
Brendan O'Mahony, Cross, Claremorris, Co.Mayo.
Tel. 092-46170

SUGARBEET SECTION
Chairman
Willie French, Loughgerald, Enniscorthy, Co,
Wexford. Tel: 054-33743
Hon. Treasurer
Padraig Walshe, Bishopswood, Durrow, Portlaoise,
Co.Laois. Tel. 0502-36144
Hon. Returning Officer
Seamus O'Brien, Knockballystine, Portlaoise,
Co.Laois. Tel. 0503- 56170

IFA EXECUTIVE STAFF
General Secretary
Michael Berkery
Asst. General Secretary
Bryan Barry
Chief Economist
Con Lucey
Director of Livestock
Kevin Kinsella
Director of Organisation
Pat Smith
Brussels Office Director
Michael Treacy,
IFA Office - 23/25 Rue de la Science, Boite 2,
Brussels. Tel. 003222303137

Financial Controller
Roger Hynes
Press Officer
Derek Cunningham

COMMITTEE CHAIRMEN AND
EXECUTIVE SECRETARIES

ANIMAL HEALTH
John Stack, Tarmons West, Tarbert, Co. Kerry.
Tel: 068-36201
Secretary: Fintan Conway

DAIRY
Michael Murphy, Coolbeggan, Tallow,
Co.Waterford. Tel. 024-97265
Secretary: Catherine Lascurettes

FARM BUSINESS
Walter Crowley, Polerone, Mooncoin, Via
Waterford, Co. Kilkenny. Tel: 051 - 895120
Secretary: Jim Devlin

FARM FAMILY
Mary McGreale, Derrygarve, Westport, Co.Mayo.
Tel. 098-26468.
Equality Office: Mary Carroll

FORESTRY
Pat Lehane, Castletreasure, Douglas, Co. Cork. Tel:
021-4892420
Farm Forestry Development Officer: Barbara
Maguire

GRAIN
Padraig Harrington, Ballingarry, Minane Bridge.
Tel. 021-4770667
Secretary: Fintan Conway

HILL FARMING
Michael Comiskey, Magurk, Leechaun P.O. Via
Sligo. Tel. 071-64245

HORSE
Timmy O'Regan, Ballygarrett Stud, Mallow,
Co.Cork. Tel. 022-26231

HORTICULTURE
John Coleman, ashgrove, Cobh, Co.Cork. Tel.
021-811624

362

DIRECTORY OF USEFUL SERVICES

NATIONAL HORTICULTURE ORGANISER:
Kieran Leddy, IFA, Irish Farm Centre, Bluebell,
Dublin 12. Tel: 01-4500266

INDUSTRIAL & ENVIRONMENT
Francis Fanning, Ahullen, Inch, Gore, Co.
Wexford. Tel: 0402-37693
Secretary: Jim Devlin

LIVESTOCK
Derek Deane, Tombeagh, Hacketstown, Co.
Carlow. Tel: 0508-71412
Secretary: Kevin Kinsella

LIQUID MILK
Donal Kelleher, Ballyphilip, Whitescross, Co.
Cork. Tel: 021-486668
Secretary: Catherine Lascurettes

PIGS
Pat O'Keeffe, Ballylough, Mitchelstown, Co.Cork.
Tel. 022-25285.
Secretary: James Brady

POTATO
John Sheridan, Drakerath, Carlinstown, Co.Meath.
Tel. 046-52329

NATIONAL POTATO CO-ORDINATOR
Malachy Mitchell, IFA, Irish Farm Centre,
Bluebell, Dublin 12. Tel: 01-4500266

POULTRY
Alan Graham, Jnr., Tullyherin, Monaghan.
Tel: 047-77819
Secretary: Ned Walsh

RURAL DEVELOPMENT
Michael Bergin, Cromogue, Mountrath,
Portlaoise. Tel: 0502-32356
Secretary: Gerry Gunning

SHEEP & WOOL
Laurence Fallon, Balladh, Knockcroghery, Tel.
0902-88232
Secretary: Kevin Kinsella

SUGARBEET SECTION
Willie French, Loughgerald, Enniscorthy,
Co.Wexfoed. Tel. 054-33743

Secretary: Elaine Farrell

WESTERN DEVELOPMENT
Con Hickey, Gurrane, Ballydehob. Tel. 028-38266
Secretary: Gerry Gunning

COUNTY CHAIRMEN

CARLOW
William Young, Kilcarrig Lodge, Bagenalstown.
Tel. 0503-21491

CAVAN
Joe Brady, Drumnagar, Tullyco, Cotehill.
Tel: 049-4330131

CLARE
Gerard Kerin, Bellharbour, via. Galway.
Tel: 065-7078005

CORK NORTH
Sean O'Leary, Gortneelig, Mourneabbey, Tel.
022-29361

CORK CENTRAL
Gerard O'Carroll, Rathanker, Passage West. Tel.
021-4841209

CORK WEST
Bernard O'Donovan, Skeagh, Skibbereen.
Tel: 028-38258

DONEGAL
George O'Hagan, Linsfort, Buncranagh, Co.
Donegal. Tel: 077-62414

DUBLIN
Joseph O'Donoghue, Evergreen Farm,
Brackentown, Swords. Tel: 01 - 8403672

GALWAY
Michael Silke, Esker, Banagher. Tel. 0509-51177

KERRY
Florence McCarthy, Killowen, Kenmare.
Tel: 064-41415

KILDARE
Michael Dempsey, Barnhill, Castledermot.
Tel: 0503-44327

DIRECTORY OF USEFUL SERVICES

KILKENNY
Ger Mullins, Doninga House, Goresbridge.
Tel: 0503-75113

LAOIS
Michael McEvoy, Graiguenahown, Abbeyleix. Tel.
0502-33408

LEITRIM
Paddy Kennedy, Breanross, Sth., Mohill. Tel.
043-24224

LIMERICK
Michael O'Flynn. Moyviddy, Newcastlewest.
Tel: 069-62054

LONGFORD
James Reynolds, Lanehill, Coolarty,
Edgewortstown. Tel: 042-23443

LOUTH
Raymond O'Malley, Millockstown, Ardee.
Tel: 041-6853963

MAYO
Michael Biggins, Ballynalty, Ower. Tel. 092-46418

MEATH
Seamus McGee, Magee's Cross, Crossakiel, Kells.
Tel: 046-43726

MONAGHAN
Seamus Traymor, Cordoolagh, Ballybay.
Tel: 042-9741131

OFFALY
Tom Loonam, Attinkee, Banagher, Tel.
0902-57197

ROSCOMMON
Eddie Fallon, Rahara Rd., Athleague. Tel.
0903-23398

SLIGO
Joe Coulter, Skreen. Tel: 071-66698

TIPPERARY NTH.
Pat Hogan, Summerville, Horse + Jockey, Thurles.
Tel: 05004-44892

TIPPERARY STH.
Tim O'Donoghue, Farranacliff, Tipperary.
Tel. 062-31287

WATERFORD
Harry Gray, Ballygarron, Bonmahon. Tel.
051-292119

WESTMEATH
Eamon Bray, Ashlawn, Ballyhealy, Delvin.
Tel: 044-64274

WEXFORD
J.J.Kavanagh, Ballinabanogue, New Ross.
Tel: 051-424771

WICKLOW
Paddy Healy, Loggam, Gorey. Tel:0402-34747.

IRISH FARMERS JOURNAL
Bluebell, Dublin 12.
Tel: 01-4199500

ORGANIC BODIES
IRISH ORGANIC FARMERS and GROWERS ASSOCIATION
Noreen Gibney, National Administrator, 56
Blessington St., Dublin 7.
Tel: 01 - 8307996
Demeter Standards Ltd.
14 Woodlet Park, Dublin 14. Tel: 01 - 2983881
Organic Trust Ltd.
Vernon House, 2 Vernon Ave. Clontarf, Dublin 3.
Tel: 01 - 8530271

MACRA NA FEIRME
Irish Farm Centre, Bluebell, Dublin 12.
Tel: 01-4508000

MET ÉIREANN
Glasnevin Hill, Dublin 9.
Tel: 01-8064200
Weatherdial:Phone 1550-123 plus

Munster	850
Leinster	851
Connaught	852
Ulster	853

DIRECTORY OF USEFUL SERVICES

NATIONAL CO-OP FARM RELIEF SERVICES
Roscrea, Co. Tipperary. Tel: 0505-22100

NATIONAL PLOUGHING ASSOCIATION
Anna May Mc.Hugh, Fallaghmore, Athy, Co. Kildare. Tel: 0507-25125

ORDNANCE SURVEY OFFICE
Phoenix Park, Dublin 8. Tel: 01 - 8206100.

REGIONAL VETERINARY OFFICES
Coosan, Athlone, Co.Westmeath.
Tel: 0902 - 75514.
Model Farm Road, Cork. Tel: 021 - 543931.
Government Offices, Hebron Road,
Kilkenny. Tel: 056 - 22977
Knockalisheen, Limerick. Tel: 061 - 452911
Fawcett's Bridge, Sligo. Tel: 071 - 42191

TAX OFFICES
Athlone Pearse Street, Athlone, Co. Westmeath.
Tel: 0902 - 21800
Castlebar Michael Davitt House, Castlebar, Co. Mayo. Tel: 094 - 37000
Cork Government Buildings, Sullivans Quay, Co. Cork. Tel: 021 - 4966077
Dublin Dublin Tax District, 1 Lr. Grand Canal Street, Dublin 2. Tel: 01 - 6474000
Dundalk Earl House, Earl Street, Dundalk, Co.Louth. Tel: 042 - 9353700
Galway Hibernian House, Eyre Square, Co. Galway. Tel: 091 - 536000
Kilkenny Hebron Road, Kilkenny, Co. Kilkenny. Tel: 056 - 75300
Letterkenny High Road, Letterkenny, Co. Donegal. Tel: 074 - 21299
Limerick River House, Charlotes Quay, Limerick. Tel: 061 - 212700
Sligo Government Offices, Cranmore Road, Sligo, Co. Sligo. Tel: 071 - 48600
Thurles Stradavoher, Thurles, Co. Tipperary Tel: 0504 - 28700
Tralee Government Offices, Spa Road, Tralee, Co. Kerry. Tel: 066 - 7183100

Waterford Government Buildings, The Glen, Waterford. Tel: 051 - 873565
Wexford Anne St, Wexford.
Tel: 053 - 63300

TEAGASC
Headquarters 19 Sandymount Avenue, Ballsbridge, Dublin 4. Tel: 01 - 6376000
Development Centre Rural Development Division, Athenry, Co. Galway.
Tel: 091 - 845200
Sheep Research Centre Belclare, Tuam, Co. Galway. Tel: 093 - 24506
Beef Research Centre Grange, Dunsany, Co. Meath. Tel: 046 - 25214
Tillage/Horticulture/Environment
Kildalton College, Piltown, Co. Kilkenny.
Tel: 051 - 643105
Tillage Research Centre Oak Park, Co. Carlow. Tel: 0503 -70200
Environment Research/Analytical
Johnstown Castle, Wexford. Tel: 053 - 42888
Horticulture Research and Development Centre, Kinsealy, Malahide Road, Dublin 17. Tel: 01 - 8460644
National Dairy Products Research Centre Moorepark, Fermoy. Tel: 025 - 42244
Dairying/Pigs/Husbandry Research Moorepark, Fermoy. Tel: 025 - 42244
National Food Centre, Dunsinea, Castleknock, Dublin 15. Tel: 01 - 8059500
National Food Centre Development Facility, Raheen, Co. Limerick.
Tel: 061 - 301155

COUNTY ADVISORY AND TRAINING SERVICES

CARLOW
The Green, Tullow. Tel: 0503 - 51210
Barrett Street, Bagnelstown.
Tel: 0503- 21267

CAVAN
Teagasc County Office, Ballyhaise.
Tel: 049 - 38300

Kells Road, Bailieboro, Co. Cavan.
Tel: 042 - 65435

DIRECTORY OF USEFUL SERVICES

Mart House, Granard Road, Ballyjamesduff, Co. Cavan
Tel: 049 - 44499

CLARE
Station Road, Ennis. Tel: 065 - 28676
Fossabeg, Scariff. Tel: 061 - 921093
Ardnaculla, Ennistymon. Tel: 065 - 71077
Cooraclare Road, Kilrush. Tel: 065 - 51189

CORK EAST
Farranlea Road, Cork. Tel: 021 - 4545055
Knockgriffen, Midletown. Tel: 021 - 4631898
Sandfield, Mallow. Tel: 022 - 21936
Chapel Street, Charleville. Tel: 063 - 81514
Bluepool, Kanturk. Tel: 029 - 50164
Carnigie Hall, Millstreet. Tel: 029 - 70031
James O'Keeffe Institute, Newmarket.
Tel: 029 - 60220
Moorepark, Fermoy. Tel: 025 - 42244

CORK WEST
Kilbarry Road, Dunmanway.
Tel: 023 - 45113
Codrum, Macroom. Tel: 026 - 41604

Aras Beanntrai, The Square, Bantry.
Tel: 027 - 50265
Connolly Street, Bandon. Tel: 023 - 41589
Coronea, Skibbereen. Tel: 028 - 21574
Agricultural College, Darrara, Clonakilty.
Tel: 023 - 33118

DONEGAL
Cavan Lower, Ballybofey. Tel: 074 - 31189
Carnamuggagh, Letterkenny.
Tel: 074 - 21053
Doonan, Donegal. Tel: 073 - 21981
Courthouse, Buncrana. Tel: 077 - 61265
Courthouse, Carndonagh. Tel: 077 - 74233

DUBLIN
Kinsealy Research Centre, Malahide Road, Dublin 17. Tel: 01 - 8460644
Corduff, Lusk. Tel: 01 - 8437703
GALWAY
Co. Advisory Office, Athenry.
Tel: 091 - 845830
C/o M. Keady, The Square, Headford.
Tel: 093 - 35563
Deerpark, Ballinasloe. Tel: 0905 - 42456

Barrack Street, Loughrea. Tel: 091 -841088
Castle Avenue, Portumna. Tel: 0509 - 41124
Upper Dublin Road, Tuam. Tel: 093 - 24506
Bridge Street, Gort. Tel: 091 - 631155

KERRY
The Pavilion, Austin Stack Park, Tralee.
Tel: 066 - 25077
Clieveragh, Listowel. Tel: 068 - 21266
Cleeney, Killarney. Tel: 064 - 32344
IRD Office, Kenmare. Tel: 064 - 41275
Courthouse, Cahirciveen. Tel: 066 - 72452
Island Centre, Main Street, Castleisland.
Tel: 066 - 41213
Credit Union House, Rathmore.
Tel: 064 - 58333

KILDARE
Friary Road, Naas. Tel: 045 -879203
Rathstewart, Athy. Tel: 0507 - 31719

KILKENNY
Kells Road, Kilkenny. Tel: 056 - 21153
Mullinavat. 051 - 898137

LAOIS
1 Park Villas, Portlaoise. Tel: 0502 - 21326
Knockiel, Rathdowney. Tel: 0505 - 46451

LEITRIM
Bridge Street, Carrick-on-Shannon.
Tel: 078 - 20028
ACC Office, Main St., Mohill.
Tel: 078 - 31076
Sligo Road, Manorhamilton.
Tel: 072 - 55107

LIMERICK
Parnell Street, Limerick. Tel: 061 - 415922
Gortboy, Newcastlewest. Tel: 069 - 61444
Kilmallock. Tel: 063 - 98039

LONGFORD
Teagasc, Town Centre, Longford.
Tel: 043 - 41021
LOUTH
Teagasc, Dublin Road, Dundalk.
Tel: 042 - 9332263
Slane Road, Drogheda. Tel: 041 - 9833006
MAYO
Michael Davitt House, Castlebar.

DIRECTORY OF USEFUL SERVICES

Tel: 094 - 21944
Bunree Road, Ballina. Tel: 098 - 22335
Newport Road, Westport. Tel: 098 - 28333
Abbey Road, Ballinrobe. Tel: 092 - 41125
Main Street, Swinford. Tel: 094 - 51157
Barrack Street, Belmullet. Tel: 097 - 81104
Mullinmore Street, Crossmolina.
Tel: 096 - 31159
Abbey St., Ballyhaunis. Tel: 0907 - 30104

MEATH
Kells Road, Navan. Tel: 046 - 21792
Willowfield, Navan Road, Kells.
Tel: 046 - 40039
Grange Research Centre, Dunsany.
Tel: 046 - 25214

MONAGHAN
Coolshannagh, Co. Monaghan.
Tel: 047 - 81188
Lakeview, Castleblayney. Tel: 042 - 9740072

OFFALY
'Sheena', Charleville Road, Tullamore.
Tel: 0506 - 21405
St. Brendan's Hse., Oxmanstown Mall, Birr.
Tel: 0509 - 20284

ROSCOMMON
Abbey Street, Roscommon.
Tel: 0903 - 25494
St Patrick's Street, Castlerea.
Tel: 0907 - 20160
Magazine Road, Athlone. Tel: 0902 - 94109
The Crescent, Boyle. Tel: 079 - 62189

SLIGO
Riverside, Sligo. Tel: 071 - 42677
Carrowanty, Ballymote. Tel: 071 - 83247
Enniscrone. Tel: 096 - 36298

TIPPERARY (SR)
River House, New Quay, Clonmel, Co. Tipperary.
Tel: 052 - 21300
Davis Road, Tipperary. Tel: 062 - 51844
Courthouse, Hogan Square, Cashel.
Tel: 062 - 61236

TIPPERARY (NR)
Castlemeadows, Thurles. Tel: 0504 - 21777

Dromin Road, Nenagh. Tel: 067 - 31225

WATERFORD
Shandon, Dungarvan, Co. Waterford.
Tel: 058 - 41211
C/o Waterford/Ross Marts, Old Kilmeadon Road,
Waterford. Tel: 051 - 75417
Main Street West, Lismore. Tel: 058 - 54181

WESTMEATH
Bellview, Dublin Road, Mullingar.
Tel: 044 - 40721
Dublin Road, Moate. Tel: 0902 - 81167

WEXFORD
Advisory and Training Centre, Johnstown Castle,
Wexford. Tel: 053 - 42622
Barretts Park, New Ross. Tel: 051 - 421404
Dublin Road, Enniscorthy. Tel: 054 - 33332
Showgrounds, Gorey. Tel: 055 - 21333

WICKLOW
Wentworth Place, Wicklow.
Tel: 0404 - 67315
Kiltegan Road, Baltinglass.
Tel: 0508 - 81200
Coolruss, Tinahealy. Tel: 0402 - 38171

INDEX

INDEX

INDEX

INDEX

NOTES

Telephone Numbers

Name	Home/Office	Mobile

Calendar 2003

January
M		6	13	20	27
T		7	14	21	28
W	1	8	15	22	29
T	2	9	16	23	30
F	3	10	17	24	31
S	4	11	18	25
S	5	12	19	26

February
M		3	10	17	24
T		4	11	18	25
W		5	12	19	25
T		6	13	20	27
F		7	14	21	28
S	1	8	15	22
S	2	9	16	23

March
M		3	10	17	24	31
T		4	11	18	25
W		5	12	19	26
T		6	13	20	27
F		7	14	21	28
S	1	8	15	22	29
S	2	9	16	23	30

April
M		7	14	21	28
T	1	8	15	22	29
W	2	9	16	23	30
T	3	10	17	24
F	4	11	18	25
S	5	12	19	26
S	6	13	20	27

May
M		5	12	19	26
T		6	13	20	27
W		7	14	21	28
T	1	8	15	22	29
F	2	9	16	23	30
S	3	10	17	24	31
S	4	11	18	25

June
M		2	9	16	23	30
T		3	10	17	24
W		4	11	18	25
T		5	12	19	26
F		6	13	20	27
S		7	14	21	28
S	1	8	15	22	29

July
M		7	14	21	28
T	1	8	15	22	29
W	2	9	16	23	30
T	3	10	17	24	31
F	4	11	18	25
S	5	12	19	26
S	6	13	20	27

August
M		4	11	18	25
T		5	11	18	25
W		6	13	20	27
T		7	14	21	28
F	1	8	15	22	29
S	2	9	16	23	30
S	3	10	17	24	31

September
M	1	8	15	22	29
T	2	9	16	23	30
W	3	10	17	24
T	4	11	18	25
F	5	12	19	26
S	6	13	20	27
S	7	14	21	28

October
M		6	13	20	27
T		7	14	21	28
W	1	8	15	22	29
T	2	9	16	23	30
F	3	10	17	24	31
S	4	11	18	25
S	5	12	19	26

November
M		3	10	17	24
T		4	11	18	25
W		5	12	19	25
T		6	13	20	27
F		7	14	21	28
S	1	8	15	22	29
S	2	9	16	23	30

December
M	1	8	15	22	29
T	2	9	16	23	30
W	3	10	17	24	31
T	4	11	18	25
F	5	12	19	26
S	6	13	20	27
S	7	14	21	28

Telephone Numbers

Name	Home/Office	Mobile

Telephone Numbers

Name	Home/Office	Mobile

THE LION – DISTRIBUTION AND FEEDING

Africa's largest and most inspiring carnivore, *Panthera leo*, is the dominant predator in most savanna ecosystems. Once found throughout Africa, except the forested parts of west Africa, the lion has been eradicated from much of its former range and is mainly confined to the larger game reserves. Outside of Africa the only wild population, numbering about 190, is found in the Gir Forest in India.

Although they have been recorded as feeding on virtually every mammal – from mouse to elephant – the lion's principal food consists of those mammals in the 100 kg to 300 kg mass range, including zebra (1), gemsbok (4), wildebeest and hartebeest. Larger prey, such as buffalo (page 1) and giraffe (2), may be of importance in some areas, while smaller species, like impala, gazelle and warthog, become prey in times of food shortage. Like all carnivores, lions are opportunists and will exploit any potential food supply, such as springbok lambs (5), during the lambing season. They will also readily scavenge carcasses like this old eland bull which died near a waterhole in the Kalahari (3). The sharp quills of the porcupine provide a good defence against lions who are tempted to have a go, but sometimes it is safer just to look (7)! However, in some areas like the Kalahari and parts of the Kruger National Park in South Africa, lions have become accomplished porcupine hunters, and operate swiftly, biting or swatting the animal's head before it has a chance to turn its back.

Lions hunt predominantly under cover of darkness and, in most cases, the prey is carefully stalked before a short chase of between 100 m and 200 m ensues. Cover provided by bushes and long grass is essential, and in open areas lions will often wait for the moon to set or retreat behind the clouds before setting off to hunt. The extent of co-operation between lions during the hunt may be high, particularly in open habitats. Larger hunting groups achieve greater success than smaller ones.

Contrary to popular belief, lions do not consciously use wind direction when hunting, but if they do happen to be downwind from their prey, their chances of success are higher. The female lions usually do most of the hunting, but the adult males have priority over the carcass.

Lions make frequent use of water when it is available (6). However, like nearly all carnivores, they are able to survive indefinitely without water, obtaining their liquid supply from the meat and blood of the prey that they capture.

1

3

4

5

6

7

THE SOCIAL LIFE OF LIONS

Of all the cats, lions are the most social. The nucleus of a lion pride is formed by a group of females who range between two and nine in number. The members of a pride do not always stay together, but frequently split up into smaller sub-prides. However, all members defend a common territory and all, at different times, associate with each other. A pride is structured in such a way that all the females belonging to it are related to one another, as female lions remain in the pride they are born into.

Frequently, two or more females give birth to cubs simultaneously. When this happens, the two groups often stay together – the different mothers freely suckling each other's cubs – so it is not unusual to see two or three litters of cubs together, all of about the same age (**3** and **6**). Cubs are born in a weak and poorly developed state (**2**), those pictured here being about one to two weeks old.

During times of food abundance, cubs are well fed and life is relaxing and easy (**4**), but when food is less plentiful the cubs may suffer, as there is little left over for them once the adults have eaten.

Young males are evicted from their natal prides at an age of about two-and-a-half years. They then go off in a group of between two and five, to become nomads. Lions are fully grown at about four years old and ready to challenge other males for the possession of a territory. This results in aggressive struggles for dominance, which frequently lead to injury or death. Those that succeed in displacing the existing males from a territory, establish a coalition of male lions, and gain mating rights to all the females in the territory (**1**). Should the females already have cubs, they will not be receptive to new mates, with the result that the males will often kill the cubs (**5**). This brings the females on heat, the final outcome of which means that the new males can sire and protect their own cubs (centrespread), and not the offspring of other male lions.

The female lion is on heat for between four and 16 days. During this period, a male is in attendance continuously as, if he leaves her side, his place will be quickly taken by another male. During the height of the mating period, lions will copulate once every 15 to 20 minutes. There is no dominance hierarchy among the males of a coalition and,

generally, all have equal access to the females, on a basis of first-come first-served.

The size of the coalition influences the length of time that males are able to hold a territory: larger coalitions generally have longer periods of tenure. Some males are successful enough to hold two prides of females simultaneously, constantly moving between the two. Usually, however, they are unable to maintain this for long, and another male coalition will eventually take over one of the prides.

Both male and female lions roar, though the males do so far more often than the females, and their roars tend to be louder. By roaring, the male lions make known their presence to other males, alerting them to the fact that the territory is inhabited and warning them against trespassing. A similar message of warning is conveyed by males spray-urinating against the bushes in their territory.

1

2

3

4

...EOPARD

...cats represent the typical carnivore, the leopard, *Panthera pardus*, ...presents the typical cat: solitary (**1**), beautiful (**2**), aloof, ferocious ...hen cornered and lightning-fast to pounce (**4**) when the moment is ...ght. Traditionally regarded as the arch-enemy of baboons, leopards, ...fact, rarely kill these large and aggressive primates, who themselves ...ometimes make a group attack on a single leopard.

...Leopard males may be from one and a half to two times the size of ...males, but size will vary in different areas. In the mountains of the ...ape Province, male leopards weigh little more than 30 kg, whereas in ...e bushveld they may weigh as much as 70 kg.

...The leopard is a survivor. Long after other large carnivores have ...en eliminated from an area, the leopard will remain. Although they ...refer the cover of rocky and mountainous areas or riverine thickets, ...opards have a wide habitat tolerance, which ranges from tropical ...rest to the fringes of deserts. Because of this, these animals have the ...idest distribution range of all the large carnivores, and are found from ...e southern parts of the African continent, northwards to the Arabian Peninsula, through the Middle East to the Far East, as far as Siberia and south-eastwards to Sri Lanka and Malaysia.

These cats are highly secretive, usually silent and nocturnal, and able to eke out an existence on small animals such as dassies, ground-nesting birds, and even mice if larger animals are absent. In protected areas, leopards usually prey on the most common medium-sized antelope such as springbok (**3**), impala or reedbuck. They are also reputed to have a predilection for dogs. In East Africa, one leopard was observed to bring back to its lair a total of 11 jackals in a period of just three weeks.

The leopard's habit of taking its kills into trees ensures that stronger predators, such as lions and hyaenas, do not rob it of its food. The strength required to hoist a 60 kg impala several metres up a tree is staggering. There is even a record of a leopard hauling a young giraffe, weighing 100 kg, into the fork of a tree.

When preparing to move a carcass, a leopard will first straddle it (**3**), then, lifting the weight with its powerful neck muscles, will proceed to carry it off to the base of a tree. With a prodigious leap, it claws its way up the tree to the first fork, and, if possible, will pull the carcass further, into the higher branches.

Leopards and cheetahs often compete for the same prey species. However, competition between the two is reduced by the fact that leopards are mainly nocturnal, whereas cheetahs are diurnal.

Male and female leopards live in separate territories, that of the male being larger than the female's. The male's territory usually overlaps those of several females, and he will mate with any one of them as they come on heat.

Cubs are born in litters of two or three, and are weaned at three months. From about four months, they accompany their mother on hunts, and remain dependent on her for up to 22 months. Female cubs may inherit part of their mother's territory when they reach breeding age, but the males in the litter must then move off to seek their own territory elsewhere.

When wounded or cornered, a leopard can become exceedingly dangerous. Many stories are told, especially among hunters, of people being seriously hurt and even killed by this animal. Leopards have been known to become man-eaters, especially in India, and there is evidence to suggest that they were important predators of our early ancestors. Man has little to fear, however, as the leopard has a naturally shy disposition and a secretive nature, and tends to avoid, rather than seek, confrontation.

CHEETAH

The cheetah, *Acinonyx jubatus*, is built for speed. Its long and powerful legs (**4**), slim body (**6**), deep chest, long tail and small head (**2**), are all adaptations to permit unexcelled speed. The cheetah is the fastest mammal on earth, capable of reaching speeds of up to 95 km per hour. In order to attain this speed, it uses up tremendous amounts of energy, causing its body temperature to rise rapidly. If it fails in its efforts to catch up with its prey after about 400 m at full speed, the animal will abandon the hunt as it is likely to suffer organ damage from the over-exertion.

In the bid to extract the fastest speed possible, the cheetah has had to sacrifice a robust skull for a small, streamlined head and for the weakest jaws of a predator its size. This makes killing larger prey difficult. Small to medium-sized mammals, such as impala, springbok (**5**), Thomson's gazelle, steenbok and hares, represent the cheetah's main prey. Its diurnal activity is probably essential for it to be able to see obstacles when moving at speed, and also ensures that

1

3

4

5

6

competition with other carnivores, which are mainly nocturnal, is greatly reduced.

After an energetic chase and kill, the cheetah is completely exhausted, and for several minutes can do little else but lie and pant heavily until it has regained enough strength to begin eating. Being the weakest of the larger carnivores, it can be easily displaced from its kill by any of the other large predators.

The cheetah is more social than the leopard, but less so than the lion. A large group of cheetahs observed in the wild is most likely to consist of a mother and her young or fully grown cubs; an adult male cheetah is unlikely to form part of the group.

Like all carnivores, cheetahs give birth to altricial young – that is, weak and poorly developed – who are dependent on parental care and protection. Litter size (between two and five) is usually larger than that of the leopard, and the mother is responsible for her cubs' welfare until they reach 18 months or more. Up to the age of about three months the cubs' backs are covered with a mantle of long, grey hair (1), which is thought to offer a measure of camouflage in the early stages of life when vulnerability to predation is high.

Once the cubs are old enough, they break away from their mother, but remain together until the females become sexually mature. At this point, they leave the group and go off alone to breed and raise their own cubs. The male cheetahs, on the other hand, form coalitions of two to three animals in the same way as male lions do. Once formed, male coalitions defend a territory. Females are not territorial and their ranges overlap with each other and with those of the males. However, in areas with migratory prey, such as the Serengeti in Tanzania, females range over much larger areas than do males.

Although not as agile as leopards, cheetahs are able to climb trees even from an early age (3), and frequently use a tree as a vantage point when looking for prey, or as a refuge from enemies (4, overleaf). However, they lack the strength of leopards and are unable to take their kills into trees.

Like most of the large carnivores, the cheetah's distribution range has declined alarmingly in recent years. They are probably extinct in Asia and most of north Africa, and are mainly confined to the larger game reserves of east, central and southern Africa. However, they are widespread over most of Namibia.

SPOTTED HYAENA

The spotted hyaena, *Crocuta crocuta*, is a much maligned and misunderstood creature. The classical view is that of the cowardly scavenger, living on the edge of the ecosystem and surviving on the pickings of the more noble carnivores, especially those of the large cats. There is no doubting the efficiency of hyaenas as scavengers; they have the most powerful teeth and jaws in the animal kingdom and are able to crunch up large bones which the other carnivores leave behind. With this faculty, hyaenas are able to get at the highly nutritious marrow locked up in leg bones. They can also digest the organic component of bone.

The spotted hyaena is far more mobile than any of the cats and can cover a large area quickly, in search of carrion. Surprisingly, they do not always wait for lions to finish eating a carcass: if there are enough of them, hyaenas may drive lions away from their kill, particularly if no large male lion is present. They easily dominate leopards and cheetahs, and have been known to drive each of the three species of large cat into a tree, as seen in (4), where a cheetah takes refuge from the hyaenas below.

But it is as active and efficient hunters that spotted hyaenas obtain most of their food. In East Africa, it is not uncommon for them to kill adult wildebeest and zebra, and, during the wildebeest calving season, they are the calves' main predators.

In the Kalahari region of southern Africa, where kills make up some 70 per cent of the hyaenas' diet, gemsbok top the list of their prey. The scimitar-sharp horns of the gemsbok are used efficiently in defence against hyaenas (1), and the adult buck is not easily overcome unless it is in poor condition. However, calves are very vulnerable to predation, and over 60 per cent of the hunting attempts on them are successful. The young animal is brought down (2 and 3) after a chase at 50 km per hour, or more, over a distance of up to three kilometres. Spotted hyaenas are also noted for their great powers of endurance. In the Kalahari, four of them were recorded to have followed a herd of eland for 23 km before eventually killing one.

In areas with large numbers of lions, spotted hyaenas take on a more scavenging role. There is always plenty of carrion available and the necessity for them to hunt is reduced.

In this species of hyaena, the female (up to 75 kg) is larger than the male (60 kg). Superficially, the female's reproductive organs resemble those of the male, this having given rise to the popular belief that the animals are hermaphrodites. Functionally, however, a hyaena is either male or female. Within their clans, females dominate the males, having priority over food and at favourite resting places. Even when mating, the males display fear of their mates.

Spotted hyaenas have an elaborate meeting ceremony. When two of them meet, they stand head to tail, lift the hind leg nearest to the other and sniff and lick each other's erected sexual organs. By exposing their most vulnerable parts to the teeth of another, they display great trust – something which unfamiliar hyaenas would never do, and which serves to cement the bonds of friendship between two that are familiar.

1

2

3

The female gives birth to only one or two cubs at a time, and these are kept at a communal den (5). Hyaena dens are equipped with narrow tunnels which are only large enough for the cubs to enter, thus providing them with ideal protection during the long periods for which the adults are away. In South Africa's Kruger National Park, some of the culverts under the tarred roads are of about the same dimensions as the tunnels of a hyaena den and have been used as such by spotted hyaenas.

Cubs are suckled until they are a year old – an unusually long time for a carnivore – and only begin to eat meat from the age of about nine months, when they are able to join the adults on the hunt. Up to this time, a mother's milk provides all the sustenance the cubs need. Because of the lengthy suckling period, the nutritional demands on the female are great, which accounts for the small litter size. It also explains the large size and dominance of females, who can better protect and provide for their young.

The whoop call of the spotted hyaena is one of the characteristic calls of the African night. Each hyaena has its own call, which is recognized by its clan members and, with practice, by the human ear. When excited on a kill, engaged in a territorial fight, or when mobbing lions, spotted hyaenas give vent to the most astonishing assortment of whoops, giggles, growls, grunts and screams which are unmatched by any other carnivore. Some of these sounds are incredibly human-like and have been interpreted by some African tribes to be the sounds of witches casting their spells on an unfortunate human.

The spotted hyaena is found throughout Africa south of the Sahara with the exception of the extreme south, where it has been exterminated, and the tropical rain forests in West Africa. In many areas, these animals are important predators and as significant as the lion in controlling numbers of prey. They are particularly efficient at weeding out the sick, the old and the slow, and so help to keep the prey populations healthy and in balance with the environment.

4

BROWN HYAENA

The brown hyaena, *Hyaena brunnea*, is smaller than the spotted hyaena, weighing about 40 kg. It is an inhabitant chiefly of the south-western arid regions of Africa, and is particularly common in the Kalahari and along the coastal strip of the Namib Desert.

Brown hyaenas better fit the title of scavenger than do the spotted hyaenas. The little hunting they do is directed at small animals, such as springhares and springbok lambs, and most hunts are unsuccessful. Killed prey forms an insignificant part of their diet, which consists mainly of mammals, such as this gemsbok killed by lions in the Kalahari (5), or often of mammals that have died through starvation and disease. Other elements of their diet include wild fruits – especially the tsama melon, insects, and ostrich eggs (2). If a large amount of food is found, often, whatever is not eaten will be carried off and stored under a nearby bush until needed. A brown hyaena has been known to raid an ostrich nest containing 26 eggs, of which it ate seven (the equivalent of 170 chicken eggs), and then scatter-hoarded the remaining 19 within a one-kilometre radius of the nest.

Being scavengers, brown hyaenas forage on their own. They are not, however, solitary like the leopard, and often several brown hyaenas will share a territory, marking it by 'pasting' secretions from the anal glands on to grass stalks, and by defecating at established 'latrines' which are formed at various points throughout the territory, but particularly around its boundary.

Usually only one female is found with her cubs at a den (1) but, on occasion, two or more females from a clan will share the den. The den is the social centre of the brown hyaena clan. It is here that the cubs and other group members spend time relaxing, playing or muzzle-wrestling (3), so contributing to the social stability of the unit.

Like the young of the spotted hyaena, brown hyaena cubs are weaned at the late age of one year (4). However, from their twelfth week of life, the adults supplement the milk diet of their cubs with food which is carried to the den. All adult members of the clan take part in this carrying procedure. Because the cubs are not solely dependent on their mother's milk, the female brown

hyaena can afford to raise a larger litter than can the spotted hyaena, and gives birth to between one and five cubs at a time. In contrast to the spotted hyaena, the female in this species is not larger than the male, nor is she dominant over him.

The striped hyaena, *Hyaena hyaena*, occurs in east Africa, the more arid regions of west and north Africa, and through southern Asia to India. Although slightly smaller than the brown hyaena, it has a very similar life-style and is predominantly a scavenger, moving around solitarily.

Brown hyaenas and striped hyaenas do not have the complicated vocal system of the spotted hyaena, and have nothing comparable to the characteristic whoop call of that species. Neither do they have the unusual meeting ceremony of the spotted hyaena, nor the associated mimicry by the female of the male's sexual organs. Generally speaking, the brown and striped hyaenas have a far simpler behavioural repertoire than spotted hyaenas because they are more solitary, do not co-operate in hunting and, although an individual will defend a territory or attack a competitor, these functions would not be undertaken by a group.

3

4

5

1

THE WILD DOG AND THE AARDWOLF

The African wild dog, *Lycaon pictus* (**5**), is one of Africa's most endangered mammals. It is a highly social species, living in packs (**1**) which range in size from a pair to as many as 50 individuals. All the adult males in a pack are related, as are the adult females, but the males and females are unrelated. Normally only the dominant male and female breed – the female producing a large litter of between ten and 21 pups – but all pack members share in raising the young by regurgitating food to them after hunting. The pups are weaned at about two months, and at three to five months leave the den with the rest of the pack to take up nomadic existence.

Wild dogs weigh between 20 and 30 kg, southern African specimens being larger than those from east Africa. They hunt in the early morning and the late afternoon, mainly medium-sized prey like impala (**3**), wildebeest calves and Thomson's gazelle. Although efficient hunters, wild dogs do not play havoc with game herds, as is often stated. In fact, they will travel large distances to find suitable prey. When a kill is made, adult members allow the pups to eat first.

Wild dogs show little fear of man and are great roamers, given to straying beyond the confines of reserves and into farmlands, so exposing themselves to the shotguns of farmers anxious to protect their stock.

The aardwolf, *Proteles cristatus* (**4**), is the most specialized carnivore. It is an aberrant hyaena, lacking the latter's powerful teeth and jaws, and weighing only 9 kg. It has a discontinuous distribution in Africa, being found only in the south and in the north-east.

In both regions, though, the aardwolf's diet consists almost entirely of snouted harvester termites of the genus *Trinervitermes* (**2**). The animals have developed a large tongue, adapted for licking up the termites as they forage above ground. If a foraging termite column is disturbed, the worker termites rush underground and the soldiers emerge, producing distasteful secretions as a form of defence. When the ratio of soldiers to workers reaches a certain level, the aardwolf is repulsed and stops feeding.

It has been calculated that one aardwolf eats up to 105 million termites in a year! These animals are, therefore, of considerable importance in controlling termite populations and should be protected.

2

3

4

5

OTHER CANIDS

Besides the African wild dog, there are nine other members of the family Canidae in Africa – four jackals (genus *Canis*), four true foxes (genus *Vulpes*), and one aberrant fox (genus *Otocyon*). The black-backed jackal, *Canis mesomelas*, (**2** and **4**) is common over the more arid regions of southern and east Africa. Like all jackals, this 6-8 kg animal is a super-opportunist, feeding on carrion whenever it is available. However, it is also an efficient hunter of rodents and of the young of small and medium-sized antelope, and if the opportunity arises, will even tackle the more vulnerable of the larger prey, such as this adult springbok, which is handicapped by sarcoptic mange (**1**). Black-backed jackals also enjoy reptiles, insects and wild fruits. Male and female pairs are monogamous and defend a specific territory.

The slightly larger side-striped jackal, *Canis adustus* (**6**), has a characteristic white tip to its tail and weighs about 10 kg. It is seen less often than the black-backed jackal and is more nocturnal. An inhabitant of the better-watered, higher rainfall areas, it has a wider distribution than the black-backed jackal. Its diet is similar, except it feeds more often on vegetable matter.

The golden jackal, *Canis aureus*, is found in east and north Africa, south-east Europe and southern Asia as far east as Burma. On the

Serengeti plains the golden jackal whelps during the rainy season, when food, in the form of migrating herbivores, is abundant, whereas the black-backed jackal whelps in the dry season, which coincides with a peak in rodent numbers and wild fruits.

The fourth member of the genus is the highly endangered Ethiopian wolf, also known as the Simien jackal, *Canis simiens*. Confined to the highlands of Ethiopia there are no more than 500 of these animals left in the wild. Threats to their survival are habitat loss, hybridization with domestic dogs, and disease, particularly rabies.

The four foxes of Africa are inhabitants of arid regions. The Cape fox, *Vulpes chama* (**5**), occurs in southern Africa, whereas the others, the pale fox, *Vulpes pallida*, Ruppell's fox, *Vulpes ruppelli*, and the fennec fox, *Vulpes zerda*, occur in north Africa, the latter two also going across into Arabia. They are all diminutive, the Cape fox at 4 kg being the largest, and the fennec at 1 kg being the smallest. Like all foxes they are adept at catching rodents.

The bat-eared fox, *Otocyon megalotis* (**3**), weighs from 4-5 kg and is predominantly an insect eater, being particularly partial to harvester termites and beetle larvae. Its large ears are sensitive to the sounds made by insects, even those moving underground. The bat-eared fox has a discontinuous distribution, being found in the arid regions of south-western southern Africa and then again in the arid north-east.

1

2

3

4

SMALLER CATS

Most cats belong to the genus *Felis*. In Africa, seven species of small, nocturnal, solitary cats are found, but as yet little is known of their behaviour.

The caracal, *Felis caracal* (**1** and **2**), is the largest of these, the males weighing about 15 kg and the females between 10 kg and 12 kg. It is found throughout Africa, except in the true desert regions and the tropical forests, and also occurs in parts of southern Asia. Its diet consists mainly of birds and small mammals, such as springhares (**1**) and dassies, but, in spite of its size, it is also able to overcome jackal, wild cat, and prey as large as adult springbok or reedbuck. The caracal is an aggressive animal and has even been known to take over a kill from a group of black-backed jackals. In the Kalahari, however, it, in turn, is often robbed of its food by brown hyaenas. In areas where the black-backed jackal has been eliminated, the caracal is believed to have increased in number, and it is thought by some that it has become a more significant predator of domestic sheep than the jackal.

The long-legged serval, *Felis serval* (**5**), weighing about 10 kg, prefers a tall grass habitat and vleis, where one of its principal prey species – the vlei rat – is found. Unlike most other cats, it is not averse to hunting in wet, swampy areas. The serval also feeds on the multimammate mouse, which it usually kills with a downward slap of the front foot.

Around 1600 BC, the ancient Egyptians began to domesticate *Felis lybica*, the 4 to 5 kg African wild cat (**4**), which has a similar habitat tolerance and distribution range to the caracal. In many of the regions where it is found, it is often the commonest of all the small carnivores. Today, however, cross-breeding between the domestic cat and the pure African wild cat threatens the species. Rats and mice comprise its basic diet, but it also eats sun spiders, locusts, small reptiles and birds. These animals are known to sit silently near the entrance of a rodent hole (**4**), ready to pounce on the occupant as it emerges. African wild cats are good tree climbers and often take refuge in trees when hunted. Some are even known to raise their young in holes found in tree trunks.

The African golden cat, *Felis aurata*, is found in the forests of West Africa, the jungle cat, *Felis chaus*, just enters north Africa, but is mainly found in the dry forests of Asia, and the sand cat, *Felis margarita*, is a desert cat of north Africa and south-west Asia.

1

2

3

4

MONGOOSES AND HONEY BADGERS

Mongooses, civets and genets, belong to the family Viverridae – the largest carnivore family, consisting of 72 species, 34 of which are found in Africa. Viverrids may be nocturnal, as are the civets, genets and the larger mongooses, or diurnal, like the smaller mongooses.

Several of the diurnal mongooses have highly developed social systems, especially evident in the banded mongoose, *Mungos mungo*, the dwarf mongoose, *Helogale parvula*, and the meerkat or suricate, *Suricata suricatta* (**1** and **4**). These tiny carnivores, weighing no more than 800 g, live in groups that vary in size from three to 30 members. Avid diggers, their diet consists mainly of beetle larvae which they dig from the ground, and of scorpions (**1**). During the forage one member acts as a guard, climbing to an elevated point and scanning the area for signs of danger. Meanwhile, the other members of the group give their undivided attention to finding food. In due course, the guard leaves his vantage point and is relieved by another. At the first sign of danger – the sighting, for instance, of an eagle, jackal or honey badger – the guard gives the alarm and the whole group acts immediately, dashing off to the nearest warren.

The yellow mongoose, *Cynictis penicillata* (**2** and **5**), is more or less the same size as the suricate but less social, usually foraging on its own. It is not as avid a digger as the suricate, and feeds more on insects that live above ground, such as locusts and termites. It also feeds on relatively large prey such as mice and small reptiles. Unlike the suricate, the yellow mongoose tends to live in areas with thicker cover, and does not, therefore, require the complex guarding system of the suricate.

The ratel or honey badger, *Mellivora capensis* (**3**), represents the Mustelidae, the second largest carnivore family, containing 67 species, which include the skunks, weasels, badgers and otters. However, only six species are found in Africa. Mustelids have a reputation for being ferocious and fearless animals, and the 10-kg honey badger is no exception. If pursued by a vehicle, for instance, it will often turn around and attack, uttering a harsh grating sound and baring its teeth. In confrontation with other animals, it tends to go for the scrotum, a method of attack which has been reported to overcome a wildebeest.

Honey badgers are found throughout Africa, except in the Sahara, and in Asia, as far as India. Their diet is diverse: they eat mice, scorpions, small reptiles and beetles, as well as large snakes and hares. They have also been known to hunt bat-eared foxes and aardwolves, and there is a record of one having robbed a brown hyaena of a steenbok kill. In the Kalahari, honey badgers are often accompanied by several chanting goshawks and sometimes by jackals, all of which collect around the honey badger hoping to snap up any of the food that it digs up. Like other mustelids, honey badgers give off a very powerful smell from their anal glands, and this is used as an effective defence against predators.